The Explosive Growth of Private Labels in North America

The Explosive Growth of

Philip Fitzell

Private Labels in North America

Past, Present and Future

A Flickinger Family Private Label Study

Global Books, LLC
New York

Global Books, LLC.
167 Madison Ave.
New York, NY 10016

Printed in the United States of America

CIP # 92-78907
ISBN # 0963292056

Fitzell, Philip B.
Explosive growth of private labels in north america/Philip B. Fitzell

Cover Design by John Cannizzo

Cover Photo Credits to A&P (Bokar, Red Circle and Eight O'Clock coffees), The Watt Design Group (Wal-Mart packaging), and Federated Foods (Red & White label label).
Photo Credits also go to: A&P, IGA, Caswell-Massey, Flickinger Co., Fortune Magazine, Business Week, USA Today. Additionally, the author directly and indirectly credits "Private Label" Magazine on the basis of his years of association with that publication. Permission granted by John Wiley & Sons, Inc., New York for quotes on pages 50, 58, taken from "Wholesaling, Principles and Practice," published by The Ronald Press Co., New York. Acknowledgment also goes to MacFarlane Walter & Ross, Toronto, Canada, for material and quotes (pages 154-55, 186) taken from "The Edible Man: Dave Nichol, President's Choice & The Making of Popular Taste."

This book is printed on "acid-free paper" to American Library Association specifications.

10 9 8 7 6 5 4 3 2 1

CONTENTS

PART III

Preface

COMING OF AGE

This author counts himself as one of the richest men alive today—though not in terms of dollar net-worth. Ask any trade editor about his, or her, salary and you will likely hear heartfelt complaints. No, my fortune sits on the experience of having lived through a virtual renaissance of private label growth in the food, drug store, and discount mass merchandise trade, since I first became involved in this business in April 1979.

Usually, after a year or two on any job, I become bored, looking for a change of pace. Not so with private label! This industry's dynamic and surprising changes, up to the present, have been like a baby growing through childhood, adolescence, and now into early maturity. Late in the 1970s, private label was in its infancy, so to speak, because it was an unknown factor, outside of the people directly involved in the trade. With my 15 years of business writing experience (including a food and beverage industry focus), prior to joining *Private Label* magazine in its start-up, I had never heard the term "private label" used. At least, it never registered in my mind.

Today, the private label phenomenon has excited, upset, or intrigued practically everyone in North America and Europe—and lately the Pacific Rim and Latin American countries as well. What is especially significant about its development, now in its young and responsible adulthood, is the fact that the brand name market leaders are paying more attention to this so-called new kid on the block. This "bargain brand," "generic," or "copycat" upstart now has all the markings of a brand. The leading manufacturers of national brands have copied its strategies—the emphasis on value in the form of bonus packs, lower pricing, or compare-and-save messages; more product content per package; upscale or premium quality and packaging; the adoption of everyday-low pricing strategies on certain products, and so on. They also have embraced category management strategies, which private label adopted throughout the 1980s, just to justify private label's position in a product category. The only difference is that the name brand manufacturers use more market research data: They can afford it.

Yes, private label is still a bit clumsy, coming out of its adolescence. Its callow days, however, are over. Private label has truly shed its secrecy and intimidation in the marketplace. It is an exclusive brand, today; it's always been. It's just that private label has suffered an inferiority complex, competing with dominant name brands that controlled consumer loyalty. Now those days are over as private label gains respect and acceptance in the marketplace.

This book traces a rich history of private label development. Private label excellence in product quality actually predates the brand leaders in a number of cases. Private label has kept small grocers profitable, while building profits for the giant chain store operators. Private label has served as a competitive incentive for brand leaders to improve their products and to sharpen their marketing efforts. Private label now helps retailers and wholesalers to be more creative in their own marketing strategies. Certainly, private label deserves more credit than it has received to date. Hopefully, this book will change some people's attitudes.

If you doubt that private label has not received its due, then please check your local library, under the subject 'private label.' If you find any books other than those by this author, "Fitzell," please let me know through the book publisher.

Much of the content in this book derives from both my direct contacts with industry sources through my work as a trade editor in this field since 1979, as well as my research efforts in writing two textbooks on the subject of private label.

In my experience, I know many people who deserve thanks for their support and cooperation in helping me form my perspective of this business. They should all be mentioned in this book. This addition, however, would bore the reader, because of its length. So I apologize for the omission. Hopefully, there will be more information published in the future, where people deserving credit for their work will be recognized. I would, however, like to thank my wife, Judith. Without her support, this book would not exist: Its composition took place during the start-up of my new business, now called Exclusive

Brands LLC, a difficult task in itself.

Also, special thanks go to the Flickinger family, which sponsored this book. The sponsors include: the late Burt P. Flickinger, Tom Flickinger, Burt P. Flickinger III, and Catherine Schweitzer. The role of the Flickingers deserve much more attention than the few footnotes or a paragraph-long mention in only a handful of books about the grocery trade. The contributions made by S.M. Flickinger early in this century, really put controlled label for the small retailer and wholesaler on the map, while also helping them, as well as many small manufacturers, survive through tough, competitive times. This industry pioneer was years ahead of his time in recognizing the value of private label in the retail and wholesale trade. Hopefully, this book sheds more light on his important contributions.

I would also like to thank Cornell University for their special research study on the role of today's brand manufacturers in the private label business. This separate project, also commissioned by the Flickinger family, is outlined at the end of this book. Finally, I would like to thank my editor Penelope Post for her many hours of work.

Today, the retailers and wholesalers who control their own exclusive brands are truly in control of their destiny. From out of anonymity, private label has come of age as a brand, an exclusive brand. It will definitely become more of a dominant force in future commerce throughout the world, as these retailers and wholesalers expand their operations globally.

Dedication

Flickinger Stores News

Journal of Household Economics

VOL. 1 AUGUST 1, 1921. NO. 1

In Which We Introduce Ourselves

The Flickinger organization is the culmination of the life work of Mr. S. M. Flickinger, whose picture is shown here. It was with reluctance that Mr. Flickinger consented to allow its use out of modesty, but it would be impossible to write a history of the organization without giving a brief sketch of his life.

Mr. Flickinger was born in Sardinia, N. Y., in the year 1864, and at the age of two years became an orphan, being from that time on cared for by foster parents, and lived on a farm until he was 21 years old, getting his education in the district school and by personal application to study during spare time.

It was his ambition to go to the city and eventually have a business of his own, that brought him to Buffalo, starting in the employ of a local retail grocer at $7.00 per week.

He applied himself so enthusiastically and conscientiously to his work that his employer voluntarily raised his pay five times during the first year.

The retail business he was with gradually worked into the wholesale grocery business, and in 1893 the business was sold to a competing jobbing house, Mr. Flickinger going with the new concern, where he stayed for about eight years.

Front page of S.M. Flickinger's first newsletter—also one of the first consumer publications ever produced by a retailer-wholesaler. 1921 (Photo credit: Buffalo and Erie County Historical Society, Buffalo, NY)

Recognizing S. M. Flickinger's Role

This book is dedicated to Smith M. Flickinger (1864-1939), a turn-of-the-century wholesale grocer, who started the concept of the voluntary group of independent grocers, working in cooperation with wholesalers to merchandise and market their own controlled-label range of products. As founder of the Red and White Stores in Buffalo, NY, Flickinger, early in the 1920s, helped to develop the first nationally-advertised control label—Red & White—for the exclusive use of retailers, who belonged to a voluntary group he organized within the United States. Eventually, he sold off his own stores to each store manager to further foster a cooperative allegiance to the Red & White store banner. Flickinger generated a spirit of trust between the retailer and wholesaler, based on honesty, fairness, and sound ethics, all tied into the Golden Rule, that is, "Do unto others as you would have them do unto you." Acting as food wholesaler, he supplied independent grocers with both manufacturers' brands and Red & White private label products, proving that the wholesaler and retailers could work together effectively.

Eventually, the Red & White voluntary group concept spread into Canada, was imitated in Australia, and nearly took root in Europe as well.

Flickinger's pioneering efforts inspired independent grocers to stay profitable with their own private label range. They were not totally dependent upon national brand merchandise, which the stronger chain store operators could sell at a lower cost, because of their large volume buying, in-house processing/manufacturing capabilities, and greater distribution efficiencies. The Red & White group members were given "ownership and control over the most complete line of grocery products and sundries in America. At that time, the bulk of their merchandise was packed under the three private labels of the Red & White system: Red & White, Blue & White, and Our Value."* Meantime, Flickinger demonstrated that a wholesaler also could be 'retailer-minded.' Initially, he operated his own stores, worked as a wholesale jobber, and licensed independent grocers in his market to use the Red & White store banner. Critics said he was trying to ride a troika, as a retailer, wholesaler, and chain store licensor.

Independent grocers today, acting on their own, through voluntary groups, or within cooperatives they own, owe a good part of their survival and inspiration to the precedents set by S.M. Flickinger. He is credited with being the father of the voluntary group movement in the United States. Unfortunately, most of the published reports about these formative years of the grocery industry in North America fail to credit, or even mention, Flickinger's role in shaping this business. More important, he helped the independent grocers to stay in business and to realize that they could compete just as efficiently as the chain stores, operating like the corporate chains, while using private label as their profit builder. Admittedly, the Red & White group also copied many of the principles practiced by A&P, the chain store market leader early in this century. Red & White's success encouraged the formation of other voluntary groups and also helped many smaller manufacturers maintain their footing against regional or national competitors. Flickinger's strategy was basically to purchase controlled products "made only by the best class of manufacturers, who are also a part of this great cooperative enterprise." Confidence was encouraged among the manufacturers, wholesalers and retailers. One method for building cooperation was "the establishment of an associated manufacturer-wholesaler-retailer group, comprising about 50 manufacturers, who met frequently with representatives of Red & White for the purpose of discussing mutual problems and thrashing out differences in a constructive way."** This effort represented one of the industry's first partnerships between manufacturer and trade customer.

*Quoted from "Voluntary Chain Marketing," a 1948 honors thesis by Burt P. Flickinger, Jr. at Harvard University, based on his personal interview with Donald S. Moore, sales manager of the S.M. Flickinger Co., Buffalo, NY, pp. 18-19.

**Ibid. pp. 18, 20.

Introduction

Defining Private Labels

Private label products cover nearly every item that consumers buy at the retail level or through food service and institutional facilities. These products are defined by their ownership and controlled distribution, where a retailer, wholesaler, cooperative, buying group, broker, marketer, exporter/importer, food service distributor or restaurant/institutional operator owns and/or controls the label or brand identity. While some of these players can also be involved in the manufacturing/processing of these products, that portion of their business represents less than 50% of their total revenues. Manufacturers who do not own private labels are described as companies generating 50% or more of their sales in manufacturing/processing activities. These manufacturers own and/or control local, regional, national, or global brands, which usually are not restricted in their distribution, i.e., competing retailers across the street from one another can carry the same brands.

Non-manufacturers can own and/or control private labels that may have the same geographic coverage as the manufacturers' brands, but there almost always is exclusivity, that is, their competitors within a marketing area cannot carry the same private label. Both this distinction of ownership (i.e., non-manufacturers) and the exclusivity of distribution within markets give private label its identity. That identity, however, has been called by many different names besides private label: house brands, control brands, distributor labels, copycats, knockoffs, generics, no name, corporate brands, retailer-controlled brands, premium brands, store brands, white labels, own labels or own brands, and exclusive brands. These identities, some purposely derogatory, are based on a number of factors and/or perspectives: the time of their appearance in history, the perception of them shared by the trade in different countries, the type of owner who controls them, the product quality level they represent, a competitor's pigeonhole description of them—usually a brand manufacturer, consumer confusion or ignorance over the terms used to describe them.

While the term "private label" serves as the basis for this book, private label still carries connotations of secrecy, because usually only the distributor's (not the manufacturer's) name appears on the private label package. The manufacturer or processor mostly remains anonymous. Yet, within the trade, private label manufacturers literally have come out of the closet in recent years, diminishing this secrecy and, in fact, manifesting pride and respect for these products. In some cases, the manufacturer's name appears on the label distribution statement, as in Wal-Mart's Equate exclusive brand for health and beauty care products. Some private labels also have added a name-brand identity on the package, so-called co-branding, for example, when a specific ingredient plays an important role in the product, i.e., NutraSweet artificial sweetener on a private label diet soft drink or the New Jersey-based cooperative Wakefern for its ShopRite brand, listing M&M candies on its Premium ice cream packaging.

In recent years, private labels overall have been significantly improved in quality and packaging enhancements, making them equal to, or better than the category brand leaders. Demeaning terms associated with private label, such as "knockoffs," "copycats" or "generics," no longer apply as they have in the past. Acceptance of private label by both the trade and consumers has grown due to a number of factors, including:

(1) The upgrade in private label packaging,
(2) The improvement in product quality,
(3) The expansion of licensing programs for private labels,
(4) The development of upscale or premium quality private labels,
(5) The debut of innovative or unique products, and
(6) The spread of private label marketing/distribution activities worldwide.

All these factors have helped to raise private label to that of a brand status in today's marketplace. Lately, there also have been product enhancements and new product developments introduced by the private label owners, cooperating with "partner" manufacturers, which also have helped elevate private label identity to the ranks of a brand. These trends now make the term private label outdated, non-representative, or not completely accurate.

While some industry players regularly use other terms, such as store brands, private brands, control brands, own brands, corporate brands, or retailer-controlled brands, this author believes that the term 'exclusive brands' offers the most comprehensive reference point for the private label business today. The distinction between exclusive brands and manufacturers' brands is still based on ownership. "Exclusive" can apply to ownership across all market segments as well as to all types of non-manufacturer owners. "Exclusive" can be applied to all quality tiers as well. "Exclusive" also covers the licensing of these products, no matter what product quality level is represented. While it can be argued that manufacturers' brands can be exclusively distributed in certain markets, or in different countries, they still have a universal base of distribution outside that area, where any retail or food service outlet can carry their brands. It can also be argued that private labels or exclusive brands can be perceived by consumers as the leading brand in a given marketplace—no different from so-called national brands—based on their commanding market share.

The Parameters of Private Label

In the 19th century, private labels in the grocery segment evolved out of bulk commodity staples, first into packaged teas, coffee, sugar, flour, spices, etc. Early in this century, private label development was expanded further into canned vegetables and fruits, frozen foods, and bakery and dairy products. Other product categories followed: paper products, detergents, deli items, soft drinks, health and beauty care products, general merchandise, and perishables such as meats, poultry, and produce. There has been a recent trend toward branding or sub-branding of these perishable products as well. With few exceptions, the packaged goods product mix has been the central focus of private label business in the retail store.

Frequently, store-prepared products, especially in the perishables area, are not counted as part of a private label program. The packaging is 'store-made,' consisting of plastic or paper wrapping with a store sticker for identity purposes. Additionally, the trend toward convenience foods and meal solutions ready for consumption or reheating has spawned more service counters within larger retail stores. They dispense foods and beverages, almost like a quick take-out restaurant, sometimes even with a chef present. These products also are not counted under private label—even though they are in many cases prepared from the store's own food stock.

In the food service-institutional market segment, private label has been packaged primarily under brands controlled by food service distributors and/or caterers. The end-user, a restaurant, fast service business, or hotel, also uses their store or company name on some packaging as well. In the trade, retailers now seek to brand the store itself, while a good portion of their product mix is displayed without packaging.

The parameters for private label have been extended virtually into every product category found in retail outlets. Private label also has tapped into untouchable product categories of the recent past: cosmetics, baby food, natural health products, gourmet delicacies, etc. Through trial and error, consumers have come to trust the quality of private labels. These shoppers recognize that what is most precious to them, i.e., a baby, or that which deserves the very best treatment, i.e., their physical appearance, can be addressed effectively with private label products. Even automobiles once carried a private label identity, but only for a short time because of a lack of auto dealership support. In 1912, for example, Montgomery Ward introduced the Assembled Car, which was renamed Modoc, selling at $1,800--a five-passenger, four-cylinder private label car. Failing to build up a dealership, the car was withdrawn in 1914. Ward also introduced its own Riverside tires about this time. Then in 1915, Ward began manufacturing farm machinery. Similarily, Sears, which opened its first retail store in Evansville, IN in 1925, unsuccessfully tried to use its Allstate brand on an automobile during the 1950s. Private label today appears in practically every type of retail outlet, including specialty stores as well as the new store formats. Its product range covers nearly the full range of products available at retail.

Scope of this Study

This book focuses primarily on the development of private label in the grocery and drug store marketplace in North America, covering the United States, Canada, and Mexico. It is a complicated story, involving many different players—often sharing diverse roles or switching roles. Each development has influenced the course of private label evolution. Synergies are discovered everywhere. Retailers, wholesalers, brokers, manufacturers, all have interacted to change and to expand private label business. This study traces these influences, including a number that have never before been published. A summary of private label activities in Mexico is included as well, especially related to the recent expansion of U.S. companies into that country and the impact of NAFTA (North Atlantic Free Trade Agreement) on trade throughout North America. Other segments of the retail and wholesale business, i.e., mass merchandisers, department stores, convenience stores, food service distributors, restaurant operators, exporters and importers are discussed as they relate to the supermarket and drug store business, in terms of competitive market position.

PART 1

The Evolution of Product Value

The 19th Century

CHAPTER 1

______19TH CENTURY VALUES______

The grocery retail trade in the 19th century evolved from a limited selection of bulk and packaged foods sold in general stores, off pushcarts, or horse-drawn peddler wagons as well as from food stands in public markets. Small mom-and-pop retail food stores emerged as well, offering more product variety. Brand identities began to appear from manufacturers as well as from retailers and wholesale grocers. Merchants were the first to use their own names as a label on clothing. Own-brand labeling in dry goods and groceries followed. The concept of branding , however, remained in its infancy, because brand awareness depended mostly on word-of-mouth endorsements, plus trust in the local merchant, trader, or peddler. Private labels initially were developed mostly by entrepreneurial retailers—individuals who exercised a pride of ownership in selling top-quality goods at a fair price. They often would make their own products and/or buy direct from the source of supply, bypassing the middlemen.

Early Private Labels Emerge

Jacob Bunn, for example, opened a grocery store in 1840 in Springfield, IL, specializing in retail and wholesale trading. Bunn developed a number of private brands—Recipe, Golden Age, Cap, Old Timer, Bunny (after himself)—names from his family, friends and nearby locations. Only two survived as private labels, Bunny and Golden Age. One of his associates at the time, Abraham Lincoln, received this distinction. Lincoln himself, early in his career, was a partner in a grocery store that failed, placing him in debt. Taking up law, he became an attorney in 1836 and one of his first clients was Jacob Bunn. Their friendship grew, when Lincoln asked Bunn to be his campaign manager while Bunn named some of his coffee products after his friends: Lincoln coffee and Mary Todd coffee. Over the decades, other entrepreneurs adopted familiar names from their environment for their private labels. Most private brands sold by Bunn are now gone, except for Wishbone, which was sold first to Manhattan Coffee Co. and its trademark eventually taken over by Lipton Tea and put on salad dressing. (Fitzell 1982)

World's Largest Food Chain: A&P

In the grocery trade, the best documented case study of a retailer's private label evolution is that of the Atlantic & Pacific Tea Company, which evolved from being an importer and merchant of teas, taken off cargo ships in New York City, into the world's largest food chain store retailer and manufacturer early in the 20th century. Its first pound of tea was sold in 1859. In the 1860s, the company began selling its own brands of tea: Cargo, High Cargo, Fine, Finest, Thea Nectar (an economy private brand).

Almost 20 years later, when coffee became a popular drink in the U.S., A&P introduced its Eight O'Clock Breakfast Coffee (1882). —(Hoyt 1969) This brand today is probably the second oldest private label still sold in the North American food-drug store retail marketplace. (Caswell-Massey may be the first—see below.)

In 1979, A&P began licensing use of the Eight O'Clock brand on an exclusive basis in markets where it did not compete for business, while its own stores also sold that brand on an exclusive basis. Today, this brand is the fourth largest selling coffee in the U.S.—predating most of the other leading brands, except Folger's (1859) and Chase & Sanborn (1863). In fact, Eight O'Clock has outlasted even the A&P brand name, which along with most of A&P's other private labels has been consolidated under its America's Choice private label program, introduced in 1994.

A&P's early success was built on a simple formula: low prices and small profits. It depended upon sales volume to carry the company. To cut costs, A&P virtually eliminated dealing with most of the middlemen—all the different levels of profit-seekers, such as bankers, importers, purchasers, speculators, wholesale tea dealers and wholesale grocers—and began to deal directly with manufacturers. By the turn of the century, A&P had grown to some 200 grocery stores with a sales volume of $5.6 million. The company soon changed from mail order "club plans" and wagon deliveries into what could be called the country's first food chain, which operated as tea emporiums, and then eventually added coffees, spices, extracts, baking powder, etc.

Its stores initially were described as "resplendent emporiums." Outside, an oversized letter "T" was ablaze with "dozens of small gas lights (that) beckoned passers-by to enter a high-window building glowing with bright red vermilion, imported from China and picked out with gold leaf. Around the windows—through which could be seen crystal chandeliers—curved arches of gas jets with glass cups glittering in red, white and blue." Inside, "walls decorated with gilt-edged Chinese panels; the ceiling a flowery canopy of fancy tin-work; the cash desk shaped like a pagoda; tea bins painted red and gold. In the center of the main floor, a cockatoo on a stand welcomed the trade." (Progressive Grocer 1971)

Late in the 19th century and early in this one, A&P's impact on the grocery trade as a pioneer developer had been significant. Credit A&P for a number of industry firsts:

(1) its discount pricing strategy,
(2) its introduction of private label products,
(3) the build-up of its own manufacturing operations,
(4) the debut of incentive marketing in the trade,
(5) its upscale store decor strategies, and
(6) its print and radio advertising.

In the latter part of the 19th century, other retailers and grocery wholesalers emerged, selling private label. Some of them were slow to adopt private label; the growth and acceptance of private label drew them into the business, as well as a realization that private label was a viable profit-builder for their business.

Oldest Existing Private Label—Caswell-Massey

From a history dating back to 1752 in Newport, RI, when Dr. William Hunter, a physician and pharmacist, opened an apothecary, Caswell-Massey Co., Ltd., New York, emerged in 1859—one year before the Civil War outbreak. Almost 20 years later, in 1877, one of the country's oldest chemists and perfumers, introduced its own Caswell-Massey brand. This brand very well could be the oldest existing private label in the U.S. food-drug store market segment.

Interestingly, for one of the oldest, still surviving, family-owned wholesale grocer, Miller & Hartman, Lancaster, PA, it took some 67 years, after its founding, before this company embraced private label. M&H began operations in 1868, renting out space in an old grain warehouse. Soon afterward, the partners, Benjamin P. Miller and John I. Hartman, moved into a stone warehouse. They supplied retailers by delivering goods—large wooden barrels of sugar, cornstarch, and rice— by horse and wagon. M&H, in fact, helped bring "frosted foods" to the retail market—an idea developed by Clarence Birdseye, who first started experimenting with the idea in 1914. With his quick freeze process perfected—placing fresh fish between two metal surfaces, around which he circulated a mist of brine chilled to minus 45 degrees Fahrenheit—Birdseye established his business, organized as the General Foods Company, which controlled all the patents on his belt froster and Quick Freeze equipment. Retailers, however, did not want to spend the money for the equipment, while consumers still regarded frozen foods with some caution. In 1929, the Postum Cereal Co. purchased Birdseye's patents, etc., renamed his product line "Birds Eye," and began marketing quick-frozen foods under that brand name. Without success, the company then approached wholesalers and institutions for large-quantity orders. Miller & Hartman, a long-time buyer of Postum cereal, agreed in 1935 to become General Foods' first Birds Eye distributor. That same year, the wholesaler introduced its own private labels in order to gain more control of the business. (Salmon 1993)

M&H executive, Dal Hartman, explains: "We could buy what we wanted and sell at prices lower than the national brands. At that time, many of the manufacturers did not advertise the way they do today. The national brands did not have the prestige they have now." M&H's oldest label "Ivy" for flour, vinegar, ammonia, and bulk syrup was joined by other identities: "Mason" for lower quality goods, "Union Jack" for its top line of canned goods, and "Bespac" household items (a label shared with a Plattsburgh, NY wholesalers, as part of a state buying group). (Salmon 1993)

One long-time and still surviving private label, "Monarch," was launched in 1881 as the "Royal Monarch" brand, covering coffee, tea and baking soda. Started by PYA/Monarch, Inc., Greenville, SC, a company serving the grocery and food service trade, this brand's identity soon afterward changed, retaining Monarch and a Lion Head symbol into the 20th century, when it changed more or less into a food service label as the company was squeezed out of the grocery trade by competition. While this private label predates Eight O'Clock coffee by a year, Monarch today is more nearly positioned as a food service distributor's brand.

In 1886, the White Swan label first appeared on grocery products, supplied by E. B. Waples and Andrew Fox Platter in their company, Waples-Platter Grocery Co. in Texas. That company was destined to become the oldest continually-operated wholesale food distributor in the Southwest. Its operation in recent years became part of the Fleming Companies wholesale business, but eventually was divested.

Entry of Food Wholesalers

Unlike the retailers,many of the independent grocery wholesalers, destined to become the industry leaders in the 20th Century, were very slow to adopt private label. Their involvement came more from their association with voluntary groups. Food wholesaling in the U.S. was taking root, notably when Wetterau in 1869, began catering to both independent grocers and the pioneers heading westward on wagon trains to settle in the West. Wetterau, Hazelwood, MO, did not develop private labels until the next century. Subsequently, this wholesaler was acquired by SUPERVALU, Inc., Minneapolis. The latter today is one of the top food wholesalers in the U.S. Its private label involvement began early in this century.

Predecessor companies of SUPERVALU, formed in 1871 as Newell and Massey, adopted the name Super Valu Stores in 1956, after numerous name and ownership changes, as well as mergers. Operating as Winston and Newell in 1928, this company joined the IGA voluntary group, two years after its formation, adopting its IGA Brand. However, some 14 years later (1942), Winston and Newell dropped its IGA franchise, forming its own group of retailers around the Super Valu and U-Save store banners. Success led to the company's renaming itself "Super Valu Stores Inc." in 1954. While the first entry into its very own private label began in the mid-1930s with coffee roasting and rebagging of commodity items, such as rice, bulk beans, candy, and the like, its full private label program was officially launched in 1954 with the Super Valu logo and the Flav-o-rite brand, plus some secondary-quality lines.

Another top U.S. food wholesaler, Fleming Companies, Oklahoma City, OK, first affiliated with the IGA group around 1927. In later years, Fleming, through acquisition of other food wholesalers and retail operations, developed its own private label lines as well. The major wholesaler, Nash Finch Co., Minneapolis, MN, began in 1885 with a small store established by the Nash brothers in North Dakota, Their partner, Harry B. Finch, joined the business in 1889. It wasn't until the 1980s, however, that its Our Family private label appeared.

Urbanization & The Industrial Revolution

Commercially, the United States was young, mostly rural, and only slowly catching up with England and its Industrial Revolution. Society was changing from an agrarian to an industrial economy. People from the farms began to settle in towns and cities. Lunch was eaten away from home more frequently, in commercial outlets. Saloons proliferated, offering a nickel beer and a free lunch. The local drugstore owner, skilled at mixing elixirs and potions, also began dispensing sodas and phosphates. So the soda fountain emerged as a viable profit center for druggists, confectioners, and other operators.

A number of inventions helped this urban retail business flourish. The first food-canning plant was opened in Boston in 1819 by William Underwood. Modern refrigeration was invented by Jacob Perkins in 1834. Thanks to James J. Ritty, the cash register appeared in 1879. Luther Childs Crowell in 1867 developed the first paper bag and the paper bag-making machine. In 1869, the first transcontinental railroad linkup was established in Utah, which opened the West.

Department and "variety" stores also catered to consumers in the cities; but most commerce occurred in the farmlands. As a result, mail-order houses like Sears, Montgomery Ward and, in Canada, T. Eaton Co., Ltd., developed as well as farmers' cooperatives. Meantime, A&P's success in developing a food store chain attracted other start-up grocery chains: The Grand Union Tea Co. (founded in 1872 as Jones Brothers Tea Co. of Brooklyn, NY); Ralphs Bros. Grocery (1873); The Great Western Tea Co. (later renamed Kroger Grocery & Baking Co.) in 1883; the Acme Tea Co. in 1894; and the Jewel Tea Co. in 1899.

From the outset, these retailers adopted private label strategies. Bernard H. Kroger, for example, sold his own coffee, tea, and spices packaged in a back room of his store, which he opened in 1883. His mother made sauerkraut and processed pickles at home for sale in the store. Kroger also takes credit for introducing the bakery concept to food stores, selling a loaf of bread at 2 1/2 cents with the quality guaranteed. By 1902, when the operation was renamed Kroger Grocery & Baking Co., he had expanded to other private labels, sourced from outside suppliers. The names he adopted were drawn from the locality—Avondale, a suburb of Cincinnati, Country Club taken from the local country club, etc. Two years later, Kroger opened what probably was the first meat department in a grocery store. (Laycock 1983)

In 1899, Frank Vernon Skiff, schooled in the grocery store trade at his father's store, rented a horse-and-wagon to sell coffee, tea, spices and extracts along with housewares to housewives in the south side of Chicago. This led to Jewel Tea, established in 1901, which also featured a line of private labels.

REFERENCES/CITATIONS

Fitzell, Philip 1982. "Private Labels: Store Brands & Generic Products." (AVI Publishing Co., Inc., Westport, CT)

Hoyt, E.P. 1969. "That Wonderful A&P." Hawthorn Properties (Elsevier-Dutton Publishing Co., Inc., New York).

Laycock, George. 1983. "The Kroger Story: A Century of Innovation." The Kroger Co., Cincinnati, OH.

Progressive Grocer Magazine, publisher, 1971, "A&P: Past, Present and Future." The Butterick Division, American Can Company.

Salmon, William A. 1993. "Building on the Past: A 125 Year History of Miller & Hartman, 1868-1993." Miller & Hartman, Inc., Lancaster, PA.

CHAPTER 2

__THE ROLE OF ENTREPRENURS__

The concept of private label emerged out of the entrepreneurial merchant's desire to offer consumers more value for their dollar.

This idea perhaps first started in the United States with clothiers, particularly Henry Sands Brooks, who opened his own retail shop in New York City in 1818, becoming one of the first to sell ready-made garments rather than the more expensive custom-made suits. Eventually, the Brooks Brothers label evolved with a Golden Fleece trademark, a symbol of the British woolen merchants, dating back to the 15th century. Mr. Brooks set numerous fashion trends in the U.S. that were inspired by European fashions: silk Foulard ties, button-down shirts, Shetland sweaters, polo coats, and Harris tweed jackets. Other specialty retailers emerged as well. One of the most famous, Tiffany & Co., opened its store in 1838. Entrepreneurs Charles Lewis Tiffany and John P. Young started with a fancy goods store, including stationery, and built a reputation for quality and craftsmanship, especially in jewelry design and silverware. The Tiffany store brand has since appeared on the finest jewelry, crystal and other specially crafted gift items. Both the Brooks Brothers and Tiffany labels have endured and today are ranked among the finest private label programs in the world.

Cash Replaces Credit

The concept of product value matured when merchants refused to compromise on quality, while offering a better price than their competitors. In the urban marketplace, consumers still liked to haggle over prices and seek good credit terms, particularly when they were short on money. A number of entrepreneurs turned the tide by emphasizing a cash-only business, where they would offer their shoppers guaranteed-value on everything they purchased. In 1858, for example, Rowland Hussey Macy, a dry-goods merchant, opened R. H. Macy & Co. in New York City, establishing a one-price policy. He introduced a cash-only trade. (This practice was developed earlier by A. T. Steward, who operated Stewart's Cast Iron Palace department store in New York in 1826, revolutionizing pricing strategies with his one-price policy and a visible price tag on all his goods.) Macy started to advertise private label hoop skirts in 1860. His strategy was to sell merchandise 20 to 50% below the competition, supported with heavy advertising and top quality goods. He manufactured his own dresses, shirts, etc., while contracting with outside suppliers for other merchandise: silk cloth, gloves, and so on. (Reilly 1966).

In 1861, John Wanamaker, a merchant based in Philadelphia, set up a men's and boys' clothing store, featuring ready-to-wear clothes at a low price. As business grew, he was able to place larger orders, setting his own terms and standards of quality, and attaching his own label on the garments. Wanamaker offered full cash refunds if customers were not satisfied.

Woolworth's Nickel & Dime Legacy

In 1879, entrepreneur Frank Winfield Woolworth opened the first Woolworth's 5 and 10¢ Store in Utica, NY, selling a variety of general, bulk merchandise attractively displayed on counter tops—obviously emphasizing price in the store identity. Woolworth was strongly influenced by A&P's success, adopting the same red store front, and adding a gold-leaf gilding in the lettering and molding plus his own 'Diamond W' trademark. That mark eventually appeared on products as packaged goods entered the product mix. Perhaps the first private label was Woolco (a company acronym) crochet cotton during World War I, when imported material was cut off from consumers. Woolworth contracted with a U.S. mill for his own product. Eventually, the Woolco brand appeared on paste and glue bottles, while other private brands also appeared: Lorraine hair nets, Herald Square stationery, Fifth Avenue linen writing paper and envelopes, etc. The latter two identities came from a widely familiar location—New York City, where the company had located its headquarters. The product mix expanded over the years, and Woolworth dealt directly with manufacturers, ordering mass quantities of goods at a low price and bypassing the jobbers.

In its undated report, "The Growing Importance of Woolworth's Private Brands," the company noted that "just 12 of our brand names presently account for 85% of total private label sales"—not including the Woolworth brand. Those dozen names were: Audition radios, musical instruments, record players, and accessories; Fifth Avenue stationery; Happy Home furnishings lines; Herald Square office and school supplies; Home Cote paints and brush accessories; Lorraine hair products; Pata Cake infants wear and accessories; Petite Belle budget hosiery for women and girls; Primrose nylon hosiery and tights; Primstyle fashion clothing; Sunny Lane candies, nuts, novelties; and TopsAll men's and boys dress and sport shirts. (Fitzell 1982)

The Woolworth legacy lasted 118 years, until the company finally closed its 413 Woolworth stores in 1997, having been unable to remain profitable in recent years. Some 572 Woolworth stores were closed in 1993. Going public in 1956, F. W. Woolworth began a diversification strategy, opening specialty Foot Locker outlets. Profits in that sector (athletic footwear and Kinney shoe stores) now guarantee a future for the company, but not under the Woolworth identity. Woolworth joins other famous retail name in the department and variety store business—W.T. Grant, Bonwit Teller, Alexander's, E.J. Korvettes, etc.—which have vanished over the years. The passing of Woolworth marks the end of one of the finest private label retail operations in the world, where its quality standards were among the highest in the industry.

The idea for a cash-and-carry grocery store was still a novelty during the first decade of the 20th century. A&P, which at the time had a full-line grocery store (300+ items), still depended on credit, delivery charges, and expensive on-premise redemption centers to handle its premium business. By 1911, A&P began to pay more attention to growing competition from cash-and-carry stores. In response, its A&P Economy Store appeared with none of A&P's fancy tea emporium décor, which helped establish its success as a chain store operation—just red paint on the store front while shelves inside were stacked almost up to the ceiling with goods. There were no longer any premium give-aways, not even a phone to take mail orders. One store manager ran each operation. The formula clicked: within a few years, A&P was opening thousands of the Economy Stores, literally on a mass-production scale.

Marion Barton Skaggs, the founder of the company that in 1926 became Safeway Stores, Inc., opened his first store, a 572-square-foot outlet, in 1915 in American Falls, ID. His father, M.B. Skaggs, a Baptist minister, built the store to help wheat farmers, who were being exorbitantly charged for the high credit tabs they ran up with storekeepers. Skaggs lived by the Golden Rule, operating under the business credo, "He who serves best, profits most." His son, "M.B." purchased the store and carried on the practice of saving on both delivery costs and the cost and loss of credit by dealing strictly on a cash basis, while passing his savings on to the farmers. He also purchased goods in greater quantities to give consumers another price break. When World War I broke out, wheat demand increased; the farmers made more money and Skaggs prospered, building his chain of stores.

Mail Order Trade Flourishes

Since a majority of consumers in both the U.S. and Canada were still farmers, they carefully watched every penny they spent. So mail order business flourished. Actually, the entrepreneurs George Gilman and George Huntington Hartford began A&P as a mail-order house, called the Great Atlantic Tea Company in 1863. Their retail business followed and eventually took over. It was Aaron Montgomery Ward who in 1872 really dedicated his efforts to the mail order trade. Ward offered a money-back guarantee on merchandise of high quality, sold at wholesale prices. For example, he commissioned the Singer Manufacturing Co. to make his own brand, The New Home sewing machine, which he sold at $26 by mail order, while the Singer sewing machine sold for $50 at retail. Recognizing this success, Richard Warren Sears, a watchmaker in Minneapolis, decided in 1886 to move to Ward's marketing area, Chicago, to form a partnership with Alvah Curtis Roebuck. Their company, Sears, Roebuck and Company, began by taking mail orders from farmers for watches, watch chains, and other jewelry items, silverware, etc., while bargaining with suppliers for the lowest price with a promise of high-volume sales. Sears' catalog,"Consumer's Guide," debuted in 1894.

Ward's success must also have influenced a Canadian, Timothy Eaton, who started as a Toronto retailer in 1883. In the following year, he dispatched his first mail-order catalog, including private label merchandise (2- and 3-cent wool gloves, etc.). By 1904, the company introduced its first trademark, "Eatonia," for shoes—a name that became so popular that a town in Saskatchewan was named after it. His store terms: cash only, no extended credit. Eaton became almost as large as Sears in terms of its mail order catalog business. His private label identities were drawn from England, such as Canterbury, Haddon Hall, and so forth. By 1917, this entrepreneur established his own product research laboratory—and then began opening factories for furniture, soft goods, stoves and refrigerators. These operations became too expensive to maintain and were sold off. The Eaton private labels at one time grew to 129 names.

The success of retail mail order business, however, stirred up resentment from local merchants. Sears, who sold to shopkeepers as well as consumers, for a time tried to appease retailer anger by leaving the identity off articles he sold, not even carrying the Sears name on packages to protect the customers. Meantime, the Sears catalog carried some manufacturer's brands, but mostly its own family of labels. Sears started with watches, then expanded into shoes, clothing, wagons, stoves, etc. No manufacturers' brand names were used, all goods were Sears items, which eventually erupted into "a blizzard of brand names." Sears also picked up on price lines as well—"Good," "Better," "Best." — (Weil 1977) Names like Acme and Kenwood appeared on hard goods lines (bicycles, clocks, ranges, etc.). By the turn of the century, Sears had sales exceeding $10 million, while Wards was close behind at about $8 million. The catalog identified Sears as the "Cheapest Supply House on Earth," and "The Great Price Maker." All merchandise was sold with a money-back guarantee. Just before the turn of the century, Montgomery Ward set up a product testing lab, while Sears Laboratories began about 1905.

Success not only breeds imitators, but also deep-seated jealousies from competitors hurt by the successful newcomers. *The American Grocer*, a trade magazine started in 1869, launched a series of articles against the A&P monopoly on behalf of the independent grocers, who were being undercut in tea prices. A&P was then called "The Great American Tea Company" (renamed "The Atlantic & Pacific Tea Co." in 1869).

REFERENCES/CITATIONS

Fitzell, Philip 1982. "Private Labels: Store Brands & Generic Products." AVI Publishing Company, Inc., Westport, CT, p. 57.

Reilly, Philip J. 1966. "Old Masters of Retailing: A History of Merchant-Pioneers and the Industry They Built." Fairchild Publications, Inc., New York.

Weil, Gordon L. 1977. "Sears, Roebuck U.S.A.: The Great American Catalog Store and How It Grew." Stein and Day/Publishers, New York, pp. 152-53.

CHAPTER 3

EMERGENCE OF BRAND NAME MANUFACTURERS

In the United States, brands were practically non-existent in the early 19th century. Brand names emerged late in the century, introduced by retail merchants, wholesale grocers, mail-order houses, and manufacturers. The manufacturers eventually took control of the marketplace on the basis of their commitment to premium giveaways, print advertising, new product development and research, and attractive packaging concepts. Socializing more away from the home or farm, consumers encountered these brands at beer gardens, hotels, bars, restaurants, soda fountains, lunch counters, expositions, county fairs, and even World Fairs. Consumers also became more conditioned to brand advertising in newspapers, magazines and on streetcars or on road and building signs. By the 20th century, it was radio advertising initially, later followed by television, that made Americans even more aware of the brands.

The U.S. Civil War (1861-65), helped establish brand recognition somewhat, as soldiers transplanted far away from home were supplied with basics like Procter & Gamble's Star candles and soap. P&G, founded in 1837, was launched as a national brand company in 1876, when Harley Procter dreamed up the ad slogan, "It floats," for Ivory soap. The first Ivory soap ad, appearing in a religious magazine, promoted laundry soap with "all the fine qualities of a choice Toilet soap." Procter emphasized the slogan "99 and 44/100 percent pure ." The ad still distinguished Ivory soap from its competitors by indicating that "Ivory Soap will 'float.'"

Advertising Helps Establish Brand Names

The brands established name recognition through advertising, often using a symbol and slogan to help consumers remember the product and associate it with the brand name. This strategy differentiated them from the competition, and as a result brand equity development began with some of today's market leaders in the forefront. For example, the Colgate-Palmolive Co., New York, which started in 1806 as a producer of commodities like soap, starch, and candles, didn't take on national brand significance until 1877 with the launch of Colgate toothpaste, which first appeared in a tube package 13 years later.

One of the most notable brand pioneers in advertising was the Lever Brothers Company in England, which started in 1885. William Hesketh Lever and his brother James packaged probably the world's first branded laundry soap, Sunlight. The product was launched with an ad campaign that played on a woman's vanity, suggesting she need not be aged by the "wash-day evil" of laundry work, if she used Sunlight. By the turn of the century, this brand was selling in Australia, Europe, South Africa, and the United States, taking on a global presence.

Numerous beverage brands emerged during this period. As far back as 1872, Schlitz was being advertised as, "The beer that made Milwaukee famous." Anheuser-Busch took on its name in 1879, after Adolphus Busch bought an interest in the Bavarian Brewery (1852) in St. Louis. The brewery already had been using an "A & Eagle" trademark on its beer packaging since 1872. Five years later, that trademark was registered with the U.S. Patent Office. (Actually, the U.S. trademark registration law was passed in 1870.) Other manufacturers also were quick to register trademarks; the Quaker Oats' Quaker man, 1877, and Procter & Gamble's Moon & Stars trademark, 1882.

The Budweiser brand was introduced in 1876 but the company had numerous other brands. It wasn't until the 1890s that "Bud" became its flagship brew. Busch was a master marketer at the time, pioneering in giveaway premiums: corkpulls, hat clips, matchsafes, watchfobs, tokens, and pocket knifes. The latter first appeared with bone and pearl handles, given out to saloon owners and customers by Anheuser Busch's traveling salesmen. By the turn of the century, the company was one of the first to use electrically-lighted "spectacular" outdoor signs—Times Square in New York City had a flashing sign of the A & Eagle logo, according to historical background information provided by Anheuser-Busch.

Similarly, Campbell Soup Co., Camden, NJ (established in 1869) first advertised its soup brand on New York City streetcars in 1899. Five years later, the Campbell kids appeared on streetcar ads.

In 1885, Dr Pepper was sold over the counter at the Morrison's Old Corner Drug Store in Waco, TX. Progressing as a brand, its message to consumers emphasized content, wheat and iron, while offering "vim, vigor & vitality."

Coca-Cola appeared in 1886 as an exotic medicinal product in the patent medicine field. Of course, bottled soda waters had been around since 1835, when Joseph Hawkins and Elias Duran, both from Philadelphia, began producing them. The soda fountain had gained in popularity for socializing, gradually helping soda water to gain in consumer acceptance. Since 1871, White Rock had built its reputation around club soda, tonic water, and sparkling mineral water. Coca-Cola, in turn, built its brand equity by advertising its product as a healthful aid to digestion and a refreshing pick-me-up carbonated beverage. Coca-Cola also established consumer recognition via impressive point-of-sale materials. The "Coke" brand identity was further hammered home by its patented Coca-Cola bottle, designed by C.J. Root in 1915.

Success Breeds Imitators

Smith Brothers cough drops were first sold out of James Smith's restaurant in Poughkeepsie, NY in 1847. Their success was quickly imitated, when competitors tried to confuse the consumer into thinking the imitative product that they produced was Smith Brothers. This competition forced the Smith Brothers to design a trademark of themselves with the words "Trade" and "Mark," each under one of the brother's pictures. In 1872, they began packaging their product, factory-filled, in paper boxes.

Many of today's familiar brand names, in a great number of different product categories, appeared late in the 19th century: Salada tea, Pillsbury Best flour, Gold Medal flour, Ralston Purina animal feed, Kellogg's corn flakes, Post Grape Nuts flakes, Folgers coffee, Maxwell House coffee, Pepsi Cola soda, Miller High Life beer, Chase & Sanborn coffee, 20-Mule Team Borax laundry booster, National Arrowroot cookies, Uneeda crackers, Gillette disposable safety razors, Del Monte canned fruit and vegetables, Wrigley gum, etc. These brands helped establish or even launch product categories. Welch grape juice, for example, was first formulated in 1869 by Thomas B. Welch from pasteurized "unfermented wine," used for his church's communion service. Charles E. Hires, who developed a formula for Hires root beer, gained national attention at the 1876 Philadelphia Centennial. His product became the first soft drink to achieve such recognition, helped by aggressive advertising and promotional support. Necco (New England Confectionery Co.), Cambridge, MA, founded in 1847, today remains the oldest multi-line candy firm in the United States. It wasn't until 1902, however that its conversation candy hearts debuted, as well as the firm's best-seller, Necco Wafers.

All these brands were quick to respond to radio, the newest advertising medium. In the 1920s and 1930s, for example, Chase & Sanborn sponsored "The Chase & Sanborn Hour," starring Edgar Bergen and Charlie McCarthy.

Some brands, such as Chase & Sanborn, also eventually became part of multi-company consolidations and/or acquisitions. C&S combined with Royal Baking Powder and Fleischmann in 1929 to become Standard Brands. Another example: C.P.C. International (now called Best Foods), Englewood Cliffs, NJ, which now controls some leading category brands that trace their origin back into the 19th century: Knorr soup (1858), Argo corn starch (1892), Mazola corn oil (1911), Hellmann's mayonnaise (1912), Skippy peanut butter (1933). Actually, the last brand had originally been formulated by Joseph Rosenfield in 1916, who seven years later received a patent for stabilized peanut butter, helping to create this product category by the early 1920s.

The 20th Century

CHAPTER 4

______AN OVERVIEW PERSPECTIVE OF 100 YEARS______

For the grocery and drug store trade, the 20th century represents a period of accelerated changes, market maturity and, through mergers, acquisitions, and expansions, a consolidation of businesses into larger corporations. In fact, this period of nearly 100 years represents an amalgamation of different players and/or trade activities, where companies have become intricately connected through parternering in different aspects of the business—retailing, wholesaling, manufacturing or processing. Richfood Holdings, Inc., Richmond, VA, serves as a good example of this trend, as reported in its 1995 annual report, subtitled, "Innovation, Efficiency and Expansion for 60 Years, 1935-1995."

During the Great Depression, 13 neighborhood grocers banded together to form Richmond Food Stores, Inc., in 1935, operating as a cooperative in order to buy direct from manufacturers and circumvent the inflated markups (20% or higher) they had been receiving from food wholesalers. Some 20 years later, the co-op's private label, Richfood, was introduced in the bread category and expanded to other product areas. By 1960, Richmond Food was a full-service food wholesaler. To boost recognition of its growing Richfood private label line, the company in 1974 renamed itself Richfood Inc. Through an acquisition, the firm became affiliated with IGA, Inc., the country's largest voluntary group of independent grocers. Through more grocery wholesaler acquisitions, Richfood developed into the fourth largest food wholesaler in the country. For example, its customer base in the Mid-Atlantic Region boasts Acme Food Stores, a division of American Stores, one of the country's largest supermarket chains. Richfood also operates its own dairy processing plant.

Every player in the business— retailers, wholesalers, cooperatives, food service distributors, manufacturers, brokers, voluntary groups, suppliers, and so on—has been significantly refocused by competitive upheavals. Additionally, in this century, foreign grocers (particularly from Canada and Europe) had begun to play a more significant role in shaping the food and drug store industry in the U.S., while at the same time bringing more aggressive private label strategies into play. As a result, the private label model overall has undergone a dramatic metamorphosis, evolving from back-room, mom-and-pop preparations into a global business, orchestrated by multi-billion-dollar retail-wholesale corporations.

Retail Chains Versus Independent Grocers

As the giant food chains emerged, private label continued to serve as a catalyst for growth. The early food chains became the biggest volume buyers and/or producers of food products under both manufacturers' brands and private label. Chains started in the 19th century, such as A&P, Grand Union, Acme, and Kroger, were joined by others: Alpha Beta (1900), Vons (1906), Ralphs Grocery (1911), Safeway (1915), American Stores (1917), and so on. Their stores started as small service-oriented groceries, evolved into cash-and carry operations, and then grew into regional supermarket chains, which could secure volume purchases of product and therefore receive price concessions from manufacturers.

For independent grocers, who had formed into voluntary groups and were working through wholesalers or retailer-owned cooperatives with their own distribution center, private labels became a critical means of survival against the growing chain store competition. Through their collective organization, often unified under controlled labels that were theirs exclusively, the voluntaries and cooperatives could cut procurement and distribution costs through carload purchases of product from manufacturers, thus realizing greater operating efficiencies, just like the chain stores. Since these groups controlled their own brands (private labels), they could:

(1) offer consumers a price advantage over the name brands,
(2) gain wider distribution of their control labels,
(3) advertise their own brands,
(4) plan merchandising and sales promotions through the group, and
(5) even extend the buying options for consumers by introducing other control brands at another quality level.

Additionally, private labels afforded the smaller manufacturers who supplied both the chains and the independents the opportunity to not only compete more effectively against the emerging, giant national-brand manufactures but also, later in the century, to expand into the export business.

Manufacturers' Brands Dominate the Market

For the most important player in this trade—the consumer—the perception of private label value began to diminish early in the 20th century, because name brand manufacturers steadily captured more shopper loyalty. Brand manufacturers developed national distribution quickly, and continually reinforced their brand equity image through advertising. The manufacturers also reinforced their growing market share:

- by innovating with new product development,
- by frequently improving their product quality,
- by introducing new refinements to the product as well as product extensions, and
- by presenting their products in more aesthetically-appealing packages.

No single retailer or wholesaler—not even the giant A&P chain or the fast-growing independent grocers, dealing through voluntary groups like Red & White or IGA—ever achieved geographic distribution equal to the name brands, at least for some, not until late in this century. Brand proliferation, however, did not eliminate the private label presence. In fact, hundreds of different private labels were developed by some of the leading grocery chains in a copycat fashion.

The biggest boost to manufacturer brands domination came from advertising, first in the growing religious and consumer publications, which started late in the 19th century, and then in radio, which appeared in the 1920s, followed by television in the 1940s. While some retailers/wholesalers, even during these formative years, did advertise their private labels in those media, the brand manufacturers carried most of the advertising clout. Overshadowed by the brands in the limelight, the retailer's store brand retreated, adopting a lower pricing image in order to attract a consumer following, while following the lead of the national brands in terms of product quality standards. Private label packaging for the most part remained static—keeping the same look for decades. As a result, the perception of quality in private labels began to wane as the name brands gained in popularity. Private label attempted to develop a copycat alternative, but could not keep pace with the changing product quality and variety, convenience features, package styling refinements, and new feature developments of the name brands.

Private label literally had to seek its own level in a whirlwind of change during the first half of the 20th century. Within the chain store operations, private label did gain strength in the bakery, meat and dairy areas. These perishable products required high-cost delivery, which was partly circumvented when the food chains built their own integrated processing and delivery systems. This strategy also gave the chains a price advantage over any brand processor.

On the manufacturing side, as competition grew among the name brands, product categories began to evolve into organized industries, particularly in the canned fruits and vegetables and the frozen foods areas. Within these industries, major branded manufacturers emerged in different product categories, creating consumer demand for their products via different advertising and promotional strategies. Generating stronger consumer demand, some brands could exercise control over the marketplace. Birds Eye, for example, would license only certain distributors on a geographic basis to carry its frozen Birds Eye brand products. To stay competitive, others had to fend for themselves if they wanted to stock frozen goods. They sought supplies via services provided by distributors and/or brokers. In this manner, they could order manufacturers' packer labels or their own private label products. This competition intensified. Yet, the brand manufacturers continued to gain market share. When Minute Maid frozen orange juice became an overnight success after its introduction in the 1940s, the pipelines could not be filled fast enough. Grocers had to seek out private label substitutes to satisfy consumer demand.

Private labels became the Cinderella of the retail-wholesale trade—hidden but still a very effective profit builder. It wasn't until the 1980s that private label attended the ball, so to speak. In the earlier decades, private label owners tried to create a brand image within their stores—stocking literally hundreds of packer labels, control labels, or private brands—most following the lead of the nationally-advertised manufacturers brands. Their private label business basically followed the market leaders. In the 1980s, nondescript generics emerged as not so much exclusive as a low-priced, standard or acceptable quality line of products for both retailers and wholesalers. As the owners of generics, the retailers, wholesalers, and brokers set all the packaging, merchandising, and marketing rules. By doing so, they began to extend that control into their first-tier store brand program in terms of better quality, more attractive packaging, and a marketing strategy. Retailers also had a new tool—scanners that tracked sales at the cash register through Uniform Price Coding (UPC). They no longer had to rely only on the word of brand name manufacturers, who could afford to buy market research data on case-withdrawals from the warehouse, tracked by a market research service. Retailers now knew first-hand what brands were selling in their stores.This data, however, was subsidized by the brand manufacturers. Throughout the 1970s and 1980s, it reported only flat private label sales in contrast to continued sales growth for the brand leaders.

Retailers As Manufacturers

For most of this century, it wasn't so much a question of the leading manufacturers' brands claiming a monopoly on quality. Retailers for decades had proven they could manufacture/process their own products alone or, through cooperatives or voluntary groups, buy top-quality goods from outside suppliers. Some retailers also had years of experience in developing their own manufacturing capability. Examples include A&P, which in the early part of the century became the largest food manufacturer in the world. Not far behind, its competitor, Safeway, in the mid-1930s operated 21 bakeries, six creameries, six coffee roasting plants, three meat distributing plants, a milk condensery, a candy and syrup factory, and a mayonnaise plant, along with a produce company for purchasing of fresh fruits and vegetables.

In the drug store segment, Charles R. Walgreen, Sr., opened his first Walgreen drug store in 1901 and, within 10 years, was producing his own line of drug products. Eventually, an ice cream plant was added. Decades later, this leading drug store chain became one of the largest private label manufacturing companies in the industry, producing more than 500 different Walgreen brand products in the mid-1970s.

Consumers Put Out of Focus

It is ironic that in the 20th century, the grocery industry's focus on serving consumers needs came full circle around to the strategies adopted by the entrepreneurs of the last century. These pioneers then offered consumers value for their dollar—low prices for high-quality goods. As business matured in the United States, competition intensified, making competition itself the center of attention. The retailers, wholesalers, manufacturers, suppliers, brokers, government agencies, literally everyone, began to pay less attention to the consumer and put more focus on keeping business and commerce fair for everyone. They felt that an even playing field would benefit consumers, giving them more purchasing options, because there would be more competition in the marketplace. So monopolies were attacked, particularly the chain food stores. Power was taken away from the retail chains and put up for grabs by the manufacturers.

It is doubly ironic that the brand manufacturers were permitted carte blanche market share monopolies in their respective product categories. Actually, consumer brand loyalty fostered by strong advertising, couponing, and promotional activities, helped these brand leaders succeed. The brand imitators or competitors also encouraged the brand leaders within different product categories to develop new, improved products and to enhance their packaging presentation as well. The national brands became the market leaders in a highly competitive marketplace. Toward the end of the 20th century, however, a number of the brand manufacturers began to abuse their power by raising prices, compromising on product quality, down-sizing packs, etc., all in the interest of raising profits for their shareholders. This trend encouraged the retailers to regain some control over what they could stock in their stores. This was accomplished by building their private label business with better packaging, improved product quality, and more aggressive merchandising and marketing efforts, while still maintaining value with lower pricing.

Private Label Gains Marketing Strength

As a result, private label—the tool that differentiated retailing entrepreneurs during the industry's formative years—resurfaced in a stronger marketing position first encouraged by the short-lived success of generics late in the 1970s and early 1980s, extended into improved first-line private label programs throughout the 1980s, and expanded more with upscale premium quality store brands in the 1990s. Through better category management strategies, the retailers and wholesalers were now calling more of the shots—and winning market share for private label. In fact, this convinced some brand manufacturers to adopt merchandising and marketing strategies practiced by the private label owners. Their marketing focus returned to giving the consumers value for their dollar, such as lower prices, bonus packs, two-for-the-price-of-one offers, and the like.

Over this Century, advertising support really gave the brand manufacturers the edge in the marketplace: Retail proprietors could not match the multi-million-dollar advertising budgets of the brands. Private label did attract a consumer following, but mostly on the basis of its lower price, promoted in the store and through newspaper or direct mail flyers. It has been argued that the pioneering merchants of the 19th century, many of whom practiced the Golden Rule, gradually were replaced by professional managers in the 20th century who were more interested in management techniques and financial backing. This transition also helped to sever their contact with the consumer. They became less interested in passing their savings on to the customer and more intent on building profits for future family owners in a company and/or its stockholders. The entrepreneurial spirit was weakened in the marketplace and only reappeared late in the century, when management strategies changed more to team-oriented management, which again fostered an entrepreneurial spirit that paid more attention to what consumers really want.

_____Early 20th Century Values (1900-50)_________

CHAPTER 5

__NEW IDEAS, NEW STRATEGIES__

At the turn of the century, consumers were still wary of peddlers, who often charged exorbitant prices, offering lame excuses for their price which only the gullible would swallow. As a result, *caveat emptor* (let the buyer beware) became the watchword in any transaction for decades. Some of the retail-wholesale entrepreneurs dealt fairly and honestly with consumers, earning their respect and loyalty by offering value: high-quality merchandise at a low price.

A Low Price, Small Profits Game Plan

Bernard H. Kroger at 23 years opened his first store in Cincinnati in 1883. His strategy was simple: buy direct from producers and sell to the consumer at lower prices than the competition. He sold on a small margin and worked toward the rapid turnover of goods. By 1902, he renamed The Great Western Tea Co., a chain of 40 stores—The Kroger Grocery & Baking Co.

One of the first wholesale grocers to abandon the *caveat emptor* policy was S. M. Flickinger, who believed in working for the buyer at retail and for his customer, the consumer. Flickinger considered his customers' interest as his own in starting up the Red & White voluntary group of independent grocers in the early 1920s. As a retailer, he serviced the consumer with top-quality products at the lowest possible price, guaranteeing the quality, or money refunded. This became a principle of private label programs in the decades that followed.

In fact, private label already had become an integral part of the value placed on merchandise purchased in stores. It certainly helped A&P, the oldest food chain in existence, build its consumer following. The founders, George Huntington Hartford and his two sons, George Ludlum and John Augustine, for example, applied the Golden Rule right from the beginning, providing "more and better foods to more people for less money." This company objective was summarized by John Hartford in a published 1944 letter to his employees. Hartford explained further that this goal was the reason why A&P produced its own private label products, becoming more proficient in procuring, processing and packing foods, while developing outside manufacturing or packer sources for its controlled brands. Hartford also emphasized the company policy: "Always do what is honest, fair, sincere, and in the best interests of our customers." A&P employees gained in their compensation and fringe benefits. Virtually no one left this company, which treated its workers so well. A&P also kept its prices at rock-bottom levels, taking the smallest profit possible, concentrating instead on building its sales volume. Why would its customers want to shop anywhere else? A&P was founded on the family ethic—focused on giving the consumer value with satisfaction guaranteed. The company for years had issued free recipes and household hints to its shoppers via *A&P Menu* and other company publications and, in 1937, launched *Women's Day*, a helpful consumer magazine that quickly become the seventh largest of its kind in terms of circulation (3 million copies per month), which survives to this date, under separate ownership.

Chain Stores Multiply

In 1900, A&P operated some 200 grocery stores with sales exceeding $5 million. This chain, which in the previous century started with tea, then added its own brand of baking powder, followed by coffee, then other grocery items, such as sugar, canned milk, bulk butter, and spices and extracts, became a sort of one-stop shopping experience for the consumer. A&P opened the new century with an expanded product mix, which included cocoa, flour, and canned foods. More products were added, such as soups, soaps, and other packaged goods. Within a dozen years, A&P doubled in size to 400 stores, generating sales of $26.6 million. Its small grocery stores stocked some 300 items, while a good part of the store shelving was taken up with premium merchandise. Premiums and trading stamps were still a vital part of the business.

Other emerging chains followed a similar growth pattern, starting with coffee and tea, spices, and extracts. Frank Vernon Skiff, who worked in his father's grocery store in Chicago, went into business for himself, first with a horse-and-wagon delivery route that became Jewel Tea. By 1901, Skiff introduced some own brand labels to the business. Together with his partner, brother-in-law Frank Ross, he watched the business grow, meanwhile also still depending on premiums like Haviland china. Skiff found that housewives resisted his door-to-door sales pitch as a peddler. So he adopted a policy of giving his customers premiums in advance, provided they promised to buy products from him. In making the transition from a service-route business to a chain store operation, Jewel president Maurice Karker in 1934 hired a business consultant to interview 18,000 Chicago housewives in order to formulate guiding principles of service, which were called the Jewel Ten Commandments:

1. Clean and white stores
2. Friendliness
3. Self-service
4. True quality
5. Freshness
6. Low prices
7. Honest weights
8. Variety of foods
9. Fair dealings
10. The Jewel Guarantee—complete satisfaction or money back with a smile.

Its private label stock was not exempt from these Commandments. (Jewel 1979)

Kroger Innovates

Bernard H. Kroger, who started the Great Western Tea Co. in 1883, entered the private label business right away by packaging coffee and tea in the store's back room. An innovator from the start, Kroger was among the first grocery stores to advertise regularly in newspapers, beginning in 1884. In the private label area, he became the first grocer to operate his own bakeries in 1901. Instead of buying bread from independent bakeries, he established his own production, allowing him to cut the price per loaf to 2 1/2 cents—a bargain, with the quality guaranteed. It cost him 2.4 cents to produce the loaf, leaving him 1/10-of-a-cent profit. Kroger also is credited with being the first grocer to establish a meat market department around 1904. (Actually, he bought out a local meat merchant, taking over his business.) Kroger also was among the first in the grocery trade to establish strict specifications for private label and to maintain his own quality assurance laboratory for testing products on a regular basis. In 1930, the company established the Kroger Food Foundation, a division staffed by some two dozen food chemists and home economists. By this time, Kroger had fully developed his manufacturing operation, which in 1932 became the Cincinnati Factory, producing peanut butter, candy, exotic coffees, teas, and spices and extracts, as well as milk and bakery products. (Laycock 1983)

Practically everything documented about the formative years of the food and drug store industry focuses on chain store developments. Very little has been written about the independent mom-and-pop retailers and wholesalers at this time, because they were so small and not yet organized into voluntary groups or cooperatives. However, A&P, the market leader, was influenced by a new concept in grocery retailing: the cash & carry stores, operated by small independent retailers. These outlets had no frills, no costly delivery charges, no premium giveaways, no trading stamps, no store servicing of gift merchandise, no phone orders, and no charge accounts. Impressed, A&P reacted by introducing its A&P Economy Store concept in 1911. It was really a no-frills box store, operated by a manager-clerk. No deliveries were made, no credit was allowed. It just stocked groceries at cheap prices. Within a couple of years of the launch, some 1,600 Economy Stores were in operation. It was the start of the biggest store roll-out in history.

Controlled Brand Distribution Idea Is Born

Of course, A&P captured most of the trade attention. Nevertheless, at this time, one of the most revolutionary developments in the grocery trade was in an incubation stage. It was an effort to solidify cooperation between the wholesaler and the manufacturer, using a controlled label. In a typewritten article, in 1951, Emil Frank of

The Frank Tea and Spice Company, Cincinnati, OH, an importer and manufacturer, indicated that the first attempt at this cooperation had begun in 1909, when an Illinois-based canning company wanted to market its brand of baked beans nationally. (Frank did not mention specific names.) An unnamed advertising agency in Chicago advised the canner that the advertising costs would be prohibitive. And so, instead, the agency conceived of the idea of having one brand advertised and controlled locally by a wholesale grocer. The Yours Truly brand became the exclusive property of the wholesalers, who would contract for carloads of the baked beans under that brand. Although the ad agency spent all its advertising allowance up front, the idea appeared viable, especially if other product lines were to be added, and additional allowances could be made available. The writer continues: "For substantial fees, in succession, they interested a coffee firm in Chicago, a milling firm in Michigan, a catsup and soup firm in Indianapolis, and a cocoa firm in New Jersey. These lines were offered to the same distributors who had agreed to sell the baked beans, and the same course was pursued, namely, to spend the money advertising locally based on a yearly contract.

"The writer's firm was the sixth one to sign up with them. A fee was paid for the right to pack the 'Yours Truly' brand of spices, extracts, and specialties. Again the fee was used for selling expense, and again the money that had been allotted for advertising was spent. Although the manufacturers had an organization, the advertising firm had sole control of the selling and merchandising." — (Frank 1951)

While the agency collected commissions on advertising, it did not manage its advertising allowances. In 1912, a manufacturer-investor gave $250,000 to the agency for this activity, but no real merchandising effort was made on behalf of the wholesaler and retailer. Result: the organization went out of business. Frank continues: "... even though it was not successful, it was a pioneering effort. The manufacturers recognized the value of cooperative effort between manufacturer and wholesaler, and the advantages of one brand distribution were often discussed. All efforts to cooperate ceased about 1913."

The concept of buying clubs years earlier had been tried in the drug store business. In 1904, local pharmacies in Toronto organized and incorporated under the name Drug Trading Company Ltd., selling all drug lines at manufacturers' list prices. In Chicago, Charles R. Walgreen, Sr., in 1911 joined with 15 other non-competing druggists on the city's South Side to launch the Velvet Buying Club. Their group was renamed Federated Drug Co. in 1914.

In the grocery business, the cooperative concept between manufacturers and wholesalers was again tested in 1912, when a tea and coffee salesman, George

Lewis, based in Chicago, organized a similar effort to Yours Truly around his Serv-us brand. The Serv-us label carried coupons good for premiums. Lewis took care of the redemption process from his Chicago office, while jobbers around the country carried small displays of premiums. Lewis collected his income from brokerage paid by the manufacturers and paid Serv-us jobbers according to their volume of purchases. Lewis got food manufacturers to agree to pack under the single brand, while giving control over the label to one wholesaler in a market. For the next nine years, until his death in 1921, Lewis carried on a successful business, using premiums and coupons along with numerous label changes. He even opened a cooperative evaporated milk condensing plant, selling stock in the concern to the jobbers. After World War I, however, a slump closed the plant. However, the focus on merchandising support was missed, even though the product quality was excellent. The manufacturers, wholesalers and retailers couldn't get together on effective merchandising strategies.

Flickinger Starts First Voluntary Group & Control Label

Credit for the first successful voluntary group movement in the United States—based upon a true partnership between wholesaler and retailer—really must go to Smith M. Flickinger, a wholesale grocer and retailer, who in 1921 acquired all the assets and debts of the Serv-Us Food Products Corp. Flickinger, orphaned at age two, was raised by neighboring farmers, who taught him the value of hard work and frugality. In 1902, at about 38 years of age, he started into the wholesale grocery business as a jobber with savings of $16,000. From its infancy, his business was unified, because Flickinger allowed his employees to become stockholders. In 1918, he opened his first Flickinger grocery store. From there, he build a chain of stores—69 stores by 1919 and 194 outlets by 1921. At the time, he also operated three wholesale jobbing houses, which served the warehousing and distribution needs of independent grocers.

Flickinger recognized the threat of the bigger food chains to the old-line wholesale grocers or independent retailers, who usually dealt with jobbers, who, in turn, tried to charge all that traffic would bear. They were dragging the independents down with them, as the big chains moved toward cash-and-carry operations, emphasizing clean stores and quick product turnover. The chains also used their own warehouses as distribution centers. From 1910 to 1930, the food chains grew to control one-third of the food distribution industry. In Buffalo, NY, his base of operations, records show that from 1918 through 1926, out of 5,125 new firms that entered the independent grocery business in that city, 83% passed from the record books. Retail grocery merchandising was called "one of the most hazardous of all businesses," according to the Statistical Survey, University of Buffalo, Bureau of Business & Social Research (1928—Volume 10, No. 4).

Flickinger capitalized on this situation. In a 1931 Buffalo, NY, newspaper interview, he remarked: "Our plan is not to go into a market and drive other people out of business, but rather to take and reorganize business concerns that are having trouble meeting the changing conditions. Our policy is to conserve, not to destroy." Against chain competition, the independent grocers, who depended on nationally-advertised merchandise for their profits, were being squeezed out of business. They needed their own private brands, just like the corporate chains, to make extra profits.

The Flickinger strategy was spelled out in the first issue (Aug. 1, 1921) of his consumer newspaper, "Flickinger Stores News: Journal of Household Economics," issued twice a month to consumers:

"Mr. Flickinger has always been an earnest student of economics as applied to the distribution of foodstuffs and realized that under the old method of distribution there was a certain percentage of waste and a duplication of effort, to bring the merchandise into the hands of the consuming public. The chain store industry was growing rapidly on account of savings affected and the retail grocer was being more and more handicapped and was rapidly dropping out of business. It was then that it was decided to go into the chain store business in connection with the wholesale business, and in 1918, we organized the Flickinger Stores, starting with one store, and gradually adding others until today we have 194 stores located in Buffalo, Jamestown, Rochester and in the small towns of Western New York and Western Pennsylvania.

"Our stock issues have all been sold to the small investor. We believe in the co-operative idea and all funds have been raised in this manner. There is no capitalist connected in any way with the Flickinger organization, our idea and plans being to have these stores owned by the people themselves.

"Our retail chain of stores has been a success from the start, its future is secure and its possibilities unlimited. Our one idea at all times is to be of service to the public, purchasing only first-class wholesome grocery products, which are passed upon by experts and passed along to the public at the smallest operating profit possible, to maintain excellent service, giving the benefit of the highest efficiency and large purchasing power direct to the consumer.

"We claim to sell all good groceries at a smaller margin of profit than any other organization, carrying the leading nationally advertised brands of foodstuffs and specializing on the Serv-us brand, which is recognized as among the best that can be produced." — (Flickinger, S.M., 1921)

To bring the same efficiencies to the independents, Flickinger first tried to convince retailers around the Buffalo, NY, area to buy dry groceries from the Flickinger Company, which would, in turn, lower the price of those goods to merchants as well as significantly cut the selling costs to customers in turn. But because of retailer loyalties to other wholesalers, there was resistance to this idea. So Flickinger created his own chain, the Serv-Us Food Stores, signing up retailers as Serv-us grocers, offering his cooperative plan to these independents in the surrounding Buffalo area. This wholesale business thrived, because he adopted the chainstore methods—encouraging retailers to devote their time to selling goods, keeping their stores clean, and applying merchandising strategies. They could let Flickinger worry about purchasing goods.

Flickinger believed in honesty, fairness and the Golden Rule. Raised on a farm, he learned the value of hard work and the importance of work ethics. He also was an idealist, according to Emil Frank in his written observations, entitled, "The First Attempt to Market a Branded Line of Food Products Packed by Various Independent Manufacturers."

Interests of Wholesalers & Retailers Gel

Frank noted that "Mr. Flickinger built the business with the thought that every policy and every move should have the best interests of the retailer and consumer at heart. About 1921," he continued, "there was a meeting held in Cincinnati, attended by a dozen of the wholesale grocers who had been interested in the old 'Serv-us' plan. Mr. Flickinger explained his plan, and the writer remembers distinctly the feeling of doubt expressed by the wholesalers present. They could not understand that the interests of wholesaler and retailer were the same and that a wholesaler could show a retailer his costs. They could not understand that supervisors could replace salesmen." (Frank 1951)

The following year, the Serv-us brand was changed to Red & White and the operation renamed the Red & White Corp., working through offices in Chicago and San Francisco. Slocum Bergren Co., Minneapolis, joined the group as its second wholesaler, followed by H. A. Marr Co., Denver; C. A. Cross Co., Fitchburg, MA; and other wholesalers in Texas, Louisiana, and the far west. Of course, it was not all smooth sailing, according to Frank. Some wholesalers thought about pulling out to start their own branch offices, "but the character of Flickinger and his associates with their ideals kept the group together," while fostering loyalty to the manufacturers. Several manufacturers, in fact, were instrumental in keeping the group together, Frank reported.

Meantime, there were still wholesalers purchasing the Serv-Us line, as part of the cooperative effort started by Lewis. Flickinger was able to convince them that their interests and the independent retailers were the same and that the wholesaler could report costs to the retailer. In effect, the supervisors at wholesale became the salesmen or jobbers. When this idea was accepted, it marked the true beginning of the voluntary chain movement in the U.S. The idea was quickly copied by other groups.

In reviewing the career of S. M. Flickinger as an industry pioneer, *The Voluntary and Cooperative Groups Magazine*, a trade publication, offered these observations on the start-up of the Red and White voluntary group:

"The name 'Red and White' originated from a secondary brand (that) Mr. Flickinger had registered. He thought the name would be appropriate for the retail stores because A&P painted its stores red, and he decided to have the retailers in his group paint their stores red and white. Later this was changed to an exterior red and a white interior.

"The first group contracts required the retailers to buy from the Flickinger Company 100% of their requirements of those items that the Flickinger Company handled, plus a pro-rata assessment for advertising. Early advertising was chiefly in the form of weekly handbills. (Such a contract is probably in restraint of trade and illegal.)

"Smith Flickinger offered his Red and White voluntary group plan to other wholesalers without any charge for the franchise. Those wholesalers, who wanted to start a voluntary group of their own, following the Red and White plan, each invested $1,500 in the capital stock of the Red and White Corporation. This was nominally to finance private label supplies. Slocum, Bergren and Wash Company of Minneapolis was one of the first wholesalers to get into the Red and White movement." (The Voluntary and Cooperative Groups Magazine 1966).

Independent Grocers Alliance (IGA) Debuts

By 1926, the magazine continued, J. Frank Grimes, an accountant, who had helped in the merger of 30 small wholesale grocers in Ontario, Canada, met executives at the John Sloan and Co., which held a Red and White franchise in Ontario. Intrigued by this concept, Grimes later met with Flickinger in Buffalo and shortly thereafter helped some 69 retailers in Poughkeepsie, NY to form the Independent Grocers' Alliance, working with William T. Reynolds and Company, a wholesaler in that city. They started with an Acorn trademark, but soon adopted their own logo for their IGA brand, covering numerous grocery items: cake flour, nut margarine, coffee, tea, canned goods, etc. Within three years, IGA retailers together grew to become the second largest sales force in the U.S. food industry, grossing $526 million in sales—second only to A&P.

The Voluntary and Cooperative Groups Magazine observed that the IGA set-up was different from Flickinger's because IGA charged the wholesalers for different services:

One IGA franchisee, for example, paid $35,000, but in return received "a competent team" sent to work on development of its group of independent grocers in that market. The magazine noted further that other voluntary groups were formed: George Greene with Clover Farms Stores, Lewis Shave with Nation-Wide Stores, Henry T. Swann with Quality Service Stores, A. E. Koeniger with United Buyers Corporation, C. C. Jolliffe with Fairlawn Stores, Freedman Dowler with National Brands Stores, etc. "All these promoters were very helpful in developing the voluntary groups field," the magazine continued, adding that "some of these set-ups were conceived in iniquity; but the men who were responsible for these things disappeared from the scene. Many small independent voluntary groups were started by wholesalers, most of whom were not thinking primarily about the welfare of the retail members, but about their wholesale grocery business. However, groups of this type have pretty well petered out." (The Voluntary and Cooperative Groups Magazine 1966).

Flickinger's group thrived. A Buffalo newspaper (June 2, 1947) reported that the group at that time operated in 33 states, plus all the provinces of Canada and Alaska, representing 6,500 stores along with 125 wholesale units. At the start-up stage, however, its Serv-us label wasn't that strong. Not only did the yellow label not hold its color, but the quality of the products was not standardized at a high level. Borrowing the name of one of his own private labels, Red and White coffee which had been introduced into his wholesale business in 1912, Flickinger replaced the Serv-us label and dropped the premium program completely. At first, Red and White was used for standard-grade products, identified with red and white squares and subsequently changed to vertical stripes. For fancy grade, he used the Checkerboard label, identified with red and green squares. Eventually that label was dropped and all Red and White products were fancy grade.

Flickinger stores, operating in Buffalo, Jamestown and Rochester, NY, were soon joined by Red & White stores in other towns. Some were company-owned, some licensed to independent grocers. When the Red & White label range was built up to a satisfactory quality standard, all the stores carried the Red & White store identity.

Private Label Equals Extra Profits

These developments marked the formation of a national chain of independent food stores under the Red & White Voluntary Chain Groups. The rationale behind owning the Red & White label was best described at the time by S.M.'s son, Glenn W. Flickinger, who explained to Flickinger store managers that it is based on making a profit:

"We are particularly fortunate in our situation for selling profitable merchandise, due to the unique position of the Red & White brand. Stores today which have to depend wholly on nationally-advertised merchandise for their profits are seriously hampered, due to the fact that a large number of them are being sold at less than the cost of doing business. This has prevailed for such a long time that that is why private brands came into the field. In looking around for ways to make extra profit, the idea of the private brand was hit upon, whereby the merchant could sell merchandise and make a living profit on it.

"Red & White originally was a private brand. Today, through the expansion of the Red & White plan of operation, it is a nationally-advertised brand, and it is the only nationally-advertised controlled brand. Red & White merchandise cannot be purchased in any other stores except Flickinger and Red & Whites, so that people in order to get this merchandise have to come back to you.

"It is advertised in *Good Housekeeping* magazine, and a large number of the Red & White items have been approved by Good Housekeeping Institute. The quality of Red & White merchandise is as fine as can be obtained. That is why it has been successful. The high selling, advertising, and promotion costs which cut into the profits of nationally-advertised brands have been eliminated and these extra costs have been changed into extra profit for the merchant." (Flickinger, G. W. 1925)

Interestingly, Glenn Flickinger encouraged store managers to adopt suggestive selling for consumers' meal solution—a term that has today became a major merchandising and marketing strategy for food retailers:

"When a woman comes into your store to buy goods, she has in mind purchasing food for an entire meal. Consequently, sell her a meal. If she buys a steak, sell her some onions, catsup, sauce, and condiments of all kinds." This strategy is now incorporated as part of category management in supermarkets. Flickinger also talked about weekly specials and "hot spots," run every Friday and Saturday. In subsequent years, the group's merchandising policy was to use its Red & White and other controlled brands as hot spots, "because we were able, first, to have a price advantage over our competition; secondly, it gave us a chance to widen the distribution on our brands and thus to increase our everyday sale at the everyday price; and lastly, it gave us an opportunity to build this business for our own." (Flickinger, G. W. 1925)

Red & White Saves Independent's Bottom Line

In a report to shareholders in 1936, the company talked about establishing strong sales on Red & White peanut butter, Brimfull soap flakes, Red & White corn flakes, and many other Red & White items. Red & White corn flakes, sold in Buffalo, for example, turned twice as many cases as did Kellogg's and Post Toasties combined. Those brands could not market large packages of their products in that market, while Red & White could.

That was under the old system, operating under provisions of the National Regulatory Agency (NRA), which established minimum prices based on a 2% profit to the wholesaler and 6% to the retailer. After that policy was declared unconstitutional (about 1936), the large selling staples and nationally-advertised brands were sold at cost or below, forcing Red & White retailers to buy from their supply houses at their invoice cost; while the retailer had no choice, but to sell to the consumer without a single cent profit. Again, Red & White merchandise came to the rescue, because it carried sufficient margin to offset the non-profit market leaders and allow both supply houses and Red &

White retailers to maintain a profit:

"We developed a compromise on our former sales policy, and our present scheme is to use two staples each week at cost for leaders. These staples are compose of sugar, lard, beans, rice, coffee, and nationally-advertised brands of proven drawing power, when sold at close prices. These will draw the people into the store. In addition, we feature no less than 10 items of our own controlled brands and very often we run considerably more... they carry from 7.5% to 15% profit to the warehouse and 15% to 25% for the retailer, with the exception of items such as flour and coffee, which never do carry those margins." (Flickinger, G.W. 1925)

Flickinger made good progress with the Red & White merchandise mix, weekly circulars, and local newspaper advertising. In 1926, about six years after launching the Red & White group, Flickinger set up a headquarters organization, forming a corporation and a staff to coordinate activities and establish policies and plans for development on a national scale. More standardization was soon introduced: a standard store front and standard headings and illustrations used in ads in newspapers and in weekly circulars. Red & White began to assume a definite personality. More supply houses were joining the group, and the organization also advertised its stores and merchandise in national magazines. A report in an address at a 1931 New York state Red & White meeting explained that:

"Every food product bearing your Red & White label that has been submitted to *Good Housekeeping* and to the *Canadian Home Journal* for testing has come through with flying colors and won the unqualified approval of these two outstanding authorities." — (Red & White Magazine 1931)

The Red & White group had drawn the attention of Canadian wholesalers, although they could not join the group because of duty charges, which prevented U.S. manufacturers and Canadian distributors from being directly connected. Flickinger, however, generously offered advice on how the Canadians could adopt the Red & White identity, thus adding an international flavor to his voluntary group. By 1930, there were 109 Red & White supply houses and branches in the U.S. and Canada—25 of them having joined in that year. By the following year, Red & White Stores were advertising their private label lines not only in *Good Housekeeping* magazine but also in the *Canadian Home Journal*, as well as on radio music programs in Canada.

Creditors-Debtors Become Partners

The grocery wholesale supply houses that joined this group discovered a uniquely innovative relationship with their retail customers. Instead of the traditional creditor-debtor relationship or exchange between seller and buyer, the voluntary chain relationship fostered a partnership, in which the supply house and the retailer supplemented each other's work and shared their gains or losses. In other words, they worked together for greater efficiency, economy and profit. It was a relationship in which the retailer would buy all of his grocery needs from a cooperating wholesaler, while also extending often to the procurement of perishables and other lines that the wholesaler did not handle. It was a concentration of purchasing power which formed the economic basis for the success of the voluntary chain. In addition, the retailer also had to cooperate with a full commitment to selling these lines, and also to charging the same prices that were advertised in newspapers and circulars.

The wholesaler, too, had to offer his retailers a general average pricing on the merchandise, which were lower than what the retailer could get elsewhere. Since most grocery stores at the time carried a majority of their stock in products not handled by the wholesaler, the latter had to take the initiative in negotiating deals with supply sources for bakery goods, butter and eggs, cheese, fresh fruits and vegetables, cured and fresh meats and other lines in order to give the retailer a better price. Additionally, the wholesaler had to handle his group's advertising efforts.

The incentive for the retailer to become a member of Red & White was described by a Canadian retailer, James Harkness from Vancouver, B.C.:

"(Before joining) we had the representatives of four jobbers calling upon us twice weekly. This provided for eight separate deliveries weekly. All this took up time. Now we do not devote time to travelers or specialty men. We have no jobber, but have our supply house. We do not buy! We just order twice weekly by mail. . . Our office duties cut to the minimum is an elimination of waste which effects a considerable saving to be credited to the retailer and, in turn, passed on to the consumer. Cooperation and loyalty make this possible.

"Someone may ask, 'Why should I give these extra savings to my customers?' I answer, 'Because such savings place Red & White members in the forefront of lowest costs and enable us to meet competition of any kind.'" (The Red & White Magazine 1931)

The Red & White private label range featured a full line of products—more than any other wholesaler or retail chain offered at the time, except perhaps A&P, which manufactured most of its own private label products. Red & White also was joined by other private labels or controlled brands, covering fancy, extra fancy, and standard grades of quality, i.e., Blue & White, Green & White, Our Value, Brimfull, Sunspun, Washo washing powder, Old Vienna malt products, etc. At one time, there were some 1,300 items in the total controlled label range at Red & White. In later years that number was pared back to between 900 and 1,000 items, appearing under the Red & White brand (420 items) and the Sun Spun and Our Value brands in the late 1950s.

The Focus on Product Quality

From the very beginning, S. M. Flickinger put a great deal of emphasis on product quality for his controlled label line. In the first issue of his consumer newspaper, "Flickinger Stores News," under a column headed, "We Want You to Know," four Serv-us products were described: Serv-us baked beans, "one brand among a few that are 'baked' and so marked on the label"; Serv-us baking powder made as "a pure phosphate powder and cost(ing) about one-half of what many other baking powders cost of equal quality"; Serv-us coffee, "a blend of some of the finest coffees grown"; and Serv-us orange Pekoe tea, "packed from the fine fragrant tea leaves of the best Ceylon variety."

An in-depth look at just what efforts were taken to insure top quality of Red & White products was presented by Asa Strause, director of the national headquarters for the group at a 1940 Red & White convention. Glen W. Flickinger, vice-president of merchandising, spoke first, announcing the introduction of Red & White hydrogenated shortening in a three-pound can as:

"The best product obtainable, fully equal to any brand on the market, (carrying) the Red & White label on it, (selling) at a price competitive with the manufacturers' brand, and (giving) the retailer a living profit."

Strause then detailed the strategy behind its development:

"Our first consideration was quality... Our first move was to call in three of the foremost manufacturers in the country and ask them to submit samples of their best-quality shortening, along with a chemical analysis of their product made by a public analytical laboratory. Due to the volume of business which would be available to them if they were successful, they very readily complied.

"Their samples, plus samples of each of their products purchased, plus samples of the heavily advertised products were sent to the Mid-West Laboratories, who are experts on baking products; and we requested them to check all these samples on the following points: flavor, plasticity, keeping quality, emulsifying properties, and color. In addition, we requested them to check the samples submitted by the manufacturers against their samples purchased on the open market to determine the uniformity of each manufacturer's product. After the chemical analysis for the above factors was made, the laboratory made a series of practical baking tests and submitted reports in detail covering these tests. The reports of the Mid-West Laboratories indicated the relative superiority of the various manufacturers' products.

"We sent samples of the product which proved superior in the Mid-West Laboratories tests along with samples of the advertised products with which our brands must compete, to the laboratory of the largest cotton seed oil producer in the world.

These products were all removed from the tin cans and placed in plain containers so that the laboratory tests would be made entirely blind. In this test, the shortening we contemplated selecting again excelled the performance of its two competitors.

"Samples were then sent to the Household Science Institute, which is a testing organization where products submitted to it are tested for household use by domestic science experts. The Household Science Institute made practical baking tests with our product along with advertised products in the following manner: baking biscuits, baking cake, baking pie crust, frying doughnuts, and sautéing meats. In every instance, our product proved itself to be fully equal to the other two brands.

"While the product in which we were interested had been subjected to, first, an outside public analytical laboratory analysis by the manufacturer, to a laboratory analysis by the Mid-West Laboratories, and also baking tests by them at our expense, to household tests in both baking and in cookery by the Household Science Institute, and to tests by the laboratory of the largest cotton seed oil manufacturer in the world, we still felt it advisable to visit each of the three plants which had originally submitted samples and, as was to be expected, we found that the product, which had withstood all these other tests, was made more expertly and more scientifically than those rejected.

"Only after this exhaustive checking was the final decision reached to offer this item to the public." Afterward, the Red & White pure vegetable shortening package carried this statement: "Our Guarantee—Every Red & White Product is guaranteed to give entire satisfaction or money refunded." (Flickinger /Strause 1940)

There was a spirit of camaraderie that developed among the Red & White wholesalers, retailers and manufacturers. From 1924 onward, except for the war years, Red & White picnics were held in Buffalo's Celeron Park annually. It became an institution with upwards of 20,000 people attending. It gave the group an opportunity to advertise the Red & White stores, their products, and the Flickinger Co. A large display of Red & White products was set up in the park.

By 1934, about five years prior to his death in 1939 at age 75, S. M. Flickinger sold off all his corporate-owned stores to the store managers, each of whom signed contracts with the company making those units Red & White stores, so that the new owners were given control within their territory in return for loyal cooperation. Flickinger wanted to continue the voluntary cooperation which had so successfully established a teamwork relationship between the wholesaler and retailer, with full confidence shared by each party.

Within four years of the start-up of the other major voluntary group, IGA, there were some 10,000 IGA food stores, operated by independent grocers, in 37 states. Their private label stock grew to some 300 items in the 1930s. The IGA concept was advertised on network radio as well as through hundreds of daily and weekly newspapers. In 1951, an IGA franchise was granted in Canada; 13 years later, it was bought out by the Canadian wholesaler involved.

Voluntary Chains Have Weaker Allegiance to Brands

In his honors thesis at Harvard University, Burt P. Flickinger, Jr., researched the subject, "Voluntary Chain Marketing," which was based mostly on personal sources since very little documentation existed on the formative years of voluntary groups. Flickinger argued that the wholesaler-sponsored voluntary chains—groups like Red & White, Clover Farms, and IGA—emphasized private labels in contrast to the corporate-owned chains and the retailer cooperative organizations, both of whom "could not expand sales of their own brands without increasing their selling costs, since they would lose the manufacturers' advertising allowances (for national brands), which were vital in paying their own advertising costs. Therefore, corporate chains and retailer cooperatives were restrained somewhat from moving rapidly into the field of private brands. Wholesaler-sponsored voluntary chains... were organized by wholesale grocers to develop better retail outlets for their own brands. The effective voluntaries carry established brands at very narrow margins with the loss covered by high margins on private brands. Their primary interest is in their own brands, because these permit a profitable mark-up and are instrumental in holding the loyalty of retail members. Retailers like a brand which competitors cannot get and which will therefore protect them against price cutting." (Flickinger 1948)

Elsewhere in this thesis, Flickinger noted that "surveys by The Food Institute indicate that control over the retailer and a more dependable income from owned brands are major factors in the tendency of voluntaries to expand, improve, and stress their private brands." He added: "Private brands have proved a bulwark of defense against corporate chain competition and over 85% (as estimated by Red & White Corp.) of the voluntaries now produce them."

Flickinger also referred to a report by Gordon C. Corbaley, "Group Selling by 100,000 Retailers" (1936), commissioned by The American Institute of Food Distributors, which indicated that from 1932 to 1936, some 64 new wholesaler-sponsored voluntaries with 6,993 more retailers had become affiliated with wholesaler grocers.

Cooperative organizations, called cooperative or voluntary chains at the time, were really either retailer-owned cooperatives or wholesaler-sponsored voluntaries. The former had probably first started with the Baltimore Wholesale Grocery, organized in 1887. In the following year, Frankford Wholesale Grocery Company was formed in Philadelphia.

Meanwhile other organizations in the drug trade had been established, such as the New York Consolidated Drug Company of Manhattan (1887) and what became one of the largest co-ops in the industry, The Philadelphia Wholesale Drug Co. in 1888.

By 1898, the Cincinnati Wholesale Grocery Company had formed as another retailer co-op in the grocery business. After a merger in 1926, this co-op had been renamed White Villa Grocers, Inc., which included more than 1,000 retailer members. Later, a number of these retailer co-ops grouped together into the National Retailer Owned Grocers Association, a federations of 100 wholesale co-ops, serving 20,000 retail outlets (Beckman and Engle, 1949).

The wholesaler-sponsored voluntary groups had gotten started in this century. The initial idea, as mentioned previously, had been introduced by a Chicago advertising agency, followed by salesman George Lewis, in 1912. Another group, the General Purchasing and Distributing Company was organized in 1916, based in San Franciso. The S.M. Flickinger Co followed along with others, such as IGA, Clover Farm Stores, Nation-Wide Stores, Quality Stores Group, etc.By 1929, the Census of Wholesale Trade reported that there were 306 wholesaler-sponsoring voluntaries in the grocery trade. (Beckman and Engle, 1949).

The Depression years helped boost the number of voluntary group wholesalers to 703 by 1939, according to the Census of Wholesale Trade. Their sales totaled $754 million, while the 222 retailer-cooperative warehouses realized sales of $223 million. Together, these two forms of co-op groups accounted for about 2% of the total wholesale trade. In the grocery trade, their market share was closer to 25% of total sales.

Why Private Brands?

With respect to the use of private brands,Beckman and Engle argued that:

(1) "It strengthens the retailer's hold upon their trade, once a reputation has been established for the brand." Advertising benefits accrue to the merchant as well.

(2) They "usually provide a larger gross margin and offer a means of avoiding direct price competition. Well-known brands of manufacturers who have not taken advantage of the resale price maintenance legislation are frequently used as 'price leader' by large distributors and therefore carry low margins. The voluntaries can advertise these national brands at competitive prices in order to combat the impression that chains sell for less, and recoup their margins by applying sales pressure to private brands of merchandise—a practice which also has been followed by many of the corporate chains."

(3) It "gives the voluntaries greater freedom in selecting their source of supply. Merchandise is purchased strictly on a basis of quality specifications rather than brand reputation, and can often be obtained at lower prices than branded goods, which have been aggressively advertised by the manufacturer." (Beckman and Engle, 1949)

REFERENCES/CITATIONS

Beckman, Theodore N. and Engle, Nathanael H. 1949. "Wholesaling, Principles and Practice" (Chapter 16, Cooperative Wholesale Distribution). The Ronald Press Co., New York, pp 270-73 (John Wiley & Sons, Inc., New York)

Ibid, pg. 276

Cook, Gordon. 1960. "The Genesis of the Voluntary Groups and the Cooperative Groups," The Voluntary and Cooperative Groups Magazine (Cook Publications, New York), April 1960, pp. 19, 82.

Flickinger Jr., Burt P. "Voluntary Chain Marketing," Honors Thesis, Harvard University (1948)

Flickinger, S.M. 1921 Flickinger Store News: Journal of Household Economics. Aug. 1, 1921, Vol. 1, No. 1, pp. 2-3.

Flickinger, Glen W. 1925. "A Short Course in Retail Grocery Store Management." (A booklet originally prepared for Flickinger store managers and applicants for a manager position., which was published for any Red and White operator). Pages 11-12.

Flickinger, Glen W./Strause, Asa. 1940. Red & White Shortening. Red & White Annual Convention. Nov. 30, 1940.

Frank, Emil. 1951. "First Attempt to Market a Branded Line of Food Products Packed by Various Independent Manufacturers."

Jewel.1979. "History of Jewel Companies, Inc." (Company Fact Sheet).

Laycock, George. 1983. "The Kroger Story: A Century of Innovation." The Kroger Co., Cincinnati, OH.

The Red & White Magazine. 1931. Vol. 3, Nos. 1, 11.

The Voluntary and Cooperative Groups Magazine 1966. "Voluntary Groups." (Cook Publications, New York), August 1966, pp. 42, 53.

CHAPTER 6

__SNAGS & OBSTACLES EMERGE__

Within the voluntary groups, the independent grocers did not own any of the wholesale business but could share in its lower-cost volume purchasing, better merchandising strategies, and cost-effective distribution strength, while spreading administrative and engineering costs just like the chain store operators. The Red & White Group set up its own brokerage operation to handle product procurement, thus saving on that expense. Previously, food brokers had acted primarily as sales representatives for the small food manufacturers, selling to small wholesale grocers. Within the Red & White Group, the brokerage handled private label products as well—perhaps a first for the industry. This arrangement, however, ran into a stone wall in 1936.

At the time, there was a feeling in the general public sector that the large food chains with their economic power represented an unfair threat to independent conventional food stores. This resulted in passage of the Robinson-Patman Act (1936), which in part made it illegal for some buyers to set up subsidiary companies to act as their broker. The argument was that this subsidiary would receive a brokerage fee while performing no service to the seller—a form of price-concession rebate. Since Red & White had adopted many of the strategies of the large food chains, it, too, came under attack. Needless to say, the Red & White Group fought against passage of the Act right to the Supreme Court, but failed to convince that judicial body.

'Section 2-C' Surgery for the Independents

The impact of the Robinson-Patman Act, especially Section 2-C (dealing exclusively with the payment of brokerage), on groups of independent grocers was argued by James A. Slocum of the Red & White Corp., Chicago, at the 1950 convention of the National-American Wholesale Grocers' Association. Slocum noted that the Act was passed to prevent price advantage to large buyers or buyers who could economically pressure sellers. Most of the Act's sections deal with price discrimination, unfair price advantage, unfair methods of getting price advantage, and so on; but Section 2-C, he argued, in effect gives brokers "a complete monopoly on brokerage income." In 1949, he continued, brokers handled some $4 billion of the total grocery business. At a 2.5% brokers fee, that represented $100 million per year. Section 2-C prevented wholesalers or retailers from tapping into this fund to lower the cost of food. At that time, the grocery food chains represented just 30% of the total food distribution business, while independent grocers, some 375,000-strong, were doing 70% of the food business.

Slocum continued:

"We [the industry and Government] went on a moose hunt. The moose was the 'gigantic A&P.' We shot at the moose and hit all the blackbirds and rabbits that were feeding on his grazing ground, and merely peppered the moose's backsides.

"The moose could buy direct. He could legally purchase at a lower price from any seller who chose to sell his production on a direct basis. If the seller used brokers, other small buyers had to buy at a higher price, which included the brokerage fee." (Slocum, 1950)

Many national manufacturers and canners, he indicated, no longer work through brokers, but instead have their own sales force. They could choose their own strategy and, through volume buying, save on brokerage; while the larger group of wholesale grocers still had to pay brokerage and were forced to pass those costs on to their retail customers. To avoid creating a brokerage monopoly in the hands of a few, Congress included the privilege of direct buying, then tagged on wording to allow a trade buyer or a buyer's representative to collect brokerage if services were rendered.

Slocum argued that the wholesalers could not compete for services rendered. The chain operators, however, were at an advantage, because they,

"Could buy big quantities and thus make net buying a fact. Practically no independent can agree to take all a plant's output, or all of a certain size, grade, or type. The chain does this with ease.

"Chains could buy total blocks of a packer's production, less brokerage, even though he used brokers. By taking it all, they got the lowest price and perfectly legally.

"Chains could develop their own brands by those first two methods, so that they were free to sell other staples at prices that made independent retailers squirm."

Private brands for the independent, he said, were not as strong as before the new laws, forcing "more and more retailers to look for profits by selling staples at the chain store price, which their wholesalers bought at 2.5% to 5% more than the chain paid."

In essence, Slocum argued, Section 2-C took away the functions of services, advertising assistance, and store operations assistance from the independent retailers.

"Many wholesalers on cost-plus plans or other pricing plans have put staples down to very low levels in an effort to help retailers. But they've been unable to meet the retailer's complete needs. Section 2-C has crippled the whole idea of wholesalers and retailers working together by denying them the right to perform the brokerage functions which they once used as an effective means of competing." (Slocum 1950).

Red & White Divests its Brokerage Business

The Red & White group was forced to spin off its brokerage business, which was re-formed outside as a separate brokerage firm called Modern Marketing Services, Inc., organized by former Red & White Corp. employees. The group decided to grant that firm a one-year licensing agreement, giving them control over advertising and sales promotions for the Red & White group.

This brokerage, of course, now represented its principals' interests, that is, the manufacturers. The Flickinger management asked its group members to continue supporting the promotion of the Red & White brand, because they felt that it still "comprised the strongest single factor in the profitable Red & White operation, either from the supply house end or the retail end." As this brokerage business developed, the firm identified itself under its owners' names, Busey, Maury and Wright, while handling Red & White brand procurement through its wholly-owned subsidiary, Red & White Distributors, Inc. The company operated buying offices in Boston, Chicago, and San Francisco, handling the Red & White private label business up until the 1950s, at which time the brokerage renamed itself Federated Foods, based in Arlington Heights, IL. That company then began developing more of its own proprietary labels, such as Hy•Top, Fine Fare, and Parade, and franchised these on an exclusive basis to retailers and wholesalers around the country. Federated was destined to become the first and one of the largest preferred brokers in the private label industry.

Unfortunately, Red & White now became less of a priority for Federated Foods. In fact, there was also less control within the Red & White group itself, where no one was willing to work together. In all fairness, the brokerage was not in a position where it could exercise power over the group. Red & White began to lose its buying power in the marketplace. In 1960, there was a reorganization and consolidation of the Red & White group, where it was felt that functions performed by the national headquarters were being duplicated at the local level, placing a financial burden on the distributors. The remaining functions were transferred to Bushey & Wright, Inc., to perpetuate the Red & White brand and other controlled brands of the group. In addition, the Red & White Foundation was established as "an irrevocable charitable trust."

IGA Holds Onto Its Brokerage Business

IGA was able to weather Section 2-C's restrictions on brokerage fees, because IGA did provide services: besides buying products, the organization also worked to develop store management (the store and stock arrangement plans, stock pricing system, credit-collection plan, inventory-bookkeeping system), as well as merchandising and advertising strategies. In his 1930 essay, "Courage To Face the Facts," IGA founder J. Frank Grimes described these services, while explaining in detail the scope and size of IGA. Grimes touched on the buying power of the organization, which sounded just like a corporate chain strategy:

> "The pooling of gigantic buying power enables the IGA to form the closest contact with manufacturers. It enables the IGA to take complete outputs of some factories and to absorb immediately any large blocks of merchandise that may be available for sale at any time. By reason of such a big national organization, we are able to operate buying offices in New York, Chicago, New Orleans and San Francisco, thus contacting producers, packers and manufacturers in this country and in other countries directly.
>
> "To illustrate: among the IGA wholesalers, there are 22 who have their own coffee roasting plants. With direct buying offices in New York and New Orleans, coffee is purchased for all of these roasters on a basis that enables IGA retailers to compete under any conditions."

Grimes also touched on the benefits of mass buying, where IGA collected brokerage fees:

> "While on most of the nationally advertised brands, no savings of consequence are being made, yet on over 90% of the wholesaler's total items, real deals have been consummated. It is of interest at this point to note that the IGA Service Allowance, comparable to ordinary brokerage, which is secured from the great majority of manufacturers, provides a sum more than enough to pay the dividends of every wholesaler. When you realize that every cent of savings, no matter how it is secured, on the purchase of groceries and grocery sundries by the wholesalers—whether it is in brokerage, service allowance, advertising allowance, special deals or what not—when you realize that every cent of this is paid back to the wholesaler each month and not one cent is retained directly or indirectly by IGA headquarters, you will begin to understand why it is that the wholesalers are so enthusiastic and making such great progress. As a result, the revenue to the wholesaler from this one source alone is many times greater than the small charges of headquarters for buying servings. The savings in freight alone to the jobber members on pooled cars of assorted merchandise are running at the rate of $15,000 per month...
>
> ". . . We cooperate with many of the manufacturers in helping them reduce their overhead—reduce their cost of production and, as a result, the IGA enjoys the benefit in lower costs. The large amount of merchandise bought through the IGA permits manufacturers to capitalize on the benefits of quantity production and organized distribution—enabling them to sell at lower prices." (Grimes 1930)

Government Outlaws IGA's Brokerage Activities

However, in 1953, IGA had to discontinue its brokerage business as a result of a Federal Trade Commission ruling that went contrary to the original intent of Section 2-C of the Robinson-Patman Act.

IGA's position was forcefully stated in a February 1952 editorial, written by Donald Grimes, then president of IGA:

"IGA headquarters until recently rendered a sales service or brokerage service for manufacturers or processors, and was paid a normal brokerage. The law states that no brokerage should be paid an organization like IGA except for services rendered, but because services were rendered by IGA, it was paid.

"This payment backs up what Wright Patman said in 1936, when he interrupted his speech promoting the Robinson-Patman Act to tell my dad, J. Frank Grimes, commonly known to all of you as the 'Chief,' that 'nothing in this Act shall hurt organizations like IGA, because they are doing such a fine job for the independents.' This writer was there and heard this statement.

"None of the payments received by IGA headquarters was used to reduce prices at the wholesale level. Never at any time was this money used to cut the price of an item at the retail level. All such monies received for services rendered were used in maintaining brokerage offices in Chicago, New York, San Francisco, and Seattle, plus the merchandising and advertising services, retail and wholesale supervision programs, store engineering, meat merchandising services, and many other functions designed to help the IGA retailer be competitive with the chains. All of these services cost considerably more than the dues received from retailers.

"However, the U.S. Courts have ruled that the four words 'except for services rendered' do not mean what they say. So IGA was forced to divorce itself from the brokerage function...

". . . It is ironic that an Act designed originally to help the independent by curbing the chains has worked to the benefit of most chains. The chains can now buy on a net basis, which means that they can take the entire output from a manufacturer or they can buy large blocks of stock, and in so doing they get their merchandise at a price with all brokerage eliminated. Many chains also have set up their own items under their own brands. Their cost figures do not include brokerage or manufacturer's profit.

"Thus the chains today, if they wanted to, could sell merchandise where brokerage is normally involved, for up to 5% cheaper than the independents. When you consider the manufactured items, they can sell their own brands still cheaper.

"The end result has been that the large corporate chains, with fewer stores, are doing 3, 4, and 5 times more business than they did before the Robinson-Patman Act was enacted." (Grimes 1952)

	1935	1952	Increase
Safeway	$293,500,000	$ 1,484,000,000	406%
Kroger	227,700,000	1,051,800,000	361
National Tea	61,600,000	405,200,000	557
A&P	800,000,000	3,400,000,000	325

Grimes backed up this statement with a chart (see above), taken from *Progressive Grocer* magazine data, showing sales growth for the leading chains.

Government Suspicions About Big Business

It is not within the scope of this book to examine in detail the growing control of government over business in the 20th century. In the previous century, individualism and free-for-all competition thrived. The growth of big business created suspicion by the public, leading to antitrust laws at the state and the Federal level, beginning with the Sherman Antitrust Act (1890), then the establishment of the Federal Trade Commission in 1914, followed that same year by the Clayton Act zeroing in on pricing discrimination, binding contracts, and the like.

With the spread of mass distribution, wholesalers became more interested in antitrust legislation. Producers adopted direct distribution, which encouraged more large-scale retail buying, making it more difficult for wholesalers to stay competitive. In one case, wholesalers protested to the FTC about a practice in the meat packing industry, where major packers like Armour and Swift plus others directly distributed meat products to retailers through branch houses and peddler cars. This effective, cost-saving method was expanded to other product lines as well: poultry and game, dairy items, canned goods, packaged and bulk grocery products, and soda fountain supplies. In 1919, after the FTC investigated these wholesaler complaints, the U. S. Department of Justice forced the meat packers to dispose of their public stockyard holdings, completely disassociating themselves from the retail meat business as well as from manufacturing, selling, jobbing and distributing unrelated commodities—the Packers' Consent Decree.

The wholesalers also rallied behind the National Industrial Recovery Act (NRA) of 1932, hoping to secure codes of fair competition to secure profit margins and prevent price cutting, selling below cost, and other unfair business practices. (The Government wanted wage and hour provisions built into the Act.) This amounted to price controls over manufacturers; but wholesalers' opinions differed, which led to the Schechter Decision by the U.S. Supreme Court in 1935, ending the NRA. (Beckman and Engle, 1949)

Anti-Chain Sentiments Grow

The voluntary groups gave the independent grocers a competitive advantage as well as new life. During the harsh Depression years, beginning in 1929, many independents were forced out of business. They naturally blamed the chains, which offered consumers lower prices backed up by more aggressive advertising and merchandising strategies. In groups such as Red & White or IGA, an option for survival was present. In fact, it's been stated that these voluntary groups even offered manufacturers wider distribution of their products than did the chain operators, who were more regional or centralized in large markets. It's obvious that the economic woes of the country during the early 1930s also played a role in the demise of many independent grocers. It's also no surprise that many of these independents were quick to support literally hundreds of anti-chain-store bills introduced into state legislatures. From 1925 through 1938, nearly 1,000 such laws were proposed, but few enacted, mainly because of the lobbying efforts of trade associations.

Early in this century, the manufacturing and distribution strengths of the retailers helped build private label business in their food store chains. In 1915, a confrontation between A&P and The Cream of Wheat Co. convinced A&P to make a serious commitment to its own manufacturing and processing of food products, where it could set its own retail prices while avoiding any selling or advertising costs. Up until 1911, A&P had only produced baking powder and extracts on its own. When A&P had lowered the price of the Cream of Wheat product by 2 cents per pack in its newer stores, the retailer ended up in court, arguing that it had the right to lower its retail price, while the manufacturer's request for a higher fixed price represented restraint of trade under the recently-passed Clayton Act (1914). The first major antitrust law, The Sherman Act, had not cover in detail the protection of the public against exploitative practices by giant corporations. Outraged by the A&P action, The Cream of Wheat Company had stopped shipping its product to A&P. This forced a court showdown, where A&P argued further that its operational costs were low enough to justify a lower retail price. The manufacturer's defense was that it had the right to establish its own pricing level and that A&P with this lower pricing in its new stores would drive other retailers out of business, monopolize the market, and thus hurt consumers. A&P lost its case. —(Hoyt 1969)

A&P Embraces Private Label

A&P then began development of its own manufacturing muscle, producing peanut butter, olives, gelatin desserts, cocoa, bread, groceries, canned salmon, evaporated milk, jams, preserves, cereals, etc. all under its new Ann Page label. Through the American Coffee Corp., A&P began to buy direct from coffee growers in Brazil and Colombia. In 1917, A&P's first bakery opened, followed by the start-up of its Atlantic

Commission Co., focused on produce purchases. In the 1920s, a revolution was underway in the food industry, in which companies moved toward improved food processing methods and more sophisticated techniques—more automation, convenience packaging, faster and more productive equipment, and so on. Many thousands of small food processors were either put out of business or consolidated into larger companies which developed national distribution.

A&P developed its own food-testing laboratories and rapidly expanded its food line, selling "A&P Exclusives" such as macaroni products, preserves and ketchup, candy, canned beans and spaghetti, salad dressing, mayonnaise, and French dressing. By the end of the decade, its A&P Products Corp. was renamed the Quaker Maid Company.

A&P's store count—mostly smaller outlets but including some larger combination stores featuring grocery items and meats, fruits and vegetables—continued to grow from 4,600 units in 1920 to more than 14,000 units by 1925. Its marketing reach in over 29 states encouraged the company to become one of the first large firms to advertise in the new medium radio.

A&P's Great Big Fall

The stock market crash of 1929 really set the tone for A&P's fortunes over the next three decades: A number of outside forces began 'crashing down' on the company. Up until 1929, A&P's sales growth had marched ahead by almost a 25% yearly growth rate. At $1 billion+ in sales, the tide began turning, thanks to mounting competitive pressures from the independent grocers.

Competition intensified more, especially for many of the independent grocers, who could not match the buying clout of the emerging chains. A&P, for example, peaked in its store count with 15,645 outlets in 1927. A&P began spreading westward to California in the next decade, while also establishing a base in Toronto, Canada. A purchasing office was set up in London, England, as well. At the time, A&P was the largest food retailer in the country as well as the largest food manufacturer.

Facing the growing chain competition, independent grocers also pooled their buying power under retailer-owned cooperatives, in which they themselves owned the supply house or distribution center, in contrast to the voluntary group, in which retailers united under the wholesaler(s), who owned the distribution center. There is very little written about the co-ops, a concept begun in the 19th century. Early in this century, a number of co-ops formed, which are still in operation today. In 1922, for example, 15 independent grocers in Pasadena, CA, formed Certified Grocers of California, Ltd., as one of the country's first retailer-owned wholesale buying cooperatives. (Its leading Springfield private label, however, wasn't launched until 1955.)

In the late 1920s, an association of buying cooperatives for independent retailers was formed as the National Retailer-Owned Wholesale Grocers (NROG), based in Chicago. The impetus, at the time, was toward group-buying, which continued to expand during the Depression. According to Flickinger's research, "NROG spread until it had more wholesale houses than any other group, and more retailers affiliated with it than Red & White, I.G.A., and Clover Farms combined... It began to develop a national line of labels and otherwise to try to parallel the organized groups of voluntaries." (Flickinger 1948) Reportedly, because of differences among the membership, the group afterward was divided into three geographic section: West Coast, East Coast, and Central states. In 1948, Shurfine Central, Northlake, IL, developed as the central states co-op. That same year, another co-op was formed, Topco Associates (then called Food Products Cooperative), Skokie, IL, owned by medium size grocery chains and grocery wholesalers. The evolution of co-ops is discussed in more detail in the co-ops section of this book.

Robinson-Patman Act Controls 'Unfair Competition'

In true competitive fashion, the independent grocers also attacked A&P and other food chains, lobbying for anti-chain state taxes imposed on the chains to allow the smaller independents to compete more effectively in their markets. Chain-store market share had climbed up to one-third or higher of total retail food sales. This activity drew the Federal government into the picture, when the Federal Trade Commission began investigating A&P and other food chains over a six-year period. By 1934, the FTC had subpoenaed various store records to prove that chains did, in fact, pay less for manufactured goods, giving them unfair advantage over the independent competition. Chain operational efficiencies very likely were not credited with being the reason for the pricing differentials at retail.

In 1935, the House of Representatives commenced its investigation of the American Retailing Federation, a new group of several chains (excluding A&P), organized to fight against anti-chain legislation. Representative Wright Patman from Texas led this investigation, which spread over the entire grocery industry, searching for misuse of allowances and quantity discounts to produce unfair deals. Since grocers were working their own brokerage terms, it was felt such abuses existed. Out of this investigation, The Robinson-Patman Act of 1936 was amended to the Clayton Antitrust Act. The new law spelled out the prohibition of anti-competitive practices, such as unfair price discrimination and inequitable quantity discounts, while also focusing on brokerage and promotional payments. Two years later, Representative Patman took it a step further with his so-called Death Sentence Bill, calling for a Federal tax levy on chain stores, the payment scaled to the number of stores per chain. This bill failed, because of strong testimony by chain representatives before the Ways and Means Committee, as well as from arguments by farmers, labor unions, manufacturers, and consumer groups, who all feared that this bill would result in unemployment, higher retail prices, and less income for themselves. Over the next 10 years, A&P faced other legal battles but endured, thanks to its conversion to the supermarket format. In 1946, the company had one-third fewer stores (5,238) than its count in 1930 (15,700+), but had doubled its sales volume. The food chain operated some 1,670 of these as supermarkets .

When it rains it pours. A&P, the market leader, ran into other obstacles. For example, in the grocery trade, a management philosophy developed that was completely opposite to A&P's high-sales, low-profits strategy. Retailers were looking for less sales volume and higher profits. A&P, however, stuck to its former strategy.

Self-Service Stores Cut Operating Costs

A&P also faced the downpour from another concept foreign to its operation: self-service stores. Alpha Beta, a California grocer, had introduced this idea in 1914. One of the company's co-founders, Albert Gerrard conceived of the idea of arranging groceries alphabetically, so that anyone knowing their A-B-Cs, could follow "The Alpha Beta System." Piggly Wiggly food stores two years later picked up on self-service in their Tennessee market, featuring turnstiles and checkout counters. In 1930, the Wegman brothers, Walter and John, who started the Rochester (NY) Fruit and Vegetable Co. in 1916, opened their first self-service grocery store, a 20,000-square-foot "showplace" store, featuring a 300-seat cafeteria, which received national attention as the state's largest retail food store—and possibly the largest in the country. That same year, King Kullen introduced its first self-service 1,600-square-foot store. Two years later, in the same New York market, Big Bear converted a large automobile factory into a self-service store, mass-merchandising both food and household goods. Later, during the Depression, in Boston, the Economy Grocery Stores (established in 1914) converted a former Ford car assembly plant into a supermarket, called Stop & Shop Supermarkets. The supermarket concept took root, featuring national brands at a low prices. While A&P had moved aggressively into a cash-and-carry format with its Economy stores, it was less receptive to the self-service concept that evolved into the supermarket. Perhaps because of its commitment to low-price private labels and the top-heavy clerk service in its stores, A&P failed to adopt the self-service format until the mid-1930s.

Intensified brand competition, the Government's crackdown on the so-called A&P monopoly—the market leader for private label, and the introduction of numerous packer label canned fruits and vegetables into grocery and supermarket outlets, all were factors that helped to weaken or dilute the private label image overall. Consumers really had no fixed image of a market leader in private label. Different quality grades of product were spread over hundreds of labels—a proliferation of identities.

Additionally, the emergence of the supermarket concept pushed private labels off track, as retailers mass-displayed national brands at a discount. A&P continued to fight for market leadership, using its private label strength, but eventually gave in to the consumers' desire for national brands. Profit-oriented management sought to cut costs, compromising on private label quality, raising retail prices and/or short-weighing product for the consumer.

There was an emergence of grocery chains either through mergers like Safeway Stores, Inc. (1915), the American Stores Co. (1917), and the Peninsular Stores, Ltd. (1931) with its Lucky Stores, or under their own power: A&P, Kroger, and Grand Union. Drug store chains also emerged: Charles R. Walgreen, Sr., started the Walgreen chain in Chicago in 1901 and Louis K. Liggett, launched the Rexall chain in 1902. Liggett organized 40 druggists into a franchise plan, offering them co-op ad money. This developed into the United Drug Co., in Boston, where Rexall products had originally been introduced early in the century.

REFERENCES/CITATIONS

Beckman, Theodore N. and Engle, Nathanael H., 1949. "Wholesaling, Principles and Practice" (Chapter 25, Wholesaling and the Government), pp. 691-702. The Ronald Press Co., New York (John Wiley & Sons, Inc., New York)

Flickinger Jr., Burt P., "Voluntary Chain Marketing" Honors Thesis, Harvard University (1948)

Grimes, Donald R. 1952. "IGA's Stand on Robinson-Patman Act," IGA Grocergram, pp. 13-14.

Grimes, J. Frank 1930 "Courage To Face the Facts" (Pamphlet published by the Independent Grocers' Alliance of America, Chicago, IL).

Hoyt, E. P. 1969 "That Wonderful A&P ." Hawthorn Properties (Elsevier-Dutton Publishing Co., Inc., New York, NY).

Slocum, James A. 1950 "In Favor of Revision of the Brokerage Clause of the Robinson-Patman Act." (Speech delivered at Convention of National-American Wholesale Grocers' Association on Jan. 31, 1950, at the Ambassador Hotel, Atlantic City, NJ).

______The Supermarket Era_____

CHAPTER 7

___SUPERMARKETS REVOLUTION-IZE THE GROCERY TRADE_____

You could consider the 1930s and 1940s as school-days for the retailers, wholesalers, manufacturers, and brokers in the grocery trade. To stay competitive in an increasingly complex marketplace, the industry players were learning strategies in purchasing, pricing, product specifications, integrated processing, profit-taking, distribution, merchandising, and advertising. They also embraced a brand-new store format called "the supermarket," which literally revolutionized the food grocery business.

Giant Chains Resist "The Cheapies"

Many chain store and independent grocery operators were quick to recognize the effectiveness of the supermarket—a self-service food store featuring grocery, meat, dairy, and produce departments. The supermarket focused on mass displays of high-sales volume products—mostly the manufacturers' popular brand leaders. Independent grocers, being less committed to any store format, were quicker to jump on the bandwagon. There was resistance, however, from the larger chain operators, such as A&P and Safeway, which had built thousands of small service-oriented stores, supported by a strong infrastructure of food processing facilities that could deliver numerous private label products to those stores. Actually, A&P was in transition, phasing out of the small Economy Store format into larger combination stores featuring better product displays. Many of these outlets had a standard display format, positioning grocery items to the left, a meat department to the right, and fresh fruits and vegetables up front. A&P was committed to food production with its Quaker Maid Company. Some independent retailers, organized into cooperatives, also thought of supermarkets as a passing fad.

". . . (Retailers) nicknamed them 'cheapies,' not only because of their low prices, but also because of their unorthodox merchandising approach. Inside, the supermarket was a world unto itself. Boxes and barrels of merchandise, displayed in self-service fashion, were strewn everywhere. Dangling banners and posters announced sensational bargains. Aisles were placed so shoppers had to pass all of the merchandise before reaching the checkout counter... Each supermarket carried a different selection of merchandise, but most featured groceries, meat, bakery goods, fruits and vegetables, dairy products, tobacco, paint, hardware, and automobile accessories." (Certified Grocers of California 1972)

A&P Sets the Industry Pace

The impact and influence of A&P on the grocery trade from the 1920s up through the 1940s cannot be overstated. This company by virtue of its size and marketing reach actually helped establish the concept of the national brand. On radio, the new medium, A&P sponsored a weekly musical program, "The A&P Gypsies." The chain opened stores on the West Coast and in Canada. Even the market leader, Dominion Stores in Toronto, was overwhelmed by this newcomer, because A&P featured meat departments. A&P was the first food chain to distribute California oranges, Texas grapefruit and Georgia peaches on a national basis; A&P was also the first to distribute fresh seafood in the Midwest. The company pioneered in self-service meats, including prepackaged meat cuts. While prepackaged bacon was an industry standard, other meat cuts helped A&P boost its meat sales—the biggest contributor to its sale volume. The company established a Super-Right quality-grade system for meat cuts of different quality grades, quality-inspection procedures, and it standardized cuts and proper trimming. Its National Meat Department centralized its buying out of Chicago.

A&P's wholesale purchasing and distribution of fresh fruits and vegetables were handled by its Atlantic Commission Company (ACCO), which operated through field buying offices, all linked to sales offices via a teletype system. ACCO cut through the middlemen in the old-line distribution system: breaking up car-lots into smaller units; cutting directly to buying at the source; shipping direct to A&P warehouses, and sometimes direct from railroad sidings into the stores, thus by-passing the warehouses. Shipments also were direct by truck from field to store, slicing up to two days off the transit time. Its work moved the food industry into prepackaged fruits and vegetables and also into using cellophane bags in order to save on handling while helping to move more produce in the stores. ACCO also developed refrigerator display cases in the stores and educated store personnel on proper handling procedures.

Likewise, in the bakery area, A&P helped improve quality and speed up fresh product delivery through its improved manufacturing and distribution system. The company strategically located ultra-modern bakeries around the country, dated all its products, and set up a Jane Parker line of goods and bakery shops, selling at full price only within 24 hours after baking. A day later, the price was reduced by as much as 40%, and on the third day, goods were thrown away. A&P additionally purchased butter directly from creameries, packing it into two grades: its top quality Sunnyfield brand and the Silverbrook brand.

Of course, the A&P story is not complete without its favorite product—coffee. Coffee represented the company's most efficient operation as well as one of its strongest contributors to profits. Its American Coffee Corp. purchased coffee directly from

Brazil and Colombia, selling the beans in its stores within 10 days to two weeks of roasting. The aroma of coffee beans became a hallmark in the A&P stores, where customers would order Eight O'Clock, Bokar, or Red Circle coffee to be ground at cash registers.

A&P's Quaker Maid subsidiary served as canner, packer, bottler, and food processor of private label products. (Later, this grocery manufacturer/processor was named after one of its most famous private labels, Ann Page.) The company's Nakat Packing Corp. provided salmon from four Alaskan canneries. A&P's White House Milk evaporated-milk condenser facilities and its National Fish Department helped to round out the range of private label products—many branded, others just sticker-labeled.

A&P's Manufactured & Controlled Brand Products

Early in its history, A&P described A&P's products to employees, explaining that the company:

". . .Entered into the marketing of its own products and became proficient in procuring, processing and packing foods, because this step would result in its stores offering better value to their customers. By going direct to the sources for many products, by manufacturing scores of others, A&P eliminates from the cost of these items many expenses that must be borne by foods of comparable quality produced by manufacturers who distribute through the general retail trade. In short, these products which carry the labels of the company are products of fine quality which arrive in your store at lower costs, and thus can be sold to your customers at lower prices. . .

"The company's products fall into two classes: those it produces in its own factories, plants, bakeries and canneries, and those it assigns to other reputable manufacturers or packers to prepare according to rigid A&P standards. In the case of each class of product, the Central laboratory establishes the high levels of quality, and is responsible for the constant maintenance of these standards by means of regularly scheduled scientific checks and tests." (A&P 1944)

The company listed its A&P manufactured products, covering coffees (Eight O'Clock, Red Circle and Bokar brands); bakery products (Marvel enriched bread; Jane Parker cakes, rolls and donuts); grocery items (Ann Page products, White House milk, Holly Carter candies); salmon (Cold Stream and Sunnybrook); fresh fruits and vegetables (Regalo); and other items.

The A&P controlled brands were described as "products packed under trademarks which A&P controls, but which are manufactured or packaged by other firms, or, when the finished product is only packaged by your company, are controlled by the company, but manufactured or packaged by outside firms or when the finished product is only packaged by A&P." They included: meats (Super-Right meats, Sunnyfield smoked and precooked hams, bacon, dried beef, lard), dexo hydrogenated shortening, canned dog food and kibbled biscuits (Daily), its butter and cheese (A&P), its eggs (Sunnybrook, Crestview, and Wildmere), its cereal products (Sunnyfield cereals and flours, Iona flours, and Daily animal feeds), and other items—A&P, Sultana and Iona canned fruits and vegetables, Queen Anne paper products, White Sail cleaning aids, etc. (A&P 1944)

In 1930, A&P's store-count peaked at 15,709 outlets, after which the company began closing stores. The Great Depression in the United States did not help sales. A&P stayed solvent with a cash surplus, because the Hartford family only leased its stores rather than carrying credit with banks for store-ownership. A one-year store lease allowed A&P to pull out quickly if a store didn't prosper. A new business philosophy emerged at that time: the focus switched to higher profits with less emphasis on building sales. Reportedly, even some of A&P's managers, when faced with an eroding market share from more competition, began to raise prices, short-weight products and use other consumer-unfriendly tactics to build profits.

A&P Relents on Supermarket Concept

It wasn't until 1936 that A&P relented, opening its first true supermarket. The company wrote about its dilemma:

John Hartford worried about the inability to close "'red ink' stores, which had grown in number by 1934. In the chain system, the decision to close such stores in great numbers is difficult. First, such stores do carry a portion of the warehouse-administrative overhead, so eliminating them shifts greater burden to the profitable stores. Secondly, there was a blow to pride and prestige that results from fewer stores and lower total volume and the effect of such a move on the employees. Finally, there was always the hope that perhaps with better merchandising, the loser can be brought back to profitability.

"These combined factors, plus growing competition from affiliated independents supplied by large wholesalers, led to declines in sales and profits from 1931-1937.

"In 1938, however, the picture turned around and A&P achieved a 12.6% increase in sales, while doubling its earnings to $18 million. It's a paradox that what changed the picture and rejuvenated the company was the effect of two forces opposed to the A&P system as it stood at the time: prohibitive chain store taxes, which ultimately forced A&P to consolidate its stores, thereby weeding out most of the unprofitable units; and the rise of the supermarket." (A&P 1985)

A&P could not ignore the King Kullen supermarket, opened by Michael Cullen in Jamaica, NY. in the early 1930s. The article continued:

"Housed in a low-rent former garage, the store was 10 times the size of the A&P stores of the day, operated on a self-service basis, offered extensive meats and produce, provided parking and emphasized low, low prices. Cullen's pricing formula—300 fast movers at cost; 200 items at 5% above cost; 300 items at 15%; 300 items at 20%.

"Shoppers stormed the store almost immediately, and sales began running steadily above $13,000 a week—at a time when the average A&P was doing $70,000 a year!

"... Once A&P began to move, the changeover resembled a landslide. In 1938, more than 500 A&P Supermarkets were opened, and as early as May, supers (in the $10,000 a week class) constituted 5% of all stores, 23% of sales, and nearly half of the company's profits. Small stores were closed by the hundreds; in one year, 1940, nearly 2,000 were closed." (A&P 1985)

Within a couple of years, the company operated more than 1,000 supermarkets. Since A&P had spent decades building its own brand equity around different private labels, the company did not abandon them, spending a good portion of its advertising and in-store promotions on brands such as Eight O'Clock, A&P, Jane Parker, Ann Page, etc. Its own brands also were supported in newspaper, radio, TV and in major national magazines, as well as the company's own *Woman's Day*. A&P's private label sales climbed from between 15 to 20% of total sales in the mid-1930s, during the Great Depression, up to 25% of all sales. The chain also began price-comparison ads, featuring private label items in one column matched against similar name brands, showing consumers in different divisions the savings—up to $2.40 for 15 items, as an example. Handbills promoted the concept: "Compare! Save 29 percent." Of course, the per-item price was less than 50 cents at that time.

A Mishandled Private Label Program

This loyalty to private label led many observers later to stereotype A&P, generalizing about the situation with the belief that a strong emphasis on private label stock could work against the retailer, using A&P as the classic case. The truth is that A&P compromised on the quality of some of its own brands, while all the time fighting to maintain profits and keep its strong manufacturing operations alive. Its weakness came not from emphasizing private label, as much as from mishandling the private label program. A&P force-fed its stores in the chain with private label stock, asking that the name brands take a secondary role. There was no effort taken in balancing the product mix within the stores.

This supermarket format, which kept getting larger and larger over the years, emphasized bargain low prices on national brand products. The concept was tougher to swallow for both chain store operators as well as the cooperative groups, each of which relied heavily on low-price private label stock and clerk service in a smaller grocery store setting. At first, the supermarket development did not bode well for private label business.

The evolution of supermarkets was hard on private label development, because the grocery chains were selling national brands at a discount. National brands seized greater control of market share. The chains, committed to private label, had to follow the trend toward discounted name-brand merchandising in the supermarkets, while also developing alternative controlled labels or private labels; they spent literally decades to establish each private label as a brand-name in the consumer's mind. In fact, some of these private labels did achieve that success. Jewel Food, for example, had more than 30 different labels—Bluebrook, Cherry Valley, Launder Maid, Yummy, Dewkist, Mary Dunbar, Old Bohemia, etc. Each label was given a prominent shelf position. Hillfarm, used on milk and dairy items, did succeed. With little or no market research intelligence, Jewel, like other retailers, thought they had to deliver the quality-levels set by the brands, but didn't utilize a wide price-differential, that is, lower the pricing of private label at retail. They wanted their private labels to look like brands and to be priced near the national brand leaders. Retaining the profit margins for private label was simply too attractive, because many products continued to be sold at a small price differential from the name brands.

Within 11 Years, Another Chain: Safeway

Safeway Food Stores, Oakland, CA, which eventually became a grocery market leader early in the century, was started as a tiny 576-square-foot, cash-and-carry store by Marion Barton Skaggs in 1915. Within 11 years, Skaggs, his five brothers and others built a grocery chain of 428 Skaggs United stores, operating in 10 states. In 1926, this group joined with Sam Seelig's chain of 322 stores, which a year earlier had renamed its stores, "Safeway." Their merger was executed by Charles Merrill, who headed up the stock investment firm that would become Merrill, Lynch, Pierce, Fenner & Smith. Merrill, who had pioneered other chain store developments in the east, saw this merger as an opportunity to develop a holding or parent company. Thus, Safeway Stores, Inc., was established, operating 784 grocery stores, 122 meat markets, six bakeries, plus other manufacturing and wholesaling activities. Its food stores measured 1,000 square feet, stocking 700 items, all operated by three or four employees per unit. Sales per store averaged about $70,000 annually.

This ambitious enterprise then embraced the Piggly Wiggly franchise system merely in order to get its feet wet with the self-service concept. Safeway was actually more interested in building its own Safeway chain. Through the early part of this century, the company can be credited with many "firsts":

- pricing fruits and vegetables by-the-pound for easier shopping comparisons,
- special merchandising campaigns to provide sales relief for farms and livestock production,
- a "buy-build-sell-lease" real estate program to reduce capitalization costs,
- the use of farm tank-to-tank trucks in hauling of milk from dairies for sanitary handling economy, and
- a guaranteed meat-trim program and retailer-owned cutting and aging facilities. (Safeway 1966)

By 1929, Safeway had established Canada Safeway Limited in Winnipeg. In the 1960s, Safeway expanded into the United Kingdom, Australia, and West Germany as well.

With its growing base of supply houses—nearly 40 processing-manufacturing facilities by the mid-1930s, that covered baked goods, coffee, dairy products, candy and syrups, and mayonnaise, it was inevitable that private label would play a major role in Safeway's development as a market leader. Certain identities were established, such as Safeway shoepeg corn, Town House sweetened grapefruit juice, and Highway canned apricots. Over the years, Safeway built up an arsenal of private labels—more than 100 different names. Eventually, this practice got out of hand.

$2.5 Billion in Safeway Brand Sales

In 1975, the company boasted that it had some 5,000 items under its own labels—about half of them could be stocked in any one store. Overall, these labels represented more than 25% of its total company sales, accounting for nearly $2.5 billion in private label sales. Safeway Brands covered both the products that it produced itself (milk, bread, ice cream, coffee, jam and jelly, detergents, soft drinks, lunch meats, and vegetable oils) and those items contracted to outside suppliers (canned fruits and vegetables, frozen foods, paper products, pantyhose, health and beauty aids, beer, wines, spirits, etc.) (Safeway 1975).

The rationale was that budget-conscious shoppers regarded these labels as brands, not carefully reading the small distribution statement on the back panel of a package. There was a profusion of names:

"Once upon a time, Safeway had more names attached to its products than anyone ever bothered to count. A budget-conscious shopper, probably unaware the items were Safeway's, could load up a 'Baskart' with Beverly peanut butter, Montrose butter, Dutch Mill processed cheese, Farm Fresh eggs, Prairie Schooner bread, Jan Arden cookies, Tea Timer crackers, Suzanna pancake mix, Golden Hearth flour, Mayday salad oil, Show Boat rice, Pennant tea, Wakefield coffee, Fair Winds tuna, Sundown fruit cocktail, Country Home corn, Anthem peas, Moneca plums, Destino tomato paste, Cascade salad dressing, Old Mill vinegar, Hy-Pro bleach, El Rapido soap, Sno-White salt, and Snow Cola soft drinks. And that Baskart would contain only a smattering of the names once used to designate Safeway products." (Safeway News 1980)

Both consumers and Safeway employees were confused. The practice also prevented Safeway from organizing promotions because there were so many different names all "disguised" as manufacturers' packer labels. Safeway finally responded by unifying all its labels under a dozen names, under its "S Brands" umbrella identity, covering items such as Lucern dairy products, Bel-air frozen items, Cragmont soft drinks, and White Magic household products.

During this era, canners proliferated in the Midwest. More than 100 firms were producing multiple packer labels for the wholesale grocers and for some chains. They also provided private labels to the chains. This period was one of rapid expansion for supermarket chains throughout the U.S. and Canada.

The grocery industry continued to grow in size, becoming more structured and competitive. With its strong manufacturing base, A&P kept its private label commitment alive. In the 1960s, its private label sales represented some 35% of total store sales—very likely the highest for a supermarket chain operation in the U.S. at that time. Competitive chains, however, were gaining strength. Independent grocers, working through cooperatives and/or wholesalers, also were building their businesses. A number of brokers helped the retailers establish private label stock. It started in basic commodity items, spread into prepared foods in canned goods, dry mixes, cereals and the like. Private label also developed in the frozen foods category, beginning in the 1930s and 1940s. Since a number of manufacturers did not produce their own product, it was handled through contractual arrangements. Frozen fish fillets grew in popularity for private label, since there were no national brand leaders in this category. Fish sticks, too, became a major product, one of the earliest prepared foods to go into private label.

Brokers Establish Private Labels

In 1936, the Robinson-Patman Act passed, prohibiting anti-competitive practices, such as unfair price discrimination and inequitable quantity discounts. As mentioned previously, this Act also scrutinized brokerage and promotional payments—no longer allowing wholesalers or retailers to act as their own brokers, that is, locating supply sources for the manufacturer or a market for the manufactured goods. IGA did not regard itself as a buyer, so it continued its brokerage service. In the Red & White private label program, set up by S.M. Flickinger, however, the retailers had their own in-house brokerage operation, which handled product procurement. But now they had to reform this operation outside the group organization as a separate business, called Busey, Maury and Wright, which over the next couple of decades managed the private label business.

Other brokers emerged as well, handling private label programs and actually providing controlled brands or packer labels produced by their principal (the manufacturer) for their trade customers (the retailers or wholesalers).

Another private label brokerage firm, serving the retail trade since 1929, after the Robinson-Patman Act, was reorganized as Alliance Associates, Coldwater, MI. Alliance developed its own niche, marketing a non-exclusive Family Fare controlled label for its customers as well as exclusive food labels, earmarked for grocery retailers as well as merchants in other market segments.

From the 1950s onward, independent brokers became significantly more important to the development of private label for smaller retail accounts—some of them destined to become market leaders. The food brokers did not start out as merchandising specialists; instead they sold products from small food-manufacturers to small wholesalers and retailers. They themselves primarily served as sales representatives. As they matured, brokers became more involved in helping customers improve their merchandising and marketing activities, too.

One of the oldest private labels, started by a broker, is the Pocahontas brand, established in produce for food service accounts about 1875. Decades later, it became available to the retail trade. In the 1930s, the brokerage firm Taylor & Sledd, Inc. (started in 1875), Richmond, VA, teamed up with Monarch Institutional Food Service to expand its product line beyond produce into other foods. And so the Pocahontas label was sold to grocery wholesalers and chain operators as a controlled label. Those accounts sometimes used it as a springboard into their own private label program by introducing their own label identities. The Pocahontas label meantime extended itself into national coverage, representing both fancy and choice grade quality, handled by franchised food-service distributors as a controlled label and by retailers and wholesalers as their own house brand.

Taylor & Sledd itself had put most of its emphasis behind being a marketing and buying group for the food service business. In the 1980s, however, the company began increasingly to emphasize its retail business.

REFERENCES/CITATIONS

A&P 1944 "You and Your Company." (A&P booklet describing company policies, the organization, its products, and its service to the consumer) The Great Atlantic & Pacific Tea Company. (November 1944).

A&P 1985 A&P Update (House Organ). Vol. 3, No. 1.

Certified Grocers of California 1972 (50th Anniversary Annual Report—1972).

Safeway 1966 ("40th Anniversary Issue," Safeway News house organ).

Safeway 1975 ("Our 50th Year," Annual Report—1975), pg. 8.

Safeway News, August/September 1980

Photographic Album 1

The A&P store (shown to the left) operated in the 19th century, selling basic commodities like teas, coffees, and sugar. Bags and barrels of coffee, taken off ships, were stacked out front, ready for delivery by horse-and-wagon to rural customers. The store worked almost like a beacon, attracting customers with its row of lanterns, its lighted 'T' logo hanging overhead, and window displays of premium chinaware and products. A&P handled both retail and wholesale trade from its stores.

This turn-of-the-century A&P store featured banners out front, advertising A&P - brand baking powder & Bocklock breakfast coffee. Its window displayed china and other premiums obtainable with the purchase of a pound of tea or baking powder.

Inside this A&P store of the 19th century, the left side stocked glassware premiums with coffee beans available underneath. The coffee beans could be taken across the aisle. for weighing on a scale. A&P Elgin brand creamery butter is at the back. Notice the colorful murals on the left and right for atmosphere.

35c Coffee.

The Great Atlantic & Pacific Tea

Store Closed ALL DAY This Wednesday
August 14th

GROCERS' DAY

SPECIAL BARGAINS FOR MONDAY AND TUESDAY

Try Our
"MOTHER'S" BREAD

Better than home-made; larger than 10c loaves elsewhere, and our special price is

7c per loaf

Get it early, as our bakers can't turn it out fast enough.

"PREMIUM" JAVA COFFEE
for two days only

20c lb.

Quaker Puffed Rice
Cerealine Cornflakes.
9c PKG.
The popular ready-to-eat cereals.

Messina Lemons. 15c

29c

55c

Armour's Beef Loaf, ready to serve cold, a 20c can 15c

Royal Jelly Powder, a
free with 2 pkgs.
each

An inside view of an A&P in the late 1920s (above) shows an expanded stock, including fresh vegetables & fruits to the left, dry grocery items stacked up to the ceiling, left and right, and a coffee grinder to the right. Butter, lard, & cheese were sold at the back and meat from a display case. Its Bokar brand (Santos coffee) is promoted in a mock-up box (3 pounds for $1).

In 1911, A&P advertised discount bargains for its own "Mother's" bread (3 cents off the 20-cent-per-loaf price) and "Premium" Java coffee (10 cents off the 30-cents-per-pound price.

George Huntington Hartford (in the portrait), founder of the A&P empire, raised his two sons, John Augustine and George Ludlum, to carry out his objective: "More and better foods to more people for less money."

TO TRY THE

WORLD'S MOST POPULAR COFFEES

Accept Kate Smith's invitation! Discover for yourself that there is a coffee that has been specially blended to suit your taste! You'll find that the coffee for you is an A & P Coffee . . . either mild and mellow EIGHT O'CLOCK, rich and full-bodied RED CIRCLE or vigorous and winey BOKAR...the three coffees whose fine, fresh flavors are better liked by more people than any other coffee at any price...A & P Coffee Service delivers these famous coffees roaster-fresh...and still in the bean. The one you choose will be ground before your eyes—exactly right for your method of making—at the very moment of purchase. Try an A & P Coffee tonight. Learn how really good coffee can be.

A&P employed celebrities like singer Kate Smith to endorse its own coffee line in ads like this one in "A&P Menu," (March 1936) a publication featuring recipes, menus and food advice.

In 1937, A&P stores began to look more like today's supermarket, featuring aisles dedicated to certain product categories. The Ann Page food line is promoted as a store exclusive on a wall sign .

Dr. William Hunter was the first physician in America to adopt the English concept of an apothecary shop, where customers could buy medicines, soaps and fragrances under one roof. Started in Newport, RI, his first shop opened in 1752. Eventually, products carried the Caswell-Massey name as well as Dr. Hunter's on a range of private labels that emerged in the 19th century, when the first Caswell-Massey store opened in New York City. These outlets stocked the apothecary line of products as well as serving sandwiches and soda. The Caswell-Massey brand is believed to be the first private label still being marketed in the drug store/food market segment in the United States.

The picture on the left shows one of the first stores in New York City, where Caswell-Massey began to include its store brand on items such as Lotus Balm for the hair, Morning Tonic, Eau de Cologne, Pure Distilled Water, etc. The tradition of "always" using "only natural ingredients and the best available" continues —it was first practiced by Dr. William Hunter in the 18th century.

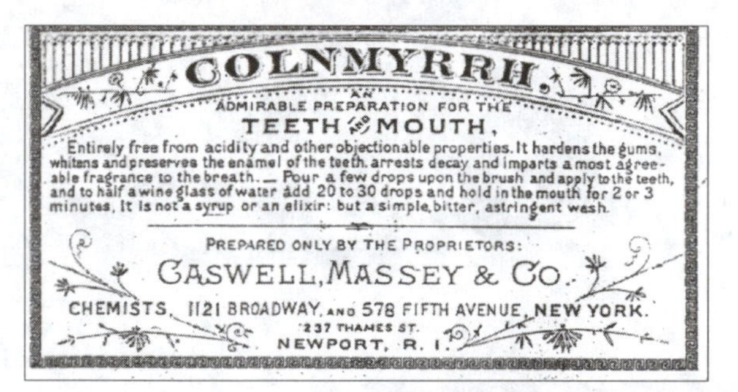

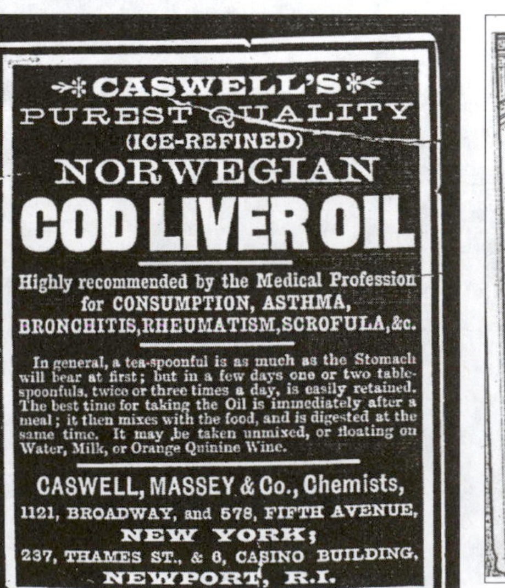

In the 1920s, The Red & White Corporation published a catalog list of items it supplied under the Serv-us and Red & White brands. Product descriptions included: tomato catsup, "pure, ripe tomatoes and spices without any artificial coloring or preservative"; and mayonnaise "with no filler or corn-starch added as is so often the case with many of the brands."

18 th century grocer Jacob Bunn sold private labels like those shown on the left. The Bunn Capitol Grocery Co. carried a number of other private brands, using names from his family, friends and nearby locations. One friend, Abe Lincoln was so honored on a coffee container. The Wish Bone label eventually ended up as a manufacturer's brand for salad dressing.

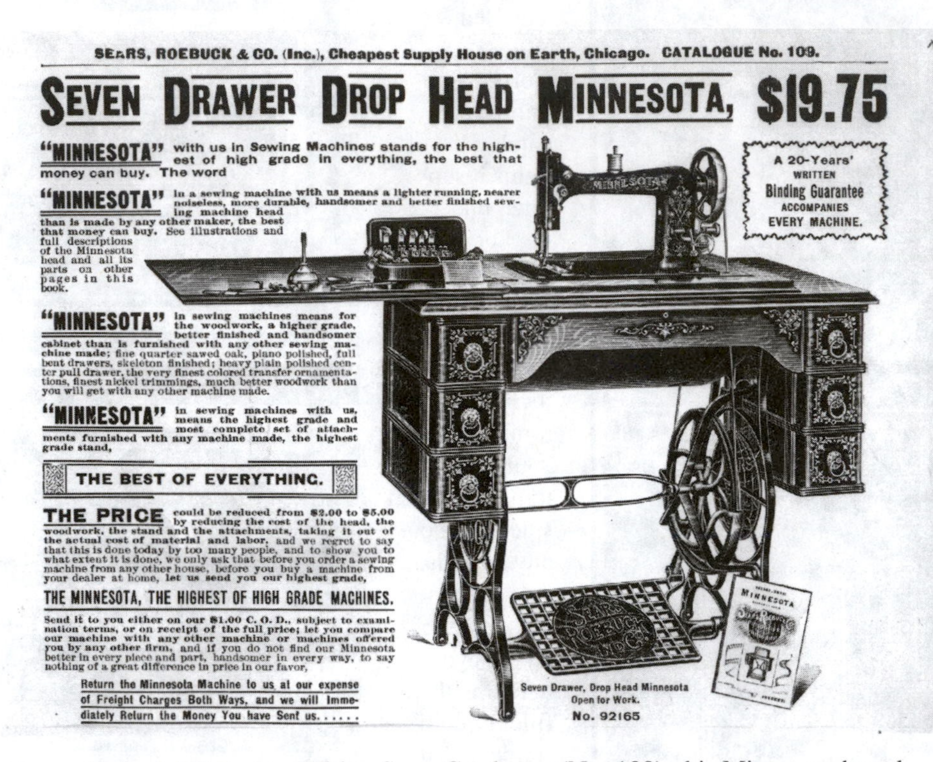

Above: In the 1900 Spring Edition Sears Catalogue (No. 109), this Minnesota-brand sewing machine was offered as an exclusive. The copy speaks for itself.
Below: This Piggly Wiggly store (1925) demonstrates the concept of self-service, in which patented swinging price tags helped consumers shop without clerks behind counters. This merchandising format also exposed shoppers to all the store merchandise.

IGA, the voluntary group serving independent grocers, began to establish its roots (and IGA Brand program) in the 1930s with stores like the one shown here.

Farmer's Co-op Enters Retail Market in 1941--Includes GLF Quality & New P & C Private Labels To Keep Competitive Pricing Alive in New York State

A farmer-purchasing-and-marketing cooperative, the Grange League Federation (G.L.F.), operated early in this century with its own flour mills, canneries, and egg auctions. In 1941, to deliver a better price to its consumers, the co-op met in Ithaca, NY to establish a separate marketing corporation, the Cooperative P&C Markets, Inc. (the P&C standing for Producers and Consumers). The following year, the co-op opened its first supermarket (12,000 square feet) in Batavia, NY. The format was self-service, featuring a complete line of grocery, meat and fresh vegetables. The stock also included G.L.F. brand and the new P&C brand. In the following decades, other private labels were introduced: Sunny Square Golden Acres, Bonny Brook, Country Manor, and Penny Curtiss. Today, The Penn Traffic Co., Syracuse, NY, operates as a $3+ billion supermarket chain, overseeing a number of store banners. (P&C Foods 1992, "50th Year" Report).

CHAPTER 8

PRODUCT/BRAND PROLIFERATION

It could be generalized that in the grocery trade, the larger manufacturers or processors emerged as the brand leaders, producing primarily their own brands, while thousands of smaller companies survived through the choice of producing their own brands, packer labels, private label business, and/or contract packing for other brand manufacturers. In the latter case, they would sometimes refer to this as "private label," since they were producing products under some other manufacturer's brand name. (This reference continues today, especially in the cosmetics market.) Under the definition established in this book, this outside business was not truly a private label. It was more a matter of being private business, which they conducted for other manufacturers/processors.

Early in this century, numerous fruit and vegetable canners began supplying fancy, choice, and standard grade products under packer labels to the grocery trade. In 1907, Minnesota Valley Canning began packing peas for the grocery trade. In the 1920s, the company introduced its Green Giant packer label, which eventually became a national brand. Some of these packer labels were changed by retailers into private labels. The idea eventually evolved of a packer label serving as the trial balloon in a product category. If the label succeeded, it could be re-identified as part of the retailer's own store brand range of products. As private label volume began growing in the 1950s, a number of manufacturers de-emphasized their packer label business and committed more to private label.

Brand Madness Spreads

The trend was toward a madness for brands as well as private label. The emerging supermarkets, some up to 50,000 square feet in size, were stocked with an enormous mix of merchandise: grocery staples, meat, bakery goods, produce, dairy items, tobacco, paint, hardware, auto accessories, etc. Within that product mix, shoppers might find up to 40 brands of peas in a supermarket. Canners multiplied like rabbits in the Midwest during the 1930s and 1940s. In Wisconsin, there were some 150 labels of canned peas sold at one time, not one of them taking more than a 1% market share. Eventually regional and national brands in the canned goods area emerged, followed by market leaders in the frozen food industry. As other product categories developed and matured, moving beyond staple items into manufactured goods, such as dry grocery foods and non-foods, and health and beauty aids, name brand leaders emerged in those categories as well. In most cases, smaller private label manufacturers followed the brand name leaders. Private label was not an innovator—products were keyed to the successful brand leaders, which pioneered quality and packaging developments in these categories.

One interesting product category where private label grew right in step with the emergence of brands is aerosol sprays—a highly diversified product area. The aerosol spray was first developed by the U.S. government during World War II, to help protect military personnel against insects in tropical war zones. This opened up the category, first to insecticides, then to paint sprays, followed by brake-cleaner sprays, other auto-cleaning sprays, and then to numerous industrial products.

Private Label Share By Departments

There really is no idea about just how pervasive private label became during the middle part of this century. One tally, completed by a National Commission on Food Marketing Technical Study, for the year 1964, found that the food chains had some 40% of their private label sales in dairy products, followed by 25% in bakery products, 10% in coffee, 9% in canned vegetables and fruits, 8% in frozen vegetables and fruit juice, and 5% in bacon. This is not surprising, since the chain operators, which founded their business on tea and then coffee, soon afterward developed their own production-processing capability in bakery and dairy, while also embracing the canned and frozen food areas for private label. (Padberg 1971)

Since the independent grocers, grouped under voluntaries or co-ops, had less interest in processing their own products, this study shows a much stronger private label commitment in canned vegetables and fruit for the voluntary retail groups (38%), for the cooperatives (38%), and the independent wholesalers (68%). Coming in second, staple dairy products registered 27% for the voluntary, 23% for the cooperative, and 13% for the independent wholesaler. Actually, the voluntaries were shown to do about twice the volume of the co-ops in private label. The voluntary and co-op private label sales together represented just 9.3% of total private label sales versus the food chains taking 88.6% of that volume overall, according to the study.

A Private Affair: Private Labels

Since most private label manufacturers were small operators, regional at best in their market coverage and either family- or privately-owned, they maintained a low profile. This may be one reason why their products were called 'private label.' Their names were not regionally or nationally recognized; indeed, their identity did not even appear on the distribution statement of a package. They remained anonymous. Other terms also came into vogue as well: buyer's labels, house brands, and distributor labels. It was a secret identity, known only within the trade. These manufacturing sources were never identified on the private label package; only the distributor's name (a retailer, wholesaler, co-op, or voluntary group) appeared on the distribution statement located on the back panel of a package. As a result, it is extremely difficult to trace the growth of private label manufacturers and their market-share development, especially in private label sales.

Many of the emerging private label manufacturing leaders, supplying different product categories, did not get started in private label until after 1950. There are exceptions, of course, such as Azar Nut in Texas, which started private label packing in the 1920s and New Jersey-based J. L. Prescott, a pioneer in private label household chemical products, which began supplying powder detergents under the Sears brand in the 1930s. It is interesting to note that in one of the early issues of *Private Label* magazine, the private label industry's first trade magazine, Prescott advertised itself in 1979 as "the greatest unknown company in our industry," announcing that it was "one of the world's largest manufacturer of private label laundry and household cleaning products." (Private Label Magazine 1979)

In the dairy category, home delivery of milk in glass bottles gave neighborhood dairies complete control over the price of milk. Yet in the late 1940s, national grocery chains began to convert to waxed paper cartons, which not only gave them a price advantage over the glass bottles, but also eventually opened up the opportunity to put their own store name or brand on the milk carton.

The supermarket retailers purchased meat from packers set to prescribed specifications for sale in the store's meat department, fully staffed with meat cutters. Shoppers ordered special cuts and weights of the product, which was then packaged and often sticker labeled, sometimes with the store identity—another form of private label.

Private Label Versus Brand Loyalty

It really wasn't until mid-century, however, that the identification of a private label industry began to take shape, as more product categories in the food and non-food grocery area opened to private label. Eventually, when one leading name brand dominated a product category, that brand identity, at least for consumers, became synonymous with the category itself. Against this developing brand loyalty, private label was said not to do well. However, two strong brands in a category allowed for some brand switching, giving private label more of a chance as another buying option for the consumer.

When several brands vied for market share in a category, private label had its strongest competitive edge up against those brands. In other words, when consumers were oriented to buy by the category instead of buying particular brand names, private label had more of a fighting chance for market share. (Consumers today are more often category buyers. Both retailers and wholesalers now plan their strategies less from a product-group focus—favoring brand leaders—and more toward a category management orientation.) At this time, however, consumers were shopping more for brands, thanks to the influence of radio and the new medium, television, as brand manufacturers began to spend millions rather than thousandsof dollars in advertising. Additionally, the proliferation of larger supermarkets, stocked with discounted branded merchandise, reinforced consumer brand loyalty.

This brand-orientation of consumers, however, did not deter retailers from promoting and building private label business. In the October 1950 issue of *The IGA Grocergram*, the voluntary group spelled out six reasons for pushing "IGA Brands" in its IGA stores. IGA did not think of its own stock as a private label:

1. Greater profits for you; greater savings for your customer.
2. Quality standards equal to or better than advertised brands.
3. Builds customer good-will and confidence.
4. Controlled label—brings customers back to IGA stores.
5. Trend is toward more controlled labels.
6. Increases over-all store volume.

That same issue of the *IGA Grocergram* also listed six ways to help IGA retailers increase the sales of IGA Brand products:

1. Have adequate stocks of all items.
2. Establish a store's quotes per item based on the store volume.
3. Preferred shelf space.
4. Mass floor displays
5. Follow through on "Feature of the Week" promotions.
6. Insist on proper shelf price. (IGA Grocergram 1950)

This scenario served as the foundation, drawing in dedicated private label manufacturers, who now supply most of the business. Today, the majority of the private label manufacturers each have sales volume under $100 million. The brand manufacturers, on the other hand, have gained the upper hand in terms of market share and, as a result, are less willing to participate in the private label business.

REFERENCES/CITATIONS

IGA Grocergram "Silver Jubilee." Sept.16, 1950

Padberg, Daniel 1971 "The Private Label Processor," Chapter 6 (sourced from National Commission on Food Marketing, Technical Study 10), Today's Food Broker. Lebhar Friedman Publishing Co., New York, pp. 54-60

_____Mid-20th Century Values (1950-80)_________

CHAPTER 9

PRIVATE LABEL GAINS STATURE

By mid-century, the leading supermarket chains were committed to private label, based upon decades of product development within their own manufacturing and processing facilities as well as on the success of their growing private label lines. So, too, were those independent grocers who had joined different voluntary groups or teamed up either separately (retailers only), or together with food wholesalers in the ownership of cooperatives. The co-ops and voluntary groups also encouraged independent grocers on their own to start up store brand programs, based upon their success with a controlled label line, while participating with a co-op or group. Additionally, private label was well-served over the next few decades by emerging brokers with off shoot private label divisions, as well as by the in-house broker organizations. The latter, initially led by Federated Foods, assigned people to, and located them within, certain accounts. These brokers helped smaller grocery retailers develop and manage private label in terms of procurement and merchandising/marketing strategies. Heretofore, only the large chain operations could afford this. Also, there were a few dedicated private label manufacturers, some having started as far back as the 19th century, who were joined by other manufacturers entering the business in subsequent years, all providing retailers and wholesalers with top-quality private label products. A good deal of credit is due these industry players for giving private label viability in the marketplace as well as a direction for growth. As this foundation solidified, drug store chains embraced private label as well, followed by the larger food and drug wholesalers, some of which had already been weaned, so to speak, on private label through their association with voluntaries or co-ops.

Private Label Stereotyped as "Cheap"

With a growing private-label presence in the marketplace, it was inevitable that competitive reactions would intensify. Some branded manufacturers and advocates of the "trusted brand leaders" from both the public and private sector inflamed their comments with vicious or highly-emotional attacks on private label. These detractors often generalized about the "cheap quality" of private label, representing it as a threat undermining the brands in the marketplace. As a result, private label was stereotyped with a stepchild status in the marketplace. Throughout the 1960s and 1970s, there were, in fact, both retailers and manufacturers who did compromise on private label quality to negotiate for better pricing. In truth, however, private label owners overall represented some well-respected industry players—retailers, wholesalers, manufacturers, and brokers—who established the highest quality standards for their own labels. In fact, there was honesty built in, because often different quality-levels of product were clearly identified under specific labels, i.e., standard grade, extra standard grade, and choice or fancy grade. For manufactured products, the private label owners insisted upon quality equal to or better than the leading brand within a given product category.

Many of these players addressed all quality levels with private label from standard grade to the finest quality. It was easy for detractors to generalize about all private label being lower quality because of its lower price. A majority of the players, however, developed first-tier, top-quality private label lines sold at a lower price than the brand leaders, thus giving consumers value for their money. Opponents argued back that only the top brands could provide value to the consumer because those brands offered better quality, which was worth the higher price. In laboratory "cuttings" of product, however, tests for quality differences in texture, color, product size, content, etc., showed that the private label version did, in fact, match the leading brand quality. The trend over the next four decades was toward improved private label quality and product selections, more advertising presence for private label, and a complete upgrade in general, making private label a major part of the food trade and a critical profit maker for the label owners.

The Role of the Chains

Supermarket chains became the market leaders in food retailing. They also were perceived to be a threat to the future of the independent grocer. Even though a number of independents collaborated in the formation of voluntaries or cooperatives which became formidable competitors against the chains, attacks on the supermarket chains continued. In 1940-41, the US Department of Justice's Antitrust Division charged market leader A&P with coercing competitors and suppliers into cutting prices to give A&P special price-treatment. Charges of trade restraint, unfair competition, and other monopolistic practices were leveled against the supermarket chain, without any consideration given the fact that A&P derived huge chunks of its profits from its manufacturing subsidiaries. The Justice Department also attacked other leading supermarket chains, such as Safeway and Kroger, for the same reasons.

In fact, it made good business sense for these supermarket chains to flex their private label muscle in order to build profits, to gain better control over pricing as an insulation against national brand price competition, to carry products and labels exclusively in their stores in order to draw in consumers, and to build customer loyalty with their own store brands.

"Low Prices Don't Hurt Anyone"

Taking its case to the public via a series of full-page newspaper ads, A&P argued that "low prices don't hurt anyone." As a result, the supermarket chain gained public support, including labor, manufacturers, farm groups, and other retailers. The

Justice Department eventually agreed to settle the matter out of court and a "consent decree" was signed in 1954, which did nothing to change A&P.

A&P began the 1950s as the largest privately-owned company in the country and the largest retail organization in the world. Its $3.2 billion in sales climbed to $5 billion+ in 1958, when the company went public. This happened because the Hartford brothers, John and George, who had taken over the family business from their father, George H. Hartford, were now both deceased, willing their 34% of the voting stock to the Hartford Foundation, while 48% was held by the Hartford family trust, with 18% left for sale to the public.

A&P was in transition, becoming more decentralized. Subsequently, this company faced nearly three decades of mismanagement. It did not stay in step with its competitors, who were introducing new products, exercising promotional deals and manufacturer allowances, and moving aggressively into the supermarket business with larger stores. Instead, A&P's management focused more on building sales and profits, and less on strengthening store morale or market share. Trading stamps, which turned into a fad in the mid-1950s, were resisted as much as possible. Much of A&P's profits ended up in the pockets of its shareholders, while its capital was misdirected into building a stronger manufacturing and distribution base—not into modernizing its retail stores. The company remained oblivious to the industry trends toward more suburban-store development, larger supermarkets, national brand promotions, new product roll-outs, greater store merchandise selection (including more non-food items), and more store services.

A&P Protects Its Private Label Interests

Additionally, A&P continued to put too much emphasis on private label, developing a protectionist policy, by giving its own brands, Ann Page, Jane Parker, A&P, etc., better shelf positioning and more promotional support than the advertised brands. A *Supermarket News* special report on the company noted that A&P's own brands—accounting for about one-quarter of its total $4 billion in retail sales—sold from 8% to 25% lower in price than the competing brands. Besides this pricing advantage, A&P also limited the selection of other brands in its stores and sometimes carried only its own private label in a product category. A&P, the article reported, operated 35 bakeries and 12 coffee roasting plants. As a result, 91% of A&P bread sales were in private label. Both the bakery-strength and the coffee business, helped A&P build customer loyalty. Its private label stock covered all the staples as well as a number of slow movers, such as aerosol insect killer, Denti-Kist toothpaste (sold mostly in the South), and in some states, its own Strathmore Club brand blended whiskey and Loch Fyne brand scotch. Baby food was considered for private label but dismissed, since its category profit-margins were small, while the brand leaders had a very strong customer loyalty. (Supermarket News 1957)

Supermarket News further indicated that A&P had paid close attention to upgrading its canned fruits and vegetables, completing three redesigns over the past 15 years. This was an area that most other private label owners only began to address more than 15 years later. Most private label packaging remained 1950-ish, so to speak. Retailers often picked up inventory stock from suppliers without too much regard for consistency of colors, registration, vignettes, design, and so on. This practice did little to promote the private label image. It was a big and costly mistake, which continued for decades.

By 1960, A&P operated some 23 manufacturing and processing plants, producing nearly 500 grocery items, plus 500 dairy and fish items. Five years later, the company spent $25 million to open its 1.5 million square-foot Horseheads, NY, plant—the world's largest food processing facility under one roof, occupying 33 acres.

It is unfortunate that A&P, under these circumstances, came to epitomize private label power in the view of the entire supermarket industry. Its example really represents more of a stubborn colossus somewhat out of control and depending too much on private label profits for survival. There are, of course,contrary illustrations in the trade, showing what private label did for the better managed retail chains, such as Safeway on the West Coast, Jewel Foods and Kroger in the Midwest, and Acme Food Markets on the East Coast. In fact, their strategies, including private label development, cost A&P its leadership role.

Jewel Foods Diversifies

Jewel Food, for example, acquired supermarkets outside its Chicago base and then broadened its merchandising mix, moving into self-service drugstores and department stores. The shop concept also was introduced within the Jewel Food Stores: Sausage Shops, Chef's Kitchens and Bakery Shops, all integrated into one store for a one-stop shopping experience. Notably, Jewel stepped into the limelight in 1960 by becoming the first U.S. food retailer to acquire a European food operation, joining with Grand Bazar department stores of Antwerp, Belgium, to form Supermarches G.B. A year later, Jewel launched another Belgium venture, Super Bazars self-service department stores, planning to integrate the Supermarches supermarket into that operation. Jewel became the largest stockholder in G.B. Enterprises, which was Belgium's largest retailer. Jewel also merged with Osco Drug that year, and next in 1962 acquired the Turn*Style general merchandise chain. Its diversification strategy continued through the 1960s: Star Market Co., Boston in 1964; the formation of White Hen Pantry convenience stores in 1965; Buttrey Food Stores, Great Falls, MT, in 1966; and 47% equity interest in Midco, S.A., now called Aurrera, S.A., self-service department stores, supermarkets and restaurants in Mexico City. By 1974, Jewel applied its European experience to development of the Grand Bazaar supermarket concept, a 66,000-square-foot food store, featuring free-standing specialty shops and a 25,000-square-foot Osco Drug store.

In effect, Jewel became almost like Procter & Gamble in that it served to school people in the trade. Jewel dispatched many people into the industry who carried its ideas into other retail operations.

By contrast, A&P, in 1973 still operated more than half its 3,614 stores in units less than 10,000 square feet. A&P also was being stereotyped as merely a private brand merchant throughout a period of rapid national brand growth. Jewel did not fight that trend. Its private label interest had followed the pattern also established at Safeway, for example: a proliferation of different store brand identities in an effort to build up brand equity in different product categories. Jewel, which tried to build market leadership in those categories and create a consumer following, did in fact succeed with some of its own brands, but eventually the company consolidated its private labels.

Acme: "The House That Quality Built"

In 1952, the commitment to private label was dramatized by Acme Super Markets, Philadelphia, with its opening of the Bakery No. 1 plant, the most modern, automated bakery (bread and cakes) in the United States. This facility was adjacent to the company's "D.C. No 1" operation, which set a new industry standard for a dry-grocery warehouse.

Acme Markets, Inc., based in Malvern, PA, is now part of one of the country's largest retail chains in both grocery and drug stores, American Stores, Inc., Salt Lake City, UT, an amalgamation of separate companies: Alpha Beta, Skaggs, Jewel, and Acme. Acme, in fact, epitomizes the classic private label strategy of giving consumers value for their dollar, starting from day-one of its operation. An historic perspective is in order. . .

"Give Away" Promotions in the 1890s

In 1891, Acme's first store was called "The House That Quality Built." In the first year of business, this operation, launched by entrepreneurs Samuel Robinson and Robert Crawford, focused on the consumer's needs in the neighborhood. Free hotcakes, buckwheat cakes, crullers and pound cakes were given out in a promotion called "A Great Give Away." Other 'Give Away' promotions followed. As the business grew and more stores were added, its name was changed to Robinson & Crawford. The owners' first newspaper ads stressed quality at a grocery store that offered "a full line of best teas, coffees and groceries at rock-bottom prices." (Acme 1991)

These entrepreneurs established themselves using the value formula of private label: the best quality at the lowest possible prices. By 1917, this Philadelphia-based chain merged with four other chains, pooling their 1,223 stores, three bakeries, five warehouses into the American Stores Company. Five years later, the company purchased a small cannery in Hurlock, MD, which marked the company's first full effort to develop distinctive store brands. Over the years, this plant processed seasonal items, such as tomatoes, apples, and other fruits and vegetables. During slow, off-season periods, the facility made pork & beans, fruit juices from concentrate and other products. Another cannery in Fair Water, WI, was purchased in 1930, bringing in high-quality peas, corn and other vegetables. This operation eventually added a freezing tunnel. American Stores even signed contracts with area growers to monitor and in some cases pick the crops. In 1924, the company acquired its Philadelphia's "D.C. No. 4" warehouse, which developed into an operation responsible for ripening bananas, candling eggs, processing fresh fish, and making and packaging mayonnaise, peanut butter, jellies, spices, and many other products. American Stores Dairy Company also began processing milk from nearly 100 small Wisconsin creameries into dairy products, especially butter, for its stores in the east.

During the 1940s, a meat packing plant was acquired to circumvent meat shortages during the World War II. Its hanging beef became well-known, but the facility also processed hot dogs, deli-meats, hams, and bacon. Over the years other sources of meat supply were added, i.e., eastern veal and lamb, western lamb and beef. The company also operated its own coffee mill in Colombia, South America.

Before the 1917 merger, each of the chains involved carried its own store brands. The Acme Tea Co., one of those chains, sold Louella butter, Victor bread, Hunter Brand canned goods, Bellgrade eggs, Dunlap's Best cornstarch, and Childs olive oil. Robinson & Crawford brought in its Gold Seal flour and butter; another chain had Mother's Joy coffee and Killarney tea. A number of those brands survived the merger; but with the canning operation underway, the ASCO brand (an acronym for American Stores Co.) emerged, covering not only canned goods but coffee, flour, and rice as well during the 1920s and 1930s. In every case, the priority set was the highest standards possible. Its Ideal brand was adopted from the 1941 takeover of Mutual Grocery Stores, based in New Jersey. That private brand eventually covered the company's entire premium brand range. (Acme 1991)

As consumers pressured the company to lower its prices, Acme's response was not to lower the quality of the Ideal range, but to introduce a second and even a third quality level of products, under such names as Farmdale, Glenside, Glenwood, Wincrest, and Fireside.

The trend was toward the introduction of private label products in other categories. The American Stores operation responded with separate identities in different categories: Princess paper products, Speed Up laundry detergents and soaps, Petagree pet food, Skyline general merchandise and health and beauty aids, Rob Roy and then Bala Club beverages, Virginia Lee and Supreme bakery goods, Home-de-Lite mayonnaise and salad dressings, Ivin's cookies, and Lancaster Brand meats. The Acme brand appeared in 1937, when the company entered the supermarket business.

Both the Ivin's and Lancaster Brand names were retained in 1981, when American Stores acquired Skaggs Companies, Inc., after which all the other private labels were consolidated under the Acme label, while the second and third level brands were re-identified as Econo Buy items. The Skyline brand also was kept until the chain acquired Jewel Companies, picking up its Osco brand for health and beauty aids and general merchandise. Through acquisition, American Stores had acquired Jewel with its Osco Drug operation.

REFERENCES/CITATIONS

Acme, 1981 . "Acme (100 Years) Markets," The Trumpeter (house organ) Commemorative Issue (1891-1991).

Progressive Grocer, 1971. "A&P—Past, Present & Future." Progressive Grocer Magazine, New York

Supermarket News, 1957. "The A&P Way (Series #13)." April 22, 1957. Fairchild Publications, Inc., Business Book Division, New York, NY.

CHAPTER 10

VOLUNTARY GROUPS & CO-OPS PERSPECTIVE

Facing strong chain store competition, the independent grocers fought for survival any way they could. One option was to voluntarily join a buying group organized around grocery wholesalers, in order to realize stronger buying power as well as greater operating efficiencies and also save time through a more organized distribution system. Two of the earliest groups, Red & White and IGA, gave the independents a chain-like appearance, including a strong controlled label line that reinforced their identity from the store facade to product packaging. The independents also could ride on the regional and national print and broadcast advertising orchestrated by the groups. These groups, in fact, spread across the United States. They also lent money to the independents to help them improve their business. In creating national distribution around the Red & White or IGA controlled labels, each group also helped the smaller manufacturers get wider distribution of their products. While major supermarket chains developed within metropolitan markets, independent grocers who were involved in the voluntary chain wholesale groups concentrated on the suburbs. Perhaps it was sheer luck, but people about this time were moving out of the cities back into the suburbs, as automobile usage increased and an improved highway system developed across the United States. Some of the alert grocery chain operators, realizing this as well, began to open stores in the suburbs; the independent grocers already had established this market as their stronghold.

Red & White Group Swallowed Up

The fortunes of Red & White and IGA differed perhaps because of the wholesalers involved in each group. Red & White had established a relationship with medium to small wholesale houses, who were eventually absorbed or consolidated into larger organizations with other flagship store interests. Even S.M. Flickinger Co., the wholesale operation that helped launch the Red & White group, was sold to a huge food wholesaler, Scrivner Inc., Oklahoma City, OK, which, in turn, was itself acquired by Fleming Companies, Inc., (same city) in 1994, thus consolidating the Scrivner operations under Fleming (an IGA owning wholesaler). Similarly, in Canada, many of the wholesale houses in the Red & White family were acquired by the country's leading wholesaler-retailer, George Weston Ltd., owner of Loblaw Companies, which converted the Red & White operations to its flagship stores. Even the Toronto-based Red & White Corporation, Ltd., had its name changed to Foodwide of Canada Limited in 1963, because of its dealings with different group store affiliates.

Near its zenith, about 1959, the Red & White voluntary group operated in 40 states as well as in every Canadian province. The group worked through 119 wholesale grocery outlets which, in turn, supplied nearly 5,000 Red & White stores. There was even an affiliation established in 1958 with Internationale Spar Centrale B.V., based in The Netherlands, a voluntary partnership of independent retailers and wholesalers operating throughout Western Europe. Plans called for developing Red & White stores in Europe, but nothing was developed. Additionally, there was an independent operation, Red & White Food Stores, established in Australia, obviously influenced by the growth of Red & White stores in the United States.

Some 10 other independent food store groups emerged as well, served by the wholesalers in the Red & White group. Flickinger, through its six major trading areas, had copyrighted group names and signs available under such names as Super Duper, R&W, Lucky Store as well as Red & White.

Red & White alluded to a published report by *Progressive Grocer* magazine late in the 1950s, which indicated that organized wholesaler-retailer teams were called the fastest growing element in the U.S. food business and the dominant force of food distribution, taking 44% of total 1956 U.S. sales in contrast to 37% for chains and 19% for unaffiliated independents.

Red & White, at this time, painted a bright future for the voluntary groups:

"Members of voluntary and cooperative enterprises accounted for 45% of the total grocery sales dollar last year. Unaffiliated independents only represented 16% of the total food dollars. Voluntary groups represented 38% of the total grocery sales in the United States—an increase of over 33% during the past 10 years. Over 90,000 stores are affiliated with voluntary and cooperative groups." (Red & White 1959)

Red & White Distributors, Inc. was operated as a wholly-owned subsidiary of the brokerage firm, Bushey & Wright, charged with procurement of the Red & White brand product line. In the controlled program, Red & White retailers and their wholesalers handled more than 410 Red & White items and a similar number under the Sun Spun and Our Value brands. Bushey & Wright also handled the packaging and label requirements for the program as well as supplying supplementary advertising and promotional material for local and national media.

Red & White Suffers Decentralization Plus Weakened Controls

Unfortunately, there were inefficiencies in the distribution system, which the group sought to correct in a reorganization plan based on a study conducted by Booz, Allen & Hamilton, business counselors. They called for a decentralized system. It was felt that certain functions at the Red & White national headquarters were being duplicated at the local level—an economic disadvantage, while other functions could be transferred to Bushey & Wright, Inc. Therefore the latter firm took over coordination of the production, quality control, wholesale distribution and retail market functions. In order to keep the Red & White and related controlled brands active over a long period of time, the group established the Red & White Foundation as an irrevocable charitable trust. It was managed by the trustee, the Continental Illinois National Bank and Trust Co., which each year paid the surplus funds it collected to the beneficiary, the University of Chicago. That money was to be used for the advancement of knowledge about food distribution and the development of techniques of operation to promote efficiency and economy.

In effect, the old Red & White Corp. of New York was dissolved and a new Red & White Corp. formed in Chicago, owned by its five top executives, which included members of Bushey & Wright. Red & White International was operated as a division of Federated Foods, Inc., with its own structure, covering the Food Service Division, the Red & White Voluntary Super Markets Division, the National Brand Sales Division, and the Hy•Top Products Division.

This action voted control of Red & White out of the hands of the group. Subsequently, it also put Red & White under a severe handicap, because the principals now in control of the Red & White brand were then developing other priorities, such as increasing regional chain store and co-op business. Tops Supermarkets, Buffalo, NY, for example, wanted to differentiate itself from the Red & White group, operating in its market. So Federated Foods assigned the Hy•Top private label to Tops. Another Buffalo supermarket chain, Harvest Markets, wanted its own label, too. So Federated, having just acquired rights to the Parade brand, assigned it to Harvest Markets. Eventually, Federated developed other proprietary controlled brands, such as Fine Fare, Leadway, Valu Check'd (generics), Better Valu, 7 Farms, 3 ring, Fiesta Fair, etc. Federated also began to manage private label programs already established by other food distributors, beginning with Piggly Wiggly, then expanding to include Malone & Hyde, IGA, Albertson's, etc. (Fuller 1996)

In the 1960s, the Red & White private label program was still Federated Foods' main business. Its sales, including both retail and food service, topped $55 million. But Federated saw the Red & White program as primarily a wholesaler label. Also, the Red & White group was slowly losing its buying power, because the members were no longer solidly behind the program. Red & White was marketed and merchandised at the local warehouse level with no concerted push from headquarters. For some Red & White members, the relationship with Federated Foods became strained, especially in securing deals from suppliers. Red & White had peaked out. As stated earlier, a number of its wholesale houses had been acquired by larger wholesalers, who switched the Red & White program over to their own private label activities.

In fact, even S. M. Flickinger Co. began to change its strategies, developing more leasing and franchising activities, as well as owning and operating supermarkets under the Super Duper identity. In 1968, for example, the company managed 96 Super Duper supermarkets, of which 23 were company-owned, while also carrying on its wholesale distribution business. By 1980, the company, through growth and acquisitions, topped $1 billion in sales. Four years later, its sales at $1.5 billion, S.M. Flickinger Co. sold out to Scrivner. In its 1983 annual report, Flickinger reported that during the past five years, private label unit sales growth—for its Red & White, Hy•Top, and Super Tru labels—expanded at an average five-year rate of 8%. Flickinger was acquired by Scrivner in 1984. That company, in turn, was taken over by Fleming Companies, which decided to end the Red & White program and other controlled labels, replacing them with its own private label programs.

Today, there are just a few scattered Red & White wholesale operations left in New England, the Carolinas, as well as some in the Midwest, and in the South. However, the concept remains as viable today as when it began.

IGA Establishes Larger, Longer-Lasting Connections

IGA truly was more fortunate than Red & White in being initially tied to emerging giant food wholesalers in the industry, including Fleming, Supervalu, Wetterau, and Nash Finch, as well as smaller but still strong and enduring regional wholesale houses—Buzzuto's in Connecticut, The Copps Corp. in Wisconsin, W. Lee Flowers & Co. in South Carolina, etc. For the most part, these wholesalers were not absorbed by larger wholesale company; they acquired other businesses or grew by themselves. More important, many of the pioneering wholesalers owe allegiance to IGA, which traces its history right back to their formative years. IGA helped them stay in business and prosper. As a result, the IGA system was kept intact. Even in Canada, Oshawa Companies, which was IGA's first Canadian franchise, took control of other IGA wholesale operations and now controls most of the IGA system in Canada. Today, some 20 owning companies (distributors), operating 65 distribution centers, serve some 3,600 IGA supermarkets around the world. IGA calls itself "the world's largest voluntary supermarket network."

The IGA story started in 1926 when J. Frank Grimes, a Chicago accountant who specialized in auditing the books of wholesale grocers, learned about the successful Red & White voluntary group. In fact, Grimes did talk with S. M. Flickinger about the concept, according to Flickinger family members. Grimes obviously was impressed. Collaborating with five associates—Gene Flack, Louis G. Groebe, W. K. Hunter, H. V. Swenson, and William W. Thompson—Grimes organized the Independent Grocers' Alliance in Poughkeepsie, NY, which was the headquarters of the W. T. Reynolds Wholesale Co. Some 69 independent retailers joined the group and at another meeting the following night in Sharon, CT, another 25 retailers joined. By year's end, there were 150 grocers calling themselves IGA retailers, which brought independent retailers together under a network of food wholesalers around the country. Within a year, IGA stores were located in 15 states. Interestingly, in 1928, Fleming Company, a regional wholesaler at the time, became affiliated with IGA. Within five years, there were more than 10,000 IGA food stores in 37 states.

IGA established its headquarters in Chicago with buying offices in New York, San Francisco, and New Orleans. The group quickly established a national advertising program of weekly radio broadcasts across the continent, in addition to regular national magazine advertising.

IGA's pooling of buying power helped the group form a close relationship with manufacturers, in fact, even taking complete control over some factory outputs as well as large blocks of merchandise available at a given time. IGA also cooperated with many manufacturers, helping them through quantity orders and organized distribution, to reduce their overhead, which allowed them to pass the savings on to IGA at a lower cost. Among the IGA wholesalers who became owners, there were 22 who operated their own coffee roasting plants. This gave IGA a strong buying base for coffee beans and, in about 1929, led to the establishment of a line of private label coffees: the White "I," higher price; Blue "G"; and Red "A" blends.

IGA Develops a Nationally-Advertised Label

The independent IGA grocers adopted an Acorn trademark, which changed soon afterward to the I.G.A. logo. From the start, IGA carried private label items with the intention of offering the independent grocers a complete line of food products under one label that could be advertised nationally. In 1929, Grimes explained the strategy, concerning IGA private label versus the nationally-advertised food items:

"Only in cases where it is found impossible for wholesalers and retailers to get their cost of doing business out of an item—only in such cases will the IGA label be put on items in competition with the well-known nationally-advertised brands." (Grimes 1931)

So the IGA brand probably first appeared on macaroni or flour, and then expanded into other items such as coffee, tea, canned goods, cake flour, nut margarine, spices, strained baby food, soap flakes, and lye. Some products were sub-branded, such as Gold Tost corn flakes, Ripe 'N Ragged canned fruits.

Since Flickinger had cornered the market with a patriotic Red & White identity on both his stores and private label packaging, IGA opted for a blue-and-white standard IGA label, along with a 16-foot painted blue-and-white exterior sign on the IGA stores.

The IGA brand products were maintained with the strictest quality standards. IGA peanut butter, for example, was strictly fancy No. 1 Virginia and Spanish peanuts. Extensive quality-control testing was maintained at the headquarters. The group garnered several awards over the years for its IGA brand items. For example, nut margarine received a Gold Medal at an international exposition in Paris in about 1929; IGA's Sunny Morn and Royal Guest collected Blue Ribbon Awards from *Spice Mill*, a coffee and tea industry publication; and *Modern Plastics* magazine gave IGA baking powder honorable mention for its lock-top lid and paper inner seal.

To help build its national image, IGA obtained IGA Brand product endorsements from numerous celebrities, such as baseball hero Babe Ruth, movie star Jackie Cooper, prize fighter Jack Dempsey, and even the dog, Pete, in the "Our Gang" motion pictures. IGA also sponsored its own radio drama show, "One Girl in a Million," staring Sally May, a winsome young night club entertainer who married Don Whitehall, son of a millionaire. IGA backed up the program with merchandising support, such as dodgers, posters, and other advertising materials. This was expanded later to sponsorship on the CBS radio network program, "Meet the Family."

By the end of 1930, IGA carried ads in 500 daily and weekly newspapers. IGA sponsored programs with *Parents'* magazine and Walt Disney Studios, in the latter case, making Pinocchio an IGA spokesman. National magazine ads for IGA products appeared in many different consumer publications, including *American Magazine, Country Gentleman, Farmer's Wife, McCalls, Pictorial Review, Saturday Evening Post.*

In 1929, IGA established its IGA *Grocergram* house organ newspaper, which soon afterward changed to a magazine format, communicating developments and ideas within the IGA system. Nearly 20 years later, IGA launched a consumer magazine, *American Family* which was sold exclusively at IGA stores, just like A&P's *Woman's Day* magazine.

Pioneering Graphic Touches

The strength of IGA came from the people within its headquarters as well as from both wholesale and retail companies. IGA, for example, innovated as early as 1931, by dispatching photographs instead of drawings for display ideas. The group also pioneered the use of full-length talking pictures in consumer-relations and sound-slide films for its personnel training program. Just 10 years after the organization of IGA, the group had its IGA label redesigned with specialty labels, featuring product vignettes that appealed to the eye. A "Ripe 'N Ragged" line of canned fruits, for example, featured product displayed in dishes ready for service on a broad black background. A thin green line, carrying the IGA medallion in red and yellow, bordered the can top, while white letters identified the fruit on a bright red band. About 1936, there were some 50 food products, numbering possibly 500 different IGA brand items. The IGA retailers followed the lead of the food chains, adding a complete line of quality fresh meats, dairy products, cheeses, more variety in fresh fruits and vegetables and a full stock of grocery items. Late in the 1930s, IGA introduced canned food such as shoestring carrots, sliced peaches, whole beets and cut wax beans in glass jars, allowing consumers to see the product before they purchased it. Its IGA TableRite meat program, a quality-assured line of products in which IGA beef selectors chose and rolled individual beef sides for delivery to IGA stores—was unveiled in 1948. (IGA 1936).

IGA's sales climbed to $2.3 billion in 1952—not too far behind A&P at $3.8 billion that same year. Red & White group registered less than $2 billion at that time.

The independent IGA grocers, too, took the initiative in promoting IGA Brand products. A group of retailers in one area, for example, once ran a co-op ads featuring the baby raised on IGA Brand strained baby food and who was the child of one of their members. Another IGA retailer in Crawfordville, AR, aggressively promoted IGA soap flakes by cooperating with a local supply depot, having them attach free wash cloths to each box as a premium give-away. Customers in the IGA store also were given free samples of the IGA soap flakes inside an envelope carrying the name and address of the retailer, to encourage them to use the product and see how effective it was.

IGA Expands Outside U.S.

In 1951, IGA granted its first Canadian franchise to Oshawa; but that franchise and others negotiated later were bought out by the Canadian wholesalers involved as a group some 13 years later. In the 1980s, IGA began its international expansion, realizing the dream of its founder, J. Frank Grimes. In 1988, C.I. Foods Systems Co., Ltd., a food wholesale firm in Tokyo, became the first international member, followed in that same year, by wholesaler Davids Holding Pty., Ltd., of Sydney, Australia.

In the 1930s, Grimes envisioned a global network of IGA stores. He did try to establish European membership, but his plans never took root: in Spain, the effort was aborted. Nevertheless, IGA continued to grow, one enduring sign of its progress being the continuation of independent store ownership passing on from fathers to sons. In a similar spirit, Grimes retired in 1951, turning control of IGA over to his son, Don, which marked a turning point for IGA. IGA went through a growth phase, under his leadership and that of two presidents who followed. But while there was growth, there also was a breakdown in the synergies established between wholesalers and the independent retailers—a problem not corrected until late in the 1970s, under the new management leadership, headed by Tom Haggai, a lecturer, author, and minister who became chairman in 1976 and president in 1988. Haggai picked up the spark generated by Frank Grimes and put IGA back on course through various programs—remodelling older stores, opening new stores, and introducing a new corporate identity program. In 1987, IGA formed an advertising committee that devised the marketing campaign, "Hometown Proud," which stressed community involvement, as a guiding IGA philosophy, in order to differentiate its retailers from their competition.

Clover Farm Evolves into Foodland International

There were, of course, other voluntary food groups formed as mentioned previously. One success story started in 1926, when George Green of Green-Babcock Company, a wholesale grocer based in Cleveland, OH, organized a national voluntary group around his Clover Farm plan. Some 33 years later, there were more than 60 Clover Farm stores, which carried the Clover Farm label, covering some 168 items. These Clover Farm stores, however, were mostly smaller mom-and-pop shops. Just like the grocery chains, this group had to adjust to the emergence of larger supermarkets. About 1957, the Clover Farm group adopted a new identity, Foodland International, to reflect its move into the supermarket business. The members, of course, kept their Clover Farm private label program, but also picked up on a Foodland program as well. It was at this time that Fox Grocery Co., Bellevernon, PA, joined Foodland International as a member.

Chauncey Freeland, now retired, worked for Fox Grocery, recalls that Fox became the driving force for Foodland International, literally putting it on the map with the buildup of some 400 stores. Other wholesalers in the group took notice and followed the Fox example. Important wholesale houses emerged, such as Hakes Foods in Iowa and Mitchell Grocery in Albertville, AL. Foodland International, Freeland indicates, grew to between 750 to 1,000 stores, encompassing some 45 wholesalers in the United States as well as three in Canada. The group maintained its own quality assurance testing facility, published a newsletter, and offered on-going promotional programs for the Foodland label. Fox Grocery carried another first-quality line, Home Best, for non-food items, and a second-tier Mrs. Lane standard-quality range. Members in the group stocked an average of 5% of their sales in private label, the commitment running from about 2% up to 10%+ per member. Fox Grocery also took some pioneering steps on behalf of private label, offering to donate so-much-per-label sold to consumers to the Children's Hospital in its marketing area—eventually some $3,000, a significant sum in the late 1950s. (Freeland 1996)

Foodland International, however, did not endure, because larger wholesalers moved in; Wetterau, taking control of Fox Grocery, then itself being acquired by SUPERVALU; Hakes taken over by Scrivner, itself acquired by Fleming Foods among many others. The larger wholesale organization, of course, carried their own store banners and private label programs, which very often survived in their takeovers.

Other reasons, of course, also dictate a change of allegiance to the voluntary group. One example is Hannaford Bros. Co., Portland, ME, which was started in 1883 by Arthur Hannaford, a farmer. Hannaford first opened a tiny wholesale fruit and vegetable shop, which eventually grew into a wholesale business that affiliated with the Clover Farm group early in the 1930s. This connection to the voluntary group helped Hannaford grow its wholesale grocery business to the point that in 1939, the company was able to purchase H.S. Melcher Co., a sponsor of the Red & White stores in Maine. Hannaford then consolidated the Clover Farm and Red & White groups under the Red & White label. The Red & White membership, however, did not work out, because Hannaford was expanding its operation into territories where other Red & White wholesalers operated. Hannaford could not carry its Red & White label into those markets, where it would lose private label exclusivity, so the company pulled out of the voluntary group entirely. Hannaford continued through a series of acquisitions and mergers, becoming the largest wholesale grocer in eastern Maine in the mid-1950s. Hannaford evolved into a multi-regional food retailer, which operated 134 supermarkets throughout Maine and New Hampshire and into parts of New York, Massachusetts, Vermont, Virginia, North Carolina and South Carolina. Recently, the company has taken the private brand used in its primary store chain, Stop 'n Save, and substituted the Hannaford name. This brand identity was registered as a federal trademark, allowing for national coverage.

One of the oldest (fifth generation) family-owned wholesale grocery businesses still in operation today, Miller & Hartman Wholesale Distributors, Lancaster, PA, mentioned earlier, in 1932 organized the Red Rose Food Stores, a buying group of 50 local retail grocers. By 1935, this group had almost 60 independent members and subsequently grew to 93 Red Rose stores. Originally paying just $1.10 per week, the independent grocers agreed to work under the supervision of Miller & Hartman, which conducted monthly meetings to keep members informed about products and prices. The group also conducted picnics, trade shows, banquets, and contests for its members. (Salmon 1993) Weekly newspaper ads carried featured items, including some of H&M's own private labels, which the store owners agreed to honor at their stores. They also had their store name and location listed at the bottom of each ad. Additionally, the store owners were provided with weekly circulars and advertising handbills, which could be given out to customers.

However, eventually, the voluntary food group Foodland International Corp., came to be managed, although not exclusively controlled, by the wholesaler, Wetterau Inc.,

Hazelwood, MO. Wetterau, in turn, was acquired by SUPERVALU in the early 1990s. Foodland licensed its registered trademark for store identification to be used in a store brands program, which less than a dozen food wholesalers, in addition to divisions in the Wetterau system, picked up on. As the Red & White group had diminished in size, Foodland had developed into the country's second largest voluntary group, overseeing more than 600 Foodland brand first-quality products in edible grocers, dairy and frozen foods. Wetterau, which had had its own private labels in the past, really became more active in private label when it became an IGA house. Subsequently, Wetterau coordinated several different controlled labels, including its own brand Foodland and IGA, either to avoid exclusivity conflicts in a market or to expand in a market new to retail customers, offering them an exclusive brand.

Federated Foods Provides Professional Support

When the U.S. Congress passed the Robinson-Patman Act in 1936, Red & White was forced to spin off its brokerage business, which initially became Busey, Maury and Wright, based in Arlington Heights, IL. In the mid-1950s, this brokerage decided to go beyond serving the wholesalers who sponsored Red & White brands, by developing its own brands for regional supermarket chains. This effort developed into a federation of some 30 private labels, franchised to different retailers, wholesalers, and cooperatives, who could market them as their own house brands. At that time, the brokerage was renamed Federated Foods. Federated also began handling the private labels of larger food wholesalers, as well as IGA business. In fact, Federated perhaps was one of the first brokers to completely manage a private label program owned by someone else. Federated took on the Piggly Wiggly private label program in the early 1960s. This brokerage evolved as a complete service organization, providing both retailers and wholesalers with such services as: product procurement and management, quality assurance, packaging, and merchandising and marketing support. The manufacturers, its principals, received the expertise of an experienced sales force, equipped with market research information and crop reports on commodities. This brokerage also began to emphasize the food service business, leading to the industry's first private label selling show late in the 1970s. By the early 1980s, Federated pioneered a similar dedicated private label selling show for its retail accounts, beginning with IGA.

Building on its effective management techniques and promotional efforts, Federated Foods evolved into a national private label marketing sales agency, operating offices in Chicago, Boston, Atlanta, Memphis, Dallas, and San Jose, CA. The brokerage managed a mobile sales force that covered every state. Additionally, Federated worked within its own in-house sales executive program, hiring professionals who could respond to the needs and requirements of suppliers—key canners, processors, freezers, and manufacturers—as well as the trade customers, i.e., retailers and wholesalers. Federated put together one of the industry's finest quality assurance programs, including on-site plant inspection; retail audits; written specifications for every product; lot selection programs; customer satisfaction programs; and compliance with state and Federal packaging regulations. The brokerage also organized a creative staff of label designers, who developed new concepts in art and photography, working toward dynamic package shelf appeal, while reflecting high-quality product content.

Federated's evolving strategy was all-encompassing. Its marketing team worked on new products, special marketing themes (retail marketing events), point-of-purchase materials, product and crop information, and follow-up assurance of product quality from suppliers. Complementing these efforts, Federated had within its staff a data processing group, which issued both standardized and customized reports, helping suppliers and distributors to better understand their business. Finally, Federated's label management team sourced labels and packaging, while managing inventories and shipments on a national scale, realizing economies and new synergies, using sophisticated computerized back-up support.

Besides its principal brands (Red & White, Hy•Top, Parade, etc.) there were a number of second quality private labels: Del Haven, Glen Park, Royal Guest, Seven Farms, Sun Spun, etc., as well as its generics line, a yellow-and-black label called Valu Check'd. Federated also managed many distributor-owned labels from major retailers and wholesalers to customers with limited market distribution.

The Role of the Cooperatives

The idea of cooperation or the sharing of ideas in an organized fashion within the grocery trade, first evolved in the 19th century, specifically in 1844 in England, where textile workers in the town of Rochdale formed a consumer cooperative society in order to supply food and other goods to their families. By 1883, a similar idea took root in Switzerland. Today, in fact, that country's supermarket business is dominated by three major consumer co-ops. From nearly the beginning of these European co-op movements, private label was made an integral part of the total business, representing from 50% up to nearly 100% of total co-op sales. (Fitzell 1992)

In the United States, during the 19th century, consumer co-ops took root almost at the same time as in England. At best, these efforts in the United States were spotty. Farmer and dairy co-ops were organized as well. Over the decades, the consumer co-ops came and went, not fully successful until the 1930s. But they still represented a very small share of total retail sales. Farmer co-ops, too, developed sporadically, dealing primarily in farm products (equipment and supplies), but also handling consumables for the families of farmers.

One notable co-op success is Farmland Industries, Inc., Kansas City, MO, which today is a $9.1 billion agricultural cooperative. Farmland is owned by half a million farmers and ranchers across the heartland of the United States, Canada, and Mexico. These producers own more than 1,400 farmer-cooperative associations which, in turn, own Farmland Industries. Farmland, founded in 1929 as the Union Oil Company, evolved into the Consumer Cooperative Association in 1936 and then adopted its present identity in 1966. There are now more than 13,000 livestock producers who also own this co-op directly.

First Grocery Co-ops on East Coast

State or regional co-ops emerged as well, where ownership was shared by local co-ops. These co-ops sometimes moved into manufacturing, processing, product procurement, and marketing of not only dairy and agricultural products, but also food and non-food groceries, paint, hardware, and other merchandise. The first co-op in the grocery business is traceable to the Baltimore Wholesale Grocery, organized in 1887 in Baltimore, MD, followed the next year by the Frankford Grocers Association, Philadelphia, PA. Grocer J. Augustus Edgar, helped spearhead this group of local retailers. They secured a warehouse and hired a manager to run the operation. Later, the group renamed itself the Frankford Grocery Company. Edgar joined the co-op in 1891 and eventually became its president—a post he held for 50 years.

Early in this century, *The Voluntary and Cooperative Groups Magazine* reported on these trends, while crediting itself with spreading the cooperative concept among wholesale food distributors. Interestingly, when that magazine's editor, Gordon Cook, interviewed S. M. Flickinger, asking about wholesale grocers serving consumer co-ops in the grocery field, Flickinger felt it wouldn't work. He did, however, believe that a wholesaler could function as a manager for a group of retailers. In contrast, Edgar had previously told the editor, Cook, that a wholesale grocer could not successfully set up a cooperative organization, both because of his self-interest and because a wholesaler was not retailer-minded. Flickinger, who had experience in both areas, proved that it could be done, following that interview. (Voluntary and Cooperative Groups Magazine 1966)

The co-op idea, in fact, spread as food wholesalers began to join forces, first to share information and eventually to develop a product procurement and distribution system for the co-op's owner-members. When a controlled label program was proposed for the co-ops, however, some participants balked, because they wanted only to share ideas and not necessarily to be tied into a specific procurement system.

To survive the onslaught of the emerging giant grocery chains, such as A&P and Safeway, the grocery independents had several options open. They could merge with other independents or acquire grocery companies and build up their own operation; they could be acquired by the chains; they could join a voluntary group owned by the wholesale supply houses such as Red & White or IGA to gain buying power; or they could organize and control their own cooperative, sharing strategies and conducting volume direct buying from suppliers to create a wholesaler profit for themselves.

Pharmacies in Toronto formed a buying club, as early as the turn of the century, incorporating that activity under the Drug Trading Company Ltd., which sold all drug lines at manufacturers' list prices. These independents eventually formed an Independent Druggist Alliance in 1933, which included the I.D.A. private label line of drug products, produced in their newly acquired Druggist Corporation Ltd. Buying clubs also were formed in Chicago: the Velvet Buying Club, which in 1914 was named Federated Drug Co. One of its founding members was Charles R. Walgreen, who started his first drug store in Chicago in 1901.

A Neglected Industry Force: The Co-op

There is little, if any, documentation available about the early history of the cooperative movement undertaken by different groups of independent grocers in the United States. In fact, throughout most of the first half of this Century, co-ops were left out of mainstream corporate thinking. They were neglected by almost everyone except the product manufacturers, who courted them as much as they did the large chain operators. The co-ops represented good business from the member stores that first numbered into the hundreds, and then for some groups into the thousands, and tens of thousands. A number of the co-ops, however, were weak in structure, being understaffed, mismanaged, and sometimes operated on individual self-interests and not on behalf of the independent grocers.

The co-op concept in grocery involved mom-and-pop grocers and small chain operators who decided to associate and cooperate within their own trading group. These retailer-owned co-ops met to share ideas, while some, quite early, also organized a control label purchasing plan for the members, who would call themselves 'Associated Grocers of...' with a geographic area made part of their identity. The members would embrace private label lines not so much because it gave them an exclusive control over their own brand of coffee, tea, canned goods, or whatever; but because the private label unified them all. They were now doing something on a united front.

The co-ops also had the example of their chief competitors, the larger supermarket chains, which were developing strong manufacturing support to assure a continuous supply of goods and to reduce their costs. Those savings were passed on to consumers. This rationale did not escape the independents, who could not afford to build bakeries, creameries, coffee roasting plants, meat distribution centers, or other production facilities. Instead, they grouped together to buy their own distribution facility, then purchased goods by the carload direct from manufacturers. Their own label gave them better control over their source of supply, i.e., a manufacturer or processor produced that brand only for the co-op. The manufacturer's own brand could be sold anywhere, which meant they would be less dependent on business from the co-op.

The controlled label gave the co-op members a better price, which they could pass on to consumers. The basis for many private label lines in the formative years for the co-ops lay in canned fruits and vegetables, and then spread to development of paper product goods, detergents, frozen foods, and other items. By controlling their own label, the co-op achieved a marketing edge, similar to what both the chain operators and the voluntary groups had achieved with their private label lines.

Retailers and wholesalers now formed co-ops across the country. In the Midwest, for example, some 100 independent grocers met in December, 1917, in Grand Rapids, MI, to discuss formation of a wholesale co-op organization. Some 27 of them signed aboard, forming the Grand Rapids Wholesale Grocery Co. Their first purchase in the spring of 1918 was a boxcar of sugar. By 1924, there were 181 members. Beginning in 1933, group advertising forged their identity. An AG emblem identified the Associated Grocers group. There were other retailers, identified under different names. Spartan Stores joined the co-op, as did other grocers in the surrounding states. The co-op began selling the Shurfine and Tastewell labels late in the 1930s or early 1940s. By 1952, the co-op had adopted the Spartan Store emblem, Spartan Stores being a secondary name used by their members in Grand Rapids. The Spartan Stores symbol in green, gold and white was used by many of the independent supermarket operators for their store identity as well as on their private label lines. Spartan Stores, Inc., today is one of the top 10 grocery wholesalers in the U.S.; its private label range extends over 1,500 products under the Spartan brand, as well as an additional 240 items under the Save Rite brand value line.

West Coast Joins Movement

On the West Coast, the independent grocers faced a major competitor in Safeway, which had 191 stores by 1920. The Safeway chain grew to 1,050 by 1925 and reached 2,675 grocery units by 1930. The independents could not match Safeway's lower pricing, its aggressive advertising and merchandising efforts. Against this formidable competitor, they organized a co-op called United Grocers, Ltd., Oakland, CA, which launched its Bonnie Hubbard label in the late teens. Bonnie Hubbard developed into a regional brand in northern California, even though it remained under the control of United Grocers. Decades later, Fleming was to acquire this operation.

In 1922, 15 independent grocers met in Pasadena, CA, to form Certified Grocers of California, Ltd. (later called CERGO). This retailer-owned wholesale buying group could buy direct from suppliers and turn over any wholesaling profits to the member grocers. They pooled their orders to buy products in carload lots. By 1926, the co-op was able to lease an 8,000-square-foot warehouse for its 123 members. In 1928, the group merged with another grocers' co-op and the following year purchased Walker Grocery Co. Private label, however, did not become integral to CERGO until 1944, with the launch of its Springfield label, followed later by other controlled brands such as Gingham, Special Value, Prize, and generic labels.

Associated Wholesale Grocers, Inc., Kansas City, KS, today claims to be the nation's oldest grocery cooperative (and the second largest retailer-owned grocery wholesaler). Its history began in 1924, when 20 independent grocers met to combine their buying and advertising power. They formally incorporated in 1926 as Associated Grocers of Kansas City. In 1953, the company adopted its present identity. It wasn't until the 1980s, however, that the company rolled out its own brands, beginning in 1984 with 150 Always Save economy products, followed the next year by the Best Choice range. AWS closed 1996 with its own brand sales topping $374 million (representing more than 1,590 items), out of total sales of $3.1 billion for the year.

Piggly Wiggly Forms "Paper Tiger" Co-op

In 1925, the essence of another cooperative effort was formed among independent grocers, who were franchisees of the Piggly Wiggly store concept. Some of these independents, in fact, owned their own local co-ops or mini regional chains. Under the tutelage of Piggly Wiggly Corp., Memphis, TN, which was reported to be the third largest grocery chain in the country at the time, the Piggly Wiggly Operators Association was formed to meet annually in order to discuss marketing strategies and share their experiences. These independents, however, did not own Piggly Wiggly Corp., so their association was at best a paper tiger co-op.

The novelty of the Piggly Wiggly concept was its self-service format, which had customers pass through a turnstile and then walk along a set shopping pattern, which took them by all the merchandise in the store, all the way to to checkout stands. This idea was developed by entrepreneur Clarence Saunders in 1916. Saunders believed he was the inventor of self-service and patented his store layout system. He also innovated in his price-marking of items, in requiring employees to wear uniforms, and in installing refrigerated cases for produce.

In a financial review of Saunders' operation, the entrepreneur was described as having

> "most of the standard traits of the flamboyant American promoter—suspect generosity, a knack for attracting publicity, love of ostentation, and so on—but he also had some much less common traits, notably a remarkably vivid style, both in speech and writing, and a gift...for comedy." (Brooks 1959)

Perhaps it was that last trait in particular that led to the naming of Piggly Wiggly as a supermarket chain.

The impact of self-service on the grocery trade was significant. Saunders franchised his concept, while also operating company-owned Piggly Wiggly stores under a corporate licensing agreement. By 1921, he had 615 owned or leased stores in 200 cities in 40 states, and the chain grossed some $60 million. The patented self-service form was licensed to others. Saunders claimed to be the sole inventor of self-service. In fact, he was probably right in arguing that he was first with a store that was fully self service, in contrast to other earlier versions, which just included self-service in their operations. However, in court cases, Saunders lost his argument to Jitney Jungle, Jackson, MI, and others. It was argued that grocer Albert Gerrard, operating in Pomona, CA, had introduced self-service into his Triangle Market in 1914 and in the following year, had, alphabetically arranged stock in his Alpha Beta stores to help shoppers locate goods by themselves.

Saunders began selling his patent for self-service in Canada, Europe, Mexico and other countries, beginning in 1919. He envisioned an international organization for Piggly Wiggly. Taking his company public in 1922, he successfully cornered the market on his stock, which he felt was underpriced, but was then delisted and eventually went bankrupt. The Piggly Wiggly Corp. survived as investors and bankers edged Saunders out, turning control over to C.D. Smith, a Memphis businessman. By mid-1923, there were 1,267 Piggly Wiggly stores in operation, 667 owned by the company, the balance franchised. That year, a large grocery chain, National Tea Co., Chicago, purchased 97 Piggly Wiggly stores.

'Guinea Pig' Strategies of Chains

Problems developed when other large chains became franchisees or owner-operators of Piggly Wiggly stores. They were attracted to the concept, but really had their own best interests at heart. Piggly Wiggly served as their test vehicle for the self-service concept. Ownership of those stores in different markets also gave the chain operators an opportunity to convert the Piggly Wiggly store over to their own chain concept. In fact, this happened more and more as the smaller Piggly Wiggly units were not as attractive as the emerging supermarket concept.

In 1929, Safeway operated 32% of the Piggly Wiggly stores in the country. By 1937, that number eroded to 10%, and by the end of the decade, Safeway was no longer associated with Piggly Wiggly.

Kroger Grocery and Baking Co., Cincinnati, actually purchased the Piggly Wiggly Corp., along with full control over its franchise system. Beginning in 1929, Kroger agreed to operate 918 Piggly Wiggly stores. Difficulties arose in that relationship, notably over competing formats. Kroger's ownership was not compatible, and the Piggly Wiggly franchisees felt uncomfortable and left the system. Eventually, Kroger converted all its Piggly Wiggly stores over to its Kroger concept.

Over the years, the Piggly Wiggly Corp. was bounced ping-pong fashion through numerous ownership changes—entrepreneurs, supermarket chains, wholesalers. Piggly Wiggly store franchisees included local co-ops, supermarket chains, and even a manufacturer, Consolidated Foods Corp., which in 1965 had to divest its retail business because of a conflict of interest, at the request of the Federal Trade Commission.

It was this changing management and its changing perspectives that slowed the development and growth of private label at Piggly Wiggly. Initially, Piggly Wiggly was a 100% proponent of national brands. In the 1930s, some private labels did emerge, because the independent operators wanted them. Some of them even developed their own private labels, such as Piggly Wiggly Carolina Company's Azalea branded line. There was a sensitivity about adopting the Piggly Wiggly name on products, because the franchise agreement, which extended to promotions, advertising, and the use of the logo on the store facade, did not mention a controlled label option.

Evolving during the early 1940s, companies in the system did pick up on a handful of different names, such as the Plymouth brand found on coffee and other products. It wasn't until the 1970s, however, that the Piggly Wiggly name appeared on the packaging, starting with aluminum foil, according to Ed Matthews, now retired from Piggly Wiggly, where he served as editor of its house organ, *Piggly Wiggly Turnstile*. The previous Piggly Wiggly president, a part-time lawyer, had been hesitant about the use of the name, but a new president, Carroll Kester, adopted this policy. Piggly Wiggly brand eventually grew to some 300+ items in the early 1980s, helped along by Federated Foods, up to the point when wholesaler Malone & Hyde took control, including management of the Piggly Wiggly private label program. (Matthews 1996)

The question to ask is: if the Piggly Wiggly co-op had adopted a strong controlled brand strategy early in its history, what would be its market position today? It's a good bet that the Piggly Wiggly name would have built a much stronger equity than it enjoys today. Its tardiness in building a strong Piggly Wiggly private label franchise put most of the work for differentiation in the marketplace on its humorous name, "Piggly Wiggly."

A National Co-op Splits into Shurfine Central & Western Family

In the 1930s, a dream materialized around the idea of forming a true national association of co-ops. This idea very likely was inspired by the success of the voluntary groups like Red & White, IGA, and Clover Farm, as well as by the growing A&P, Kroger, and Safeway chains. The National Retailer-Owned Grocers co-op (NROWG), was discussed in 1926 at a retail grocers' convention in Omaha, NB, when a group of wholesalers began formulating strategies to compete against chain competition. The following year, they incorporated NROWG as a cooperative for exchanging information about buying procedures and discounts offered around the country.

As Shurfine International, Northlake, IL, tells it: "...the wholesale grocers felt a need to become affiliated in order to do collective buying and earn maximum discounts offered by the manufacturers....A buying office was opened in Chicago in July 1934; this organization was better known as NROG (National Retailer Owned Grocers, Inc.)." They acquired the Shurfine brand from the Grocers Cooperative Bakery, Minneapolis, MN, using that identity on bread products, beginning in 1932. Success led to the formation of a brokerage business and further expansion of the Shurfine brand as well as other brands. "It should be pointed out," Shurfine continues, "that the decision for opening up a buying office did not meet with unanimous approval as there were those who felt the buying activity as well as the brokerage operations interfered with local operations. As time passed, this disagreement developed into dissension and the cooperative efforts began to suffered." In 1938, the co-op also was ordered by the Federal Trade Commission, acting on the Robinson Patman Act of 1936, to end the co-op brokerage business, if it wanted to continue on a cooperataive basis, and to concentrate business on a buy-and-sell basis. After WWII (1948), members on the West Coast (mostly larger combination store operators), who had incorporated their organization under the Pacific Mercantile Co., took over their San Francisco branch office for the co-op. The East Coast members, mainly small neighborhood grocery operators, organized under the name Eastern Division, NROG, while the central states members grouped together as the Central Division, NROG. While there was more private label activity conducted in both the East and Central regions, the central area overall represented the largest sales volume. In 1948, NROG was splintered apart, because of differences of opinion among its members.

One might ask why the different co-ops formed over the early decades of this century did not grow and prosper at the pace set by the food store chains. One answer could be found in the strategy they adopted. The co-ops paid their members rebates from the surplus earnings they made, instead of reinvesting that money in upgrading and modernizing their operations. When they did decide to improve the business years later, they faced inflated costs, when things had become more expensive. Conversely, the more aggressive chain store organizations immediately reinvested their earnings in building toward their future needs, i.e., modernizing their stores, distribution warehouses, and manufacturing facilities. If they didn't spend the money this way, the government taxes on their surplus would have consumed profits.

The NROG group was broken into three geographic regions: West Coast, East Coast, and central states. The western group, which traces its origins to the Pacific Mercantile, was formed in March 1934 in San Francisco as a retailer-owned wholesale buying group, and after separating from the Chicago group, continued up until 1963, when it was renamed "Western Family," taking its name from an old magazine distributed by the group. The central group was renamed "Central Retail Owned Grocers" in 1954 and some 10 years later adopted its Shurfine private label as the corporate name, Shurfine-Central. The co-op was owned by stockholders who represented regional distribution warehouses, which are owned and operated by independent retailers. They carried the Food King standard quality range after 1956, and then developed upwards of 15 different names to cover different product categories: Soflin paper products, Embassy appliances and gloves, Energy charcoal, MC2 detergents, Viktor aluminum foil and plastic bags, Sheerfine pantyhose, Shurfine foods, Shurfresh perishable products, etc. These labels were consolidated under first-quality Shurfine and Shurfresh labels, and secondary quality Thrift King. In the early 1950s, Shurfine-Central became the first user of regional TV, sponsoring a feature length movie. (Fitzell 1982) In 1984, the co-op added voluntaries to its membership; then in 1990, supermarket chains joined Shurfine as well. In 1991, foreign trading partners were added as members. The diversity of clientele-spread to new business: bakery, deli, meat and produce all with the Shur-fresh brand program.

Retailers Establish Topco Associates

In 1944, the retailer Alpha Beta, La Habre CA, helped form the Food Products Cooperative, Inc. as a national cooperative buying association with other independent retailers. The members teamed up to pack quality merchandise under the brand name, Food Club, for selected food chains looking to pool their volume requirements in order to compete against the national grocery chains. It was a time of wartime shortages, during which its many members needed canned and frozen foods supplies. Four years later, this co-op renamed itself Topco Associates, Inc. (Topco), Skokie, IL. At that time, the co-op also began experimenting with frozen foods, under the Top Frost label. This label along with Food Club represented choice and fancy products; but the co-op also packed good products under other labels: Elna, Dartmouth, and Gaylord-Topco. (Cramer 1973)

Alpha Beta, of course, had previously stocked private label (even going back to the original stores that made up the chain). As Alpha Beta, its first private label was Big 7 label, representing the name taken from the group of seven stores which made up the Alpha Beta chain. During the Depression, the chain launched its Sunrich standard quality items, which featured a colorful vignette against a black background.

This line, however was discontinued when the chain moved aggressively into the Topco program in the late 1940s. And when Alpha Beta was acquired by American Stores in 1961, its Topco line was discontinued in favor of the American Stores private labels.

"Give Me What You Give Topco"

Topco was formed by supermarket chains and grocery wholesalers who wanted centralized services to handle purchasing, product development, quality standards, and distribution control. Topco set its Food Club quality standards to meet the minimum standards established by the US Department of Agriculture; and in fact, its quality control people often would visit its suppliers' plants to assure that those standards were met. An industry cliché developed: "Give me what you give Topco."

In the late 1950s, Topco set the standard in other ways, developing private label outside the commodities area: paper goods, formulated products, nonedible items. Without an industry standard, Topco targeted the leading brand in a category for the quality standard. Eventually, the co-op developed an arsenal of controlled labels, which included: Top Frost frozen foods, Food Club dairy and processed foods, Topco household products and health and beauty aids products, Top Crest general merchandise, and Top Fresh produce. For lower quality, Topco developed the Gaylor and Valu Time brands, as well as Dog Club pet foods, Top Spread margarine, and Beacon beauty aids. A subsidiary, Kingston Marketing, handled the first-quality Kingston label and Dartmouth, the lower quality label, for large regional chains.

A turning point came in 1971 with the U.S. Supreme Court ruling in a landmark Topco Case, stating that the cooperative could no longer grant exclusive geographic franchises to its members. This ruling actually helped Topco focus its operation, moving aggressively in product development and marketing, as well as opening its services to associate members, who could participate in some of its programs.

Topco also developed rigid specifications and testing techniques to maintain product quality for its private labels. In the 1970s, Topco described these procedures:

"Topco buyers and technologists spend much of their time in the field working with sources of supply, first to develop the desired products and then to ensure their consistent quality. A constant flow of samples both from the producers and the retailers is subjected to tests both in Topco labs and, where required, in outside laboratories.

"Topco, like other strong distributors of their own brand products, is an important ally and outlet to its many sources of supply. Some of these sources are large enough to produce and market products successfully under their own brands. In many cases, however, they are small and medium-size producers, who do not have the financial strength or organization to market their own brand products effectively in competition with giant competitors. Topco's staff works with these smaller sources to develop, produce and package products which do compete successfully in the marketplace." (Topco 1970)

This cooperation explains how private label worked for all parties involved. It was truly a partnership based upon cooperation, which is the essence of the cooperative movement. This joint effort really helped retailers, wholesalers, and manufacturers build their private label business.

Wakefern & Roundy's Start Co-ops

It was in the same spirit that eight grocers in the Newark, NJ area in 1946 pooled their resources by banding together as a unified, high-volume purchaser. They set up a 5,000-square-foot warehouse in Newark under the Wakefern/ShopRite cooperative, shipping out 10,000 cases of groceries per week. By 1954, the co-op, Wakefern Food Corp., Elizabeth, NJ, introduced frozen orange-juice concentrate under its ShopRite label, thus starting what subsequently became an impressive rang of private label products, including a number of controlled labels as well. The co-op, however, never tried to substitute private label for a national brand, but always attempted to give consumers a choice.

Today, Wakefern Food Corp., now based in Edison, NJ, calls itself the largest retailer-owned cooperative in the country. It operates 2.5 million-square-feet of warehouse space, supplying upwards of 25,000 items of goods as well as more than 3,500 private label products to 190 ShopRite stores in New Jersey, New York, Connecticut, Pennsylvania, and Delaware. Privately-held, Wakefern's total sales, at the warehouse level, are now estimated at close to $4 billion. Private label share of those sales at retail are estimated to be well above the industry average—perhaps 30+% of total sales. Its store brands include: ShopRite, Farm Flavor, Flavor King, Very Best, Value Pak, and Chef's Express.

Another major retailer-owned cooperative, Roundy's, Inc., Milwaukee, WI, was formed in 1953, when Roundy, Peckham & Dexter Co., an 80-year-old wholesaler, sold its assets to hundreds of retail grocers in Wisconsin. That wholesaler traced its roots to the start-up of Smith, Roundy & Co. in 1872. The company grew to become one of the largest importing and jobbing grocery houses in Wisconsin, owning the Red Cross Coffee and Spice Mills. Its business spread to the neighboring states of Michigan, Minnesota, Iowa, and Illinois.

At the start of this century, Roundy, Peckham & Dexter Co. began handling "controlled labels," including Curtice Brothers, Hart, Flag, and Flickinger's California Fruits. It wasn't until 1922, however, that the company really started its own private label business, beginning with Roundy's salt. Charles J. Dexter, president, in 1929, at the age of 84, developed an idea to promote the Roundy's label. He established the Roundy's Food Studio, where talks and demonstrations on wholesome food preparation were given. Social clubs, church groups, and other organizations met for the Roundy program and afternoon lunch. These groups could conduct their own business meetings or social functions there. After the meeting, they would be presented with a company cookbook, containing recipes, which used Roundy private label products. For nearly eight years, the Food Studio was Roundy's primary source of private label advertising and promotion.

When the co-op was formed, the Roundy's label grew in consumer acceptance. The group operated a modern coffee roasting plant, a fixtures facility, a packaging plant, and cash-and-carry warehouses, as well as an institutional business. Through acquisitions and growth in later decades, Roundy's has become one of the top five co-ops in the U.S. today. (Engelman 1985)

Staff Supermarkets Debuts Co-op Label

The co-op experience also helped whet the appetite of independent retailers' for their own private label program. Some retailers, including major privately-held chains, entered a co-op by this means. Staff Supermarket Associates, Inc., another co-op begun late in 1959 in New York City as a retailer-owned buying group, worked to help small grocery retailers to compete effectively against the giant chains. This group operated without warehouses, shipping products direct from the manufacturers to the member chains—up to 18 at one time, mostly located in the Northeast and Midwest. Together, they exercised more buying power with their own controlled Staff label as well as other private labels, such as Brookville extra standard quality products and both Corky and Prize Pet for pet products, adding generics late in the 1970s.

In 1959, Schnucks Markets, St. Louis, picked up the Staff controlled label grocery and frozen foods. Its success led Schnucks to develop its own label first as an experiment with Schnucks brand box potato chips, starting in 1960. Schnucks at that time also began development of a controlled label dairy program with Quality Dairy, O'Fallon, IL. This program was among Schnucks' first cost-plus contracts with a supplier, a buying method it continues with many suppliers up to the present. The chain also considers this move "pivotal in that it enabled Schnucks to make gains in the competitive pricing of milk against national chains, which had gained a packaging advantage in the late

1940s." Previously, Schnucks couldn't get waxed paper cartons at a price savings over glass bottles. So the chain had worked with Aro Dairy Co. to act as its supplier as well as to other independent grocers. When demand grew too great for that local dairy, Schnucks augmented the milk supply with Quality Dairy. (Casey 1989)

Staff also added another independent, Wegmans, Rochester, NY, to its buying group, but that privately-held regional supermarket chain in 1979 dropped the Staff program then developed its own private label buying-program and introduced the Wegmans brand chainwide.

REFERENCES/CITATIONS

Brooks, John 1959. "A Corner in Piggly Wiggly" (Annals of Finance). The New Yorker Magazine, June 6, 1959.

Casey, Marie 1989. Schnucks, "1939-1989: Fifty Years of Friendliness." Schnuck Markets, Inc., St. Louis, MO.

Engelman, Lydia 1985. "The History of Roundy's. Food For Thought." (Company newsletter) December 1985.

Fitzell, Philip 1992. "Private Label Marketing in the 1990s." Global Book Productions, New York, NY.

Fitzell, Philip 1982. "Private Labels: Store Brands & Generic Products." AVI Publishing Company, Inc., Westport, CT.

Freeland, Chauncy 1996. Phone Interview with former employee of Fox Grocery Co.

Fuller, Mike 1996. Phone interview with former executive at Federated Foods.

Grimes, Frank J. 1931. "Courage to Face the Facts." Independent Grocers' Alliance of America, Chicago, IL.

International Super Marketing 1959. Red & White Corp.

IGA 1936. IGA Grocergram. IGA Inc., Chicago, IL

Red & White 1959. "The Red & White Story." International Super Marketing (house organ). May 1959, pg. 8.

Salmon, William A. 1993. "Building on the Past: A 125 Year History of Miller & Hartman, 1868-1993." Miller & Hartman Inc., Lancaster, PA.

Topco 1970. "This is Topco." (Company pamphlet). Topco Associates Inc., Skokie, IL

The Voluntary and Cooperative Groups Magazine 1966. Industry Pioneers. Cook Publications, Hackensack, NJ.

CHAPTER 11

____PRIVATE LABEL FROM A MANUFACTURING PERSPECTIVE___

Low-Profile Independent Grocers

There has been very little written about privately-owned grocers and wholesalers, because they prefer to maintain a low profile. Nevertheless, independent grocers on their own also have excelled in the supermarket chain business, while also helping to advance private label development. Many of these grocers resorted to manufacturing their own products, which helped to build a private label presence for them. The families Butt, Meijer, and Wegman serve as excellent examples.

From 1950 onward, supermarket chains experienced significant growth, a number of companies already established as public firms, others heading in that direction. Yet private family ownership was the course set by others. While in later years chains such as Publix in Florida, Vons in Southern California, Stop n' Shop in Boston, and Fred Meyer in Portland, OR, turned to public ownership, a number of highly-successful privately-owned chains endured, becoming market leaders in their own right. The families mentioned above are cases in point. Private label played a significant role in establishing their leadership in the marketplace.

Texas-Grown H-E-B

In 1905, Mrs. C.C. Butt Staple and Fancy Groceries opened for business in Kerrville, TX. Its format featured open cracker barrels and ceiling fans. It wasn't until Florence Butt's son, Howard Edward Butt, took charge after World War I that this grocery chain began to develop. By 1928, H.E. Butt began a major expansion, growing through the Great Depression not only with new stores, but also with its own Harlingen Canning Company, which produced "Texas-grown, Texas-packed" goods. Later, other manufacturing plants were established, including a milk plant, meat plant, ice cream plant, pastry bakery, photo-processing lab, and a bread-tortilla-bun bakery. Today, this large chain of 270 one-stop shopping stores features a consolidated operation, including a drug store, butcher shop, fish market, florist, delicatessen, bakery, and department store. H-E-B has taken a leadership role in private label development as well, establishing stringent quality standards and creative packaging, and jalso excelling in category management strategies.

Wegman Sets Standards

In 1915, the grandparents of Robert B. Wegman, who decades later became chairman and CEO of Wegmans Food Markets, Inc., opened a small grocery store in front of their home in Rochester, NY. The next year, their sons, Walter and Jack, were operating the Rochester Fruit & Vegetable Company. By 1930, they drew national newspaper headlines with the opening of the largest retail food store in New York state and possibly the country: a 20,000-square-foot "showplace" store, featuring a 300-seat cafeteria. They eventually converted to a self-service format in 1949 and made a full commitment to a private-label buying program in 1979, when the Wegmans brand was introduced throughout the chain.

Today, this 50-plus store chain, operating in New York and Pennsylvania, has its own centralized meat distribution and bakery facility, plus an egg farm. Additionally, the company operates a building and garden supply chain and 51 Chase-Pitkin outlets. In recent years, Wegmans has received numerous kudos from the press as well as industry-wide recognition for its market leadership, including outstanding work in category management. This has helped dedicated private label manufacturers as well, developing more sophisticated marketing strategies in partnership with Wegmans. The firm's 100,000-square-foot superstores today feature a distinctive Market Cafe restaurant that offers food service ambiance and chef-prepared foods. The chain has made grocery shopping fun; some observers, in fact, believe Wegmans' merchandising strategies, with deli and produce in particular, make it the best operated grocery chain in the country, if not the world.

Meijer Combines Food & General Merchandise

In 1934, the Dutch immigrant, Hendrik Meijer opened his first grocery store in Greenville, MI. He quickly gained a reputation for low prices, quality merchandise and courteous service. The Meijer supermarket chain evolved into a one-stop shopping concept in 1961, when Meijer added general merchandise to his product mix.

Today, this chain has positioned itself as a foods and general merchandise retailer, operating close to 100 Meijer combination stores, plus about 80 gas stations in five midwestern states: Michigan, Illinois, Indiana, Ohio, and Kentucky. Its outlets range in size from 122,000 to 250,000 square feet, encompassing some 25 departments. Most of the stores stock more than 100,000 different products, including more than 12,500 different private label products, covering fashions, hardgoods, and grocery items, which encompass almost every department: deli, bakery, bulk foods, service meat and seafood departments, pharmacies, photo labs, video shops, etc. Some larger stores include a Grand Food Fair combining several ethnic and specialty food restaurants, including Fred's American Grill, Wonton's, and The Pizza Pan.

Meijer now puts more emphasis on new product introductions, such as premium Angus beef, Meijer-brand fat-free products (Hidden Fudge and Devil's Food Cake cookies), and other items. Overall, the buildup of new Meijer-brand items has increased the chain's corporate brand product count to an amazing 22,000 items.

Size, size, size. The supermarket chains continued to increase in square footage through the 1950s and 1960s . Kroger, for example, stocked an average range of 5,000 to 8,000 items per store. By the 1980s, its SKU (Stock Keeping Unit) count had grown to between 18,000 to 20,000 items. This growth was fueled by the move toward one-stop shopping. Supermarket operators also began to diversify, adding drug-store chains, sometimes in combination with their supermarkets. Kroger acquired Sav-On Drugs in 1960; Jewel merged with the 280-store Osco Drug in 1961; American Stores took control of the 40-store Rea & Derick drug chain in central Pennsylvania in 1964, and so on.

Consolidations Affect All Players

With this trend came a greater consolidation of the entire business, affecting not only the companies but also their private label identities. When companies merged or acquired other firms, private label programs at each operation were combined under a single identity. Of course, this strategy also applied to house-cleaning a plethora of labels. As early as 1946, for example, Kroger consolidated 45 different private brand identities under its Kroger name, which represented its first-quality lines. The chains were moving toward fewer private labels in order to better control and manage their stock. They were forced to consolidate these labels as private label emerged in new product categories. The growing trade demand from chains, independents, and buying groups brought more manufacturers, mostly smaller companies, into this business.

The trend at mid-century was toward consolidation for the manufacturers' brands as well. These companies were learning how to fight more intensely for shelf space via advertising and promotional efforts. Deadbeat brands, which did not sell, had to be weeded out. Of course, some retailers were smarter than others with respect to managing shelf space for the brands as well as for private label in their supermarkets . Private label did not necessarily receive first-child preferential treatment, except perhaps for those retailers who manufactured or processed their own products. But these operators insured that the quality of the products they produced was first rate. In fact, a chain like Kroger had established its Kroger Food Foundation in 1930 to monitor product quality and test foods in its laboratory. Years earlier, Kroger also had home economists test recipes and prepare information leaflets for consumers giving cooking advice. In the 1930s, the chain established cooking schools. Its Food Foundation also formed the

Homemakers Reference Committee, including some 750 homemakers who received samples of Kroger brand products and competing brands to test under actual home conditions.

With this kind of support, there's little question that Kroger's private label quality standards were among the highest in the industry. In fact, the company had resisted the supermarket concept for as long as possible because it viewed itself as a bare-bone, bargain house that emphasized price. Koger's policy was to emphasize product quality in its stores. Early in the 1960s, the company revitalized its entire manufacturing operation with modern plants while combining small facilities into larger regional operations for greater efficiencies. An improved interstate highway system made a more centralized operation possible.

Retailers, of course, couldn't produce all their private label stock in-house. As many more items entered the private label range, retailers were required to buy from outside sources. In the evolution of private label into different product categories, the trend in the United States was more toward smaller manufacturers/processors, leaving the national brand business, with its high costs of product development and marketing, to the larger manufactures. In the smaller Canadian market, national brand manufacturers were more receptive to private label and generic business, because this helped them boost their overall sales volume.

Dedicated Private Label Manufacturers

In the manufacturing segment, more dedicated private label business developed as product categories became better defined. This resulted from the growth of competition, the emergence of more retailers and wholesalers, the continued research and development of products by brand leaders, and the enhancement and sophistication of packaging. Brokers also helped smaller manufacturers realize they could develop private label business with smaller retail chains and independents. Large supermarkets were organized into departments and service areas (meat, seafood, bakery), creating specific product aisles or sections in the supermarket: the cereal aisle, the health-and-beauty-aids aisle, the canned foods aisle, and so forth. Private label now fit in almost everywhere because of the growing acceptance of its quality. There was a time not too long before, when the cereal aisle had belonged only to Kellogg's, and the aspirin in the health-and-beauty-aids aisle was dominated by the Bayer brand. Now manufacturers came to recognize the potential in this burgeoning private label business.

Private label owners did not compromise on quality because they could not afford to put a store name or their own brand name on a product that would be noted as inferior. Likewise, the manufacturers couldn't afford to stop a production line for their name brand and switch to lower-quality ingredients or materials for a private label run. It was more cost-effective just to divert a finished product onto another packaging line, filling/wrapping the product under a customer's label.

Private Label Takes Its Share in Product Categories

Opportunities for private label entry began to spring up in new as well as existing product categories. There are many interesting stories, showing how private label gained a toe-hold up to near-domination in specific product categories.

—Aerosols

The aerosol industry, as mentioned earlier, emerged during World War II, when the U.S. Government commissioned the development of a practical pesticide spray to be used by servicemen in tropical war zones. A heavy-walled cylinder similar to a fire extinguisher was developed, using natural pyrethrin (made from chrysanthemum flowers) with Freon 11 and 12 as the propellant. This development led late in the 1940s to the first large-scale use of insecticide sprays for the consumer market. Crown Cork & Seal working with Newman Green developed a light-weight, three-piece aerosol can that was affordable. With its growing popularity, the aerosol product field turned into a playground of different packaging presentations. Spray paints were put into the aerosol can, followed by different auto spray products (brake cleaner, etc.) as well as other industrial products.

Private label business in this product category emerged late in the 1940s via custom filling. Spray cans were packed under different marketer's labels. One manufacturer, Spray On Products, a contract packer, was acquired by Sherwin Williams, Solon, OH, in 1964. This firm rolled out a full line of aerosols, covering every product category except pharmaceuticals, personal care, and food items. More recently, the operation, called HomeLine Products Specialty Division, was reidentified as Diversified Brands. In 1996, its parent company (CGS) agreed to purchase Grow Group, Havre De Grace, MD, which produces aerosol products and household and professional cleaning products, thus making Sherwin Williams' operation a major private label supplier of aerosol products under its newly-organized Cleaning Solutions Group (CSG).

—Pet Foods

Doane Products, Joplin, MO, a dry dog- and cat-food manufacturer, started into business in 1960, just about the time that market leader Ralston Purina was moving from pellet-with-flakes or meal-formulated pet food into an extruded product. Doane was in the vanguard of extruded pet foods for private brands, first picking up private label business for agricultural co-op and feed mills, followed soon afterward by supermarkets such as

FedMart on the West Coast; H.E. Butt in Texas; and HyVee in Iowa. From the beginning, Doane emphasized modern manufacturing technology, never compromising on quality for a lower price. There are still pieces of the private label business that the company will not bid for. While Doane remains an imitator of the brand leader, that is changing lately. Its partnership with a major buying group has resulted in some unique super premium products: lamb and rice dinners and super-premium kitten food-products made for private label in supermarkets to compete against specialty pet stores and mass merchandisers. (Weber 1996)

—Ready-To-Eat Cereals

Malt-O-Meal Co., Minneapolis, MN, which began its business in 1919 as a farina-based cereal manufacturer, distinguished itself from the market leader, Cream of Wheat hot cereal, by making its product with toasted malt. However, it wasn't until the 1960s, that Malt-O-Meal entered the private label business, offering puffed wheat and puffed rice in bags. Then the company expanded into five basic Read-To-Eat (RTE) cereals: corn flakes, raisin bran flakes, bran flakes, crisp rice, and sugar-frosted flakes. The hot cereal part of its business remained flat, while cold cereal products came to represent two-thirds of its sales. Eventually, private label business comprised 70% of its total sales.

At the beginning, private label market share in the RTE cereal market remained modest, that is, less than 5% up until 1989 when it climbed to 8.5%. The problem initially was that the price spread between the brands and private label was practically negligible. An Acme Store in Philadelphia, for example, sold its brand of private label next to Kellogg's at 2 cents per package less, while merchandising the private label product with compare-and-save shelf signage. Grand Union stores in New Jersey carried private label toasted oats at 2 cents per package higher than Cherrios. Consumers just weren't excited about a 2-cent savings, and they were certainty not willing to trade over to a higher-priced store brand from their favorite cereal. Retailers could not make any above-average margin on a product that barely moved off the shelf. Private label was also hurt by offering different package sizes, i.e., 18-ounce versus a 20-ounce brand leader package, which confused consumers even more.

Then a funny thing happened on the way to the supermarket. The brand leaders began to raise their prices, two or three times a year, throughout the latter part of the 1980s. The price spread between private label and the brands grew to 50% or more. Consumers began trying—and liking—the private label product; as a result, its market share grew. The brands really helped to build a private label presence in the RTE cereal category. (Guy 1996)

—Coffee Filters

The 1970s saw yet more product categories opened up for private label. In the United States, nearly the entire market was skewed to percolator coffee makers. By contrast, in Europe, it was mostly drip coffee makers. Melitta, the market leader in Europe, traced its history back to 1904—but predominately as a branded company.

In 1972, Mr. Coffee introduced coffee filters to the U.S. market. Rockline Industries, Sheboygan, WI, started in this business and almost immediately began serving private label accounts. The company made sales calls to non-food, food, and grocery buyers at retail; but nobody wanted the private label product. They were too busy or had too many private label SKUs to handle already. Rockline, however, persisted, and made headway with Safeway Stores plus a few other retail accounts, willing to put in a linear foot of shelf space devoted to filters in their coffee aisle. They found the profit margins on private label too attractive to give up—30 to 50% or more. Soon the word got out and the coffee buyer, the non-foods buyer, the grocery buyer—everybody wanted private label coffee filters.

A problem arose over pricing. Mr. Coffee had a 58% market share with its fluted filters. But the brand sold for something like $2.29 per package in the supermarket, while Walgreens Drug Stores carried the same product for 69 cents. Consumers began to think that the supermarket was an expensive store. When private label filters were introduced at the lower price, consumers assumed thatthe paper quality was inferior. It wasn't: Rockline could not afford to change its production runs in order to lower the paper grade for private label or even for generics, when that business developed late in the 1970s.

Rockline innovated in this product category, introducing coffee filters packaged in poly bags and was the first to introduce unbleached coffee filters and to use a dispenser box that made filter separation easier. The company continues to be a dedicated and successful private label manufacturer, now controlling about 80% of the private label business in coffee filters. (Rudolph 1996)

From the 1950s onward, supermarket chains experienced significant growth, some becoming public companies, others continuing under private ownership, and still others switching back and forth, depending on acquisitions or whatever. Such companies included: Publix in Florida, Vons in Southern California, Hinkey-Dinkey in Omaha, NB; Borman's Farmer Jack in Detroit, MI; Steinbergs in Montreal; Stop n' Shop in Boston, MA; Big Bear in Columbus, OH; Fred Meyer in Portland, OR; Weingartens in Houston, TX; Schnucks in St. Louis, MO.

There was, in effect, greater consolidation of the business, not only affecting companies but also private label identities. The supermarket chains moved toward fewer labels for better control over their own lines. As private label lines emerged in other product categories, the demand brought in more manufacturers, mostly smaller companies.

In the drug-store segment, both Rexall and Walgreen developed franchise programs. Walgreen moved into self-service stores in 1949. Other chains emerged. Revco Drug Stores, Winesburg, OH in 1956, was positioned as a discount drug chain. Its Revco label appeared in 1960. In 1971, Revco purchased Private Formulations to guarantee an adequate supply of vitamins and food supplements. Its manufacturing muscle grew—there was another plant in California and acquisition of Barre-National, a producer of liquid generic drugs, in 1977, followed later by Carter-Clogan Labs, maker of human and veterinary injectibles.

Another discounter, Rite Aid Corp., Shiremanstown, PA, began in 1962 with only a small private label effort. Private label benefited in this segment with the expansion into larger stores or combination food or home improvement stores. Osco Drug, under Jewel Companies, provided Osco-brand health and beauty aids, film, and its Velvetouch brand hosiery to Jewel outlets.

A Question of Quality

Private label often has been stereotyped as being of inferior quality, perhaps because it is perceived not to be a national brand which consumers have been told through advertising represents the best quality available in the marketplace. Since there had been no rallying cry for private label prior to the 1980s, it was really up to the individual supermarket chains to tell consumers about the top quality of their private labels. The chains, however, had numerous labels, so the perception of a single, strong brand chain-wide was not easily achieved.

From the late 1950s forward, a number of factors came into play, helping private label sales to establish new product category roots and to grow and spread from the chains into smaller retail organizations and become more prevalent in the marketplace. It was principally the influence of the larger supermarket chains, such as Safeway, Kroger, American Stores, Jewel, National Tea, A&P, and others which helped private label gain in stature and recognition. These chains maintained a strong, impressive private label business mainly because of in-house manufacturing support, which they had enjoyed for decades. In addition, more products were introduced under private label in diverse product categories, private label itself was reinforced and the chains moved further toward a consolidation of labels. Brand equity was being established with fewer private labels. In the past, these labels had proliferated and often changed after chains were merged or acquired.

In many ways, it also could be said that consumers took an active role in helping private label come into its own. Shoppers were becoming better educated, more informed and more vocal about the products they purchased and the prices they paid. The Baby Boomers, people born after World War II, started to shop with their critical eye set increasingly on product quality and variety; convenience products; and low prices. The retailers who paid attention to these needs became the market leaders—especially those chains that put strong emphasis on both their in-house manufactured products and on private labels contracted with outside manufacturers. A case in point was Kroger, which quickly established market leadership nationwide in the second half of this century.

Kroger maintained a strong commitment to top-quality private label products, such as its line of Country Club packaged foods and Kroger-brand French coffee, both of which can be traced back to the start-up days of Barney Kroger at the turn of the century. It is no accident that Kroger has delivered the highest quality standards for its own brands ever since and as a result has taken over as the leading supermarket chain in the United States today.

By the 1950s, Kroger's Food Foundation—its scientific testing laboratory division —set up auditing procedures where the company's private label products were compared with national brands and competitors' private labels. The Foundation monitored products from outside suppliers. Additionally, its own manufacturing facilities since the mid-1940s were backed up with stringent quality control procedures as well as equipment engineering functions.

The Foundation developed into a Corporate Quality Assurance Department in 1961, handling product evaluations of food and non-food items in its labs, staffed by food scientists and technicians. Their responsibilities included the assurance that Kroger meet its goals in product quality (measuring up to or surpassing national or regional brands); regulatory compliance; and facility sanitation. This department worked with the Kroger buyers and outside suppliers. It also helped develop private label products along with procedures set up by the Kroger manufacturing facilities.

Kroger's New Product Development Strategies

Early on, Kroger established itself as any top national brand manufacturer would do, adopting the same research and development techniques and following through with merchandising and marketing support, which, of course, was limited to its own chain of stores. Kroger has explained its strategy in new product development:

"While Kroger's development of some products, such as yogurt, has been at the forefront of the industry, most private label products respond to established consumer interest. The first step is to bring in a sample of a successful product made elsewhere and analyze it thoroughly. 'We break the product down and see what it is made of, how it is made, and from this analysis we give our product development people a starting formula from which they can make a similar product,' explains an R&D technologist.

"Next, the product is analyzed by a group of highly-trained technologists to determine what it might still need to make it acceptable. They might say, this is close, but we think you need more cloves, or salt, or sugar, or spice or whatever, the technologist explains.

"Eventually, the new product is ready for its most critical test: it goes to a consumer tasting panel for blind tests in comparison with the most popular national brand product. 'One doesn't have to be a dead ringer for the other one,' says an R&D researcher. 'There can be a difference. But both products have to be equally acceptable to the consumer. The testers have to say they would buy one as quickly as they would the other. At this point, we have a product that is ready to go to market.'

"Precise specifications for the new product must then be worked out. Detailed records specify the percentages of raw materials in the formula and the exact manner in which each is to be added. Kroger scientists set standards for the product's color, consistency, and other physical properties and list its raw materials, which is important to suppliers as well as Kroger staff people manufacturing the new item.

"... The exact specifications are a quality insurance policy, enabling technologists to spot-check the item a year, or several years later. 'This becomes a standard,' says a Kroger quality assurance official, 'guaranteeing us that the product is still what we said it was when we put it on the market.' " (Laycock 1983)

More Than 30% of Kroger's Sales in Private Label

Kroger's commitment to private label, as far as can be determined, has been very strong for decades. Late in the 1950s, private label represented an estimated one-third or more of its total store sales. That ratio has not changed by much up to the present, even though Kroger usually does not count a number of its own manufactured products as part of its total private label product mix.

In the 1960s, Kroger maintained three quality-tiers of private label, allocating budgets to support these products in its different geographic divisions. The budgets were tied to personnel budgets to create an incentive to sell private label. Every employee was apprised of the importance of private label to Kroger's bottom line.

The chain maintained a flexible budget, however, when a division while committed to sell "X" dollars of Kroger Manufactured Products (KMP) did not necessarily have to deliver those sales in a specific product line. If KMP salad dressing, for example, did not sell, the sales could be made up with another KMP product.

In contrast, Kroger's strong competitor, A&P, took a different approach with its private label. Throughout the 1960s, A&P had adopted a centralized management strategy: "X" cases of an A&P product had to be sold and that product was forcefully jammed down the throats of store managers, who had to sell it even if it meant at a marked-down price.

Kroger's sales strategy included working with the stores on promoting KMP items within the divisions, providing compare-and-save signage, shelf sets, and a percentage of advertising and display allowances.

Eventually, Kroger assigned category buyers the task of promoting KMP items. Yet the company continued to dispatch field reps to organize promotions and displays, running the Kroger brand business just like a manufacturer's brand.

Kroger's Leadership Role in Perishables

Over the years, Kroger has taken the initiative in some key private label categories, namely dairy, eggs, produce, and meat. As far back as 1947, the company pioneered by opening its first egg processing plant in Wabash, IN. Eggs were collected directly from farms, graded and packed under USDA supervision, and then rushed to the Kroger stores within days. This process included a candling inspection, where eggs are passed over a strong light to check on their interior quality .

Kroger also took another first step in the 1970s, based on consumer research which showed that shoppers were looking for more than just a prepackaged plastic-wrapped item within a limited product selection. Consumers wanted more choices, more product variety, and more size-options. Kroger responded by offering tropical fruits, oriental vegetables, and up to 10 varieties of lettuce. The move toward wider selection of perishable produce began. The chain would dispatch produce buyers into the crop-growing areas around the country to purchase fruits, vegetables, or flowers. Its Wesco Foods buying organization tracked down different sources in order to provide choice product year-round, including buying products from South America to New Zealand.

In the dairy area, Kroger built up an impressive network of dairy plants—14 located around the country, charged with keeping Kroger stores supplied with fresh milk, ice cream, yogurt, cottage cheese, etc. Its Heritage Farms, for example, supplied 200 stores with Heritage Farms brand dairy products.

In the 1970s, when consumers started to demand dating of perishable products on grocery store shelves, Kroger took a leadership role by voluntarily stamping a "sell by" date on its milk products. Eventually, more than 2,000 items were open-dated to assure customers of product freshness. In 1970, Kroger also began processing its own cheese. By 1974, the company had opened one of the country's largest and most modern cheese plants in Rochester, MN.

In the dairy area, Kroger continued to innovate, working during the 1980s with Corning Glass Works to develop a method to convert whey—a by-product in cottage cheese productions difficult to dispose of—into a sweet syrup used to produce baker's yeast.

When cattle feeding and breeding methods were less sophisticated in the 1930s, consumers had to settle for a tougher grade of beef. At the time, Kroger's Food Foundation established special research fellowships at the Mellon Institute of Industrial Research in Pittsburgh, PA, which studied the natural processes by which enzymes break down fiber in meat as it ages. This lengthy process was costly: And so Kroger-funded scientists, working with the Food Foundation, perfected a method to speed up the aging process, using a special sterilizing lamp, developed by Westinghouse. The lamp killed bacteria and mold, allowing the meat to be hung in rooms where warm temperatures speeded up the aging process without spoilage. This led to Kroger's famed Tenderay beef, which was widely practiced until beef feeding and breeding methods improved, and meat no longer needed this special treatment.

On two occasions, proposals were made by others to alter the beef grading system, thus allowing lesser quality beef to be classified as Prime and Choice. Kroger always opposed these changes and succeeded in 1982 in an effort to prevent a lowering of the grading standards. Its stores now regularly stock some 200 different kinds and cuts of meat. (Laycock 1983)

A Key To Success: Strong Management

The fortunes or misfortunes of a company, as we have seen, often can be traced to the strength of its top management. During the 1960s, the supermarket industry was undergoing dramatic changes and adjustments, as many family-owned businesses evolved rapidly into larger, more diversified organization; and mergers, takeovers, and foreign expansion became popular. The industry was changing rapidly. Acme and Alpha Beta joined forces in 1961; Safeway moved into England in 1962 and into both West Germany and Australia in 1963; Buttery Foods and Jewel Companies merged in 1966; Ralphs Grocery became a Federated Department Stores division in 1968; and then Vons came under the control of Household Finance Corp. Consumerism became increasingly a marketing reality as such issues as civil rights, the environment, trading stamps, became central.

For some companies, the transition through these changes was smooth under the leadership of executives like Quentin Reynolds, who became president at Safeway in 1966; John R. Parks, who was elected president of Acme in 1965; Donald S. Perkins, who was made president, while George L. Clements became chairman and CEO at Jewel in 1965. For others, however, the course turned bumpy. IGA's founder Frank Grimes, retiring, turned control over to his son, Don, in 1951, after which, with subsequent presidents, IGA lost its spark and its growth momentum up until the 1970s, when Tom Haggai became chairman and later president. Similarly, A&P, in making the transition from a private, family-owned business to a public company late in the 1950s, underwent two decades of stagnation, as management turned away from John Hartford's mandate—"quality food at the lowest price"—toward more emphasis on building corporate profits for the Hartford Foundation. It wasn't until the 1980s, under the control of Tengelmann in Germany and a new chairman and CEO, James Wood, that A&P began its comeback. Wood, reporting to stockholders in fiscal 1981, pointed to six basic factors that had contributed to A&P's "downward spiral of performance" since 1971:

(1) small stores poorly located throughout most of its trading areas,
(2) store closings that produced a senior work force with higher cost per man-hour than competition,
(3) a manufacturing orientation that over-emphasized private label,
(4) inadequate remodeling and new store development programs in markets with future growth and profitability,
(5) inconsistencies in staff development and training, and
(6) an outmoded management information and control system.

In 1965, at a cost of $25 million, A&P had opened a 1.5-million-square-foot, food processing facility in Horseheads, NY. It was the world's largest plant of its kind under one roof (33 acres). The company also opened a 70,000-square-foot delicatessen kitchen and a $16 million bakery in Flushing, NY. While competition was moving toward superstores and large combination food-and-non-food formats, A&P concentrated more on the profitable area of manufacturing. In 1970, three additional manufacturing plants were acquired. By the end of the decade, the company had 17 factories, while most of its stores still were under 10,000 square feet each. Wood closed down or sold most of the factories, keeping the coffee operation intact. He also cut back on the private label commitment, bring it down from a high point of more than 33% of total sales to about 18%. After reorganizing the company, embarking on an new acquisitions course, and developing new store formats, A&P more recently has moved private label share back toward 25% of total sales. Of course, this indicates that A&P's problem wasn't with private label itself (except when the company may have compromised on quality), but in other weaknesses within the company.

Dedicated Private Label Brokers

Private label first became the business of big chains, which could afford volume buying of these products. Private label also was fitted into the strategies of voluntary groups and co-ops, serving the independent smaller grocery chains. Eventually, private label began to work for almost anyone in the business, as brokers contributed their support, sometime even developing their own control labels for exclusive use in different markets.

Federated Foods was one of the first brokers to explore private label development for smaller food retailers and wholesalers. This firm emerged as a national private label marketing sales agent for both the retail and food service industries, representing hundreds of private label suppliers in food and non-food products. Federated also developed one of the industry's finest quality assurance programs, covering on-site plant inspection, retail audits, written specifications for every product, lot selection programs, customer satisfaction programs and compliance with state and Federal packaging requirements. In fact, Federated set the highest quality standards in the industry. Competitors looked at its strategies and followed suit. Federated developed consistency in quality. Its different controlled labels were given exclusively to customers in different marketing areas. Its income derived from brokerage paid by suppliers, while the retail customers were invoiced directly by the suppliers whereby any allowances or deals accrued directly to that customer. Besides owning and managing several brands made available to distributors, Federated now also manages many distributor-owned labels. Additionally, the company helps its customers organize their private label marketing events.

By 1965, it's estimated that Federated was billing about $55 million in private label, including both retail and food service accounts. The brokerage since has grown to more than an estimated $1 billion. Federated's success stems from its construction of a full-service national sales agency which took the initiative for private label accounts. In the 1980s, for example, as national brand manufacturers were moving toward direct consumer promotional spending with coupons, cash rebates, and contests, Federated inaugurated perhaps the private label industry's first cash rebate program on a national scale for its Hy•Top and Parade disposable diapers, offering consumers up to a $5 refund with the purchase of three packages ($3 for two packages or $1 for one package). Federated also toyed with the idea of bounce-back coupons on similar private label products. The agency began orchestrating its private label promotions around national trade events, such as a frozen food month, a dairy month, etc. Early in the 1990s, Federated was acquired by private investors operating under a holding company.

Starting in the 1950s, more independent food brokers took on private label business for their customers while serving their principals, the manufacturers or processors. Since starting up its Hyde Park private label program in the mid-1960s, for example, Malone & Hyde, Inc., Memphis, TN, a major wholesale grocer in the Southeast, relied specifically on local brokers to market the private label program in its nine autonomous divisions. Eventually, M&H consolidated its Hyde Park program along with its more recently acquired Piggly Wiggly private label program under Kitchen Products, a division of Federated Foods, which worked out of M&H's headquarters. Kitchen Products was charged with handling sales, marketing, quality assurance, and label control. Purchasing of product, however, was handled by M&H.

Different Strokes For Different Brokers

There were, of course, other specialized private label brokers similar to Federated Foods, although each developed its own strategy in serving its clients. One long-time firm, Alliance Associates, Coldwater, MI, began in 1929 under the name Jobber Services. After enactment of the Robinson-Patman Act, Alliance evolved into a private label broker for specific products, becoming fully committed to this business during the 1970s. Alliance has developed both exclusive (Nature's Classics, American Feast, Walton's Farm, etc.) and non-exclusive (Family Fare) controlled labels for its customers. This firm also has helped retailers outside the grocery trade, that is, mass merchandisers, drug store chains, warehouse club store operators, and limited assortment store retailers expand into private label.

Another account-specific broker, Continental Companies, Concord, CA, in 1963, began specializing in both branded and private label frozen food accounts. Continental pooled both into consolidated orders, filling truckloads at a minimum cost, thus saving time for its customers. Continental's attempt to expand beyond frozen foods into dry groceries was unsuccessful, leading to its acquisition by Federated Foods in 1991.

Beginning in 1966 as an item broker for retailers and wholesalers, Herb Pease Sr. evolved into a program broker, organized under Marketing Management Inc. (MMI), Ft. Worth, TX. Its exclusive brands, made available for retailers and food service clients, include: Real Value, Hyper Value, Best Way, and Budget Buy.

MMI over the years provided strong support to the industry. In 1981, MMI organized its Service Purchase Program, which guaranteed its principals expanded private label sales, while reinvesting a sizable portion of its commission from those sales to the customer accounts assigned to the program, giving them merchandising and marketing support materials to help build their private label sales. MMI has attracted major customers such as Fleming, Shurfine-Central, Bruno's, and Thriftway. In 1989, MMI funded the launch of this industry's Quality Assurance Association, Ft. Worth, TX—a group of quality assurance professionals, including wholesalers, retailers, food service distributors, brokers, cooperatives, government/regulatory personnel, manufacturers, independent laboratories, and students. The group is dedicated to promoting quality assurance in all aspects of private label products.

In 1968, Clem Perrucci began as a field broker for California canners, developing his Cal Growers brokerage business in San Jose, CA. Cal Growers acquired the rights to the Thorofare label from Farm House Foods Corp., Milwaukee, WI, in 1982 and has since evolved more into an account specific brokerage, eventually picking up the SUPERVALU account and other business.

In the mid-1970s, Peter Schwartz, who worked for Alliance Associates, was selling the New York City-based grocery chain, Bohack's, on the idea of a private label program at the same time that Milt Sender, who worked for Staff Supermarkets, was pitching Bohack's to join the Staff co-op. Bohack's actually introduced Schwartz and Sender, who discovered they were making fairly similar presentations. The meeting led to a partnership between the two men, which developed into Daymon Associates, New York (now Stamford, CT). Their second account, Ralphs Grocery, Compton, CA., which signed in the same decade, first became interested in private labels in the 1950s, when private label brokers sold the chain on canned goods and other foods. Subsequently, all the private label buying decisions were placed into the hands of the grocery buyers. Consequently that business was handled as an afterthought—after all the national brand product procurement was completed. Daymon proposed that Ralphs start a private label program, recommending the items to stock, and establishing quality standards that must be equal to or better than the national brand quality while also returning a better gross profit rate than the national brand.

Daymon began adding other accounts, including Wegmans in Rochester, NY; Bi-Lo in Mauldin, SC; Hannaford Brothers in Scarborough, ME, etc. In the process, it has become the country's largest account specific broker, in-house broker or as Daymon prefers to call itself, private label marketing/sales agent. Its billings now are estimated at in excess of $5 billion.

As the supermarket business consolidated, many of the smaller independent brokers were squeezed out of business, replaced by the larger account specific brokers, who encouraged private label program development. Overall, these brokers have contributed significantly to the sophistication and growth of private label business in both the retail and wholesale food industries.

Early Market Research Efforts

What helped to blur the perception of private label growth at this time were the syndicated market-research reports, starting with data first generated in the 1970s. Selling Areas-Marketing, Inc. (SAMI), New York, organized by Time Inc. in 1966, wanted to boost advertising at its owned-and-operated station, WOOD-TV in Grand Rapids,

MI. A broadcasting consultant felt that if a way could be found to get a fast and digitized measure of Grand Rapids food store sales, that city could then serve as a test market for name brand manufacturers, who would buy more advertising spots on the station. At the time, most food retailers already were using the computer to control their inventories from delivery to the warehouse through to its movement to the stores.

A computer-based system was developed to barcode brands by product, sizes, flavors, and case packs in order to track sales volume and market shares for individual items. Clients purchased the service based on the specific brands and items they wanted to have measured. The more brands included in the report, the higher the price members of the service paid. To get food operators to share their data with SAMI, the latter paid them 25% of its gross revenues and began issuing reports that showed the operators the market's total sales volume and their share in that marketing area. Three years later, SAMI started to track private label sales on a biannual basis. But at best, its private label sales tracking was merely a token recognition of this business.

Subsidized by name brand manufacturers, this research painted a flat growth trend for private label throughout the 1970s and 1980s, by simply drawing on stock removed from retailers' warehouses as a measuring stick. It did not cover direct store deliveries from the manufacturer. This data also was projected from the database collected in SAMI's major marketing areas. On its 20th anniversary, SAMI was issuing reports every 28 days on the movement of all brands and items in 475 different product categories in 54 major markets, which the company claimed accounted for 88.4% of national food store sales. (SAMI 1985)

In January 1987, when in-store scanning had developed in supermarkets, Information Resources Inc. (IRI), Chicago, began its InfoScan reports, tracking private label sales—projecting data collected mostly from major markets onto the national picture. Nielsen Marketing Research, Northbrook, IL, also began reporting on private label, called "controlled brand," and generics in 1987. These data have shown growth, but not as dramatic as what has been reported individually by leading chains, co-ops, voluntary groups, and independent chains. This divergence continues to this day.

REFERENCES/CITATIONS

Guy, Pat 1996. Phone interview at Malt-O-Meal Co., Minneapolis, MN.

Laycock, George 1983. "The Kroger Story: A Century of Innovation." The Kroger Co., Cincinnati, OH, pg. 78.

——- pp. 87-101.

Rudolph, Ralph 1996. Phone interview with CEO at Rockline Industries, Sheboygan, WI.

SAMI 1985. "Twenty Years with SAMI: 1966-1985." Selling Areas-Marketing, Inc., New York, NY.

Weber, Dick H. 1996. Phone interview with executive at Doane Products Co., Joplin, MO.

_____LATE 20TH CENTURY VALUES (1980-Present)__________

CHAPTER 12

AN INDUSTRY EMERGES

There continues to be an erroneous belief, held by many, that the private label business represents only a copycat strategy for retailers interested in building profits for themselves and tricking consumers into thinking that they are buying the leading manufacturers brands because of similarities in packaging. A review of the previous chapters in this book shows that private label, in fact, has a long, rich history; private label has achieved top-quality levels; private label has been innovative; private label has frequently given the consumer the lowest price possible; and private label has offered support to leading retailers in their build-up of supermarket chains, while also helping smaller independent distributors stay profitable.

Retailers have copied the look of leading-brand containers and packaging graphics because that format represents the reference point that consumers have established in their minds for a certain product. Private label owners could not afford the expense of building their own brand equity references through multi-million-dollar advertising campaigns and frequent, attractive packaging strategy changes. They had to follow the market leaders in each product category, achieving leadership only in those areas where a retailer maintained strong manufacturing and/or processing support or where a category had little or no manufacturer-brand activity.

As more players entered the private label business, it was inevitable that quality standards would be compromised by some companies. There never was any governing agency that set the highest standards for private label. For decades, it has existed at different quality levels; so, more or less anything goes. This unwritten rule opened the door for generic products in the late 1970s, followed by upscale premium private label products late in the 1980s. The most successful private label owners were those who made the strongest commitment to supporting the private label program. Those who paid lip service or gave barely a token effort did not succeed in private label.

The Industry's First Trade Publication and Trade Association

It is at this point in the history of the business that private labels began to coalesce as an industry. In the past, private label existed and prospered, but was never regarded as an industry per se. With numerous small manufacturers addressing their own product niche, they really had nothing in common with one another. There never was talk about a sector of the marketplace called "private label"—not until April 1979, when a trade magazine was established, *Private Label,* followed in November 1979 by the launch of a trade association, the Private Label Manufacturers Association (PLMA), both based in New York City. This author had the good fortune to participate in and work with both the magazine and PLMA from their start-ups.

In fact, prior to joining *Private Label* magazine in March 1979, this author had never heard the term "private label," and certainly did not know what it meant! That is punctuated with an exclamation point, because my experience in business and trade writing traces back to 1964. This ignorance about the subject, prompted me to learn more about this business and eventually to write two textbooks on the subject: "Private Labels: Store Brands & Generic Products" (published in 1982 by AVI Publishing Co., Inc., Westport, CT, now out of print) and "Private Label Marketing in the 1990s" (1992—available through Global Books LLC, New York, NY).

Private Label magazine was started by publisher E. W. Williams, who traced his business writing experience back to the 1920s. Indeed, Williams often heard about private label as owner of the magazine *Quick Frozen Foods* which covered a market segment where private label had developed strong representation. In later years, two other U.S.-based private label trade magazines were launched by other parties. Only one, *Private Label News*, started by Marci Smith of Certified Publications, Doylestown, PA, survives with its emphasis expanded from a new-products-news focus more into general news and features about the industry. The other publication, *Store Brands*, published by Charleson Publishing, Princeton, NJ, was short-lived, very likely from little advertising support.

Late in 1997, this author, through his company, Exclusive Brands LLC, New York/Paris, launched a quarterly business magazine, called *Exclusive Brands*. This publication focuses on the global private label business, covering all aspects of the trade and all the players involved in this business internationally.

On October 23, 1979, Williams, together with the editor-publisher of *Private Label*, Ralph Selitzer, and this author, staged an organization meeting for what was to become PLMA. This organization was formed from a group of about 20 industry representatives, which was comprised mostly of manufacturers but which also included two independent private label brokers (Herb Pease, Sr., and Greg Phillips) and a quality assurance test laboratory representative (Dr. Herbert Shuster). The manufacturers who were present at The Chemist Club in New York City for the first meeting had never met each other before. They more or less came out of the woodwork, making their presence known to others in the trade outside their sphere of business, for example, peanuts, cooking oils, detergents, vitamins, cereals, etc. It was an historic meeting because PLMA was destined over the next 15 to 20 years to emerge as an international organization, its membership company numbers surpassing 2,000, including manufacturers and associate members (brokers, suppliers, publications, etc.).

PLMA Stages Trade Shows

The PLMA organizational meeting set plans for its first annual meeting to be held March 27-28, 1980 at the St. Louis (MO) Marriott Hotel. Remarkably, that event, attracted 320 industry people from 34 states, the District of Columbia, and Canada, including 195 manufacturers, 70 retailers/wholesalers, and 55 brokers, consultants, and other guests. The keynote speaker for the event was Esther Peterson, Special Assistant to the President for consumer affairs. The meeting also included numerous sessions, including 36 other speakers and panelists. PLMA elected its slate of officers, and voted Ralph Selitzer its first president.

PLMA's first officers:

Joseph Conte (Witco Chemical Corp.'s Ultra Division) as chairman; William L. Robbins (American Safety Razor Co.) as first vice-chairman; and Don Spellman (J.L. Prescott Co.) as second vice-chairman.

PLMA board members in three-year terms:

Arthur R. Berman (Richheimer Foods Co.),
Frank O'Neill (B.H. Krueger Inc.),
Ralph Behr (Food Oils Corp.),
Gregory Phillips (Aid Pak Co.),
Donald S. Schnitz (Ralston Purina Co.), all to three-year terms.

Two-year board members:

Lon M. Lonker (Certified Chemicals, Inc.),
Gerald McPeak (General Tea Corp.),
Daniel C. Funk (Triple C Food Products Corp.),
L. Stephen Weiss (Carnegie Labs Division of Rexall Drug Co.),
Neal E. Schmidt (Zoecon Industries).

Elected to one-year term:

Anthony Siciliano (Commodore Foods, Inc.),
David A. Horwitz (Life Laboratories, Inc.),
Wayne Dunlap (The Merit Group, Inc.),
Sydney Schaffer (Landon Co., Inc.),
Al Silverman (Konishiroku Photo Ind. USA Inc.).

PLMA also recognized Herbert V. Shuster (Herbert V. Shuster, Inc.) and E. W. Williams (Private Label Publishing Co.) as ex-officio officers.

The first PLMA Trade Show & Educational Conference was held September 22-24, 1980 at the Ramada O'Hare hotel in Chicago. That event included 56 exhibitor booths with 383 registrants attending from 30 states plus Canada and Puerto Rico. The keynote speaker was Ralph Nader, the noted consumer advocate. (PLMA 1980).

PLMA's current president, elected in 1982, is Brian Sharoff, who together with a staff of meeting organizers have made PLMA one of the most successful trade associations in the United States. PLMA's educational programs and trade shows, all dedicated to the private label business, have helped the industry take shape and mature in every aspect of private label development: product sourcing, quality assurance controls, packaging design and strategies, legal issues, merchandising, and marketing.

In 1979, when *Private Label* magazine first solicited for advertising most of the manufacturers, suppliers or service companies had never before promoted their private label products or activities. Often, the magazine had to create ads for these companies. They had no one in their companies doing this type of work, not to mention any outside advertising agency support. As a result, the magazine can be credited with helping the industry find its identity and grow, through communications and published information about the players, the product categories that private label addressed, and the general trends in the business with respect to the private label program.

The magazine and PLMA together put private label on the map, making it a respectable, recognizable sector of commerce. It took time but private label, despite many pressures exerted by the industry leaders (which continue today), did become a full-fledged industry. The road was rocky. For example, this author, attending the major supermarket trade show in the early 1980s, the Food Marketing Institute's Annual Convention & Exposition, met with angry or rude reactions by exhibitors on the FMI trade show floor. There was not a single sign, nor mention of the private labelindustry, anywhere. Any such concern was conducted not in public view. Today, FMI hosts a Private Label Pavilion, started in 1995, at the same annual convention. The 1997 show drew as many as 30 private label exhibitors to the Pavilion.

The Private Label Program

The concept of an organized program devoted to private label really took shape when dedicated private label brokers began to develop and manage such a program, which covered every aspect of a product's life. Many different styles of management evolved, from a single manager, buyer, or coordinator up to committees; the most successful programs were those where top management took an active interest in making private label a success.

In 1973, for example, P&C Food Markets, Syracuse, NY, made a strong commitment to private label, based on top management approval. At that time, it stocked some 60 private label items excluding perishables like ice cream, milk, bread, meat, etc. It was unusual for a supermarket chain to have an organized private label coordinator. Usually, buyers in different product areas did their own thing with private label. P&C appointed a dedicated private label manager, Joe Gallagher (now retired), to whom the buyers were free to suggest new items. But the manager selected the packers of those items. Gallagher remembers that it was unusual to have a former USDA inspector working as an employee and checking all the private label shipments. The chain's policy—unlike its competitors—was not to buy cheap. "Our competitor," he recalls, "did lower the private label standard to accommodate a special price promotion, i.e., four items for a dollar. We never did that."

Within eight or nine years, P&C's private label line grew to 1,000 items. The chain also innovated by introducing the depiction of product contents on its own can labels. In all cases, the quality would be as good as or better than the brand leaders. Gallagher worked with the broker, Alliance Associates, tapping into its expertise on label definitions, truth-in-packaging laws, etc. The company also supported its program with four major promotion each year such as double-truck sales. (Gallagher 1996)

Private label generally was viewed as a program encompassing the procurement of products; quality specifications; packaging requirements; quality assurance; legal matters and government regulations; merchandising and marketing support; and export activities. Since no guidelines existed on how a private label program should be organized, different strategies evolved. This could involve selected buyers, who took on private label responsibilities in their respective product categories; an executive in procurement, managing the overall activity; a private label manager selected to coordinate the program; committees formed to help direct private label business, etc.

Private Label Philosophy Emerges

From the 1970s onward, more organized efforts were undertaken by retailers and wholesalers to consolidate, control, and expand these programs. Many factors came into play, including the nature of the organization itself (some companies being more aggressive than others), the people involved (savvy merchandising and marketing personnel recruited from larger companies or from the manufacturing sector), a management style (dictated from the top down); the structure of the program itself, including licensing deals; the company track record in private label (for some new and unfamiliar, for others, stretching back to the last century). While the degree of commitment also varied considerably, an implicitly-shared private label philosophy emerged around such principles as:

- *Product Quality* —high standards measured against the brand leaders in a product category,
- *Quality Assurance* —established product specifications that were kept consistent,
- *Legal Safeguards* —protecting against copyright and trade-dress infringement,
- *Product Pricing* —set below the competing brand-leaders in a product category,
- *Product Selection* –high-traffic categories and popular product sizes that delivered sales and profits,
- *Brand Identity* —establishment of a brand equity rather than a mere copy cat strategy following the category brand leader,
- *Packaging Strategies* —position of the product at different quality levels with image, appearance, and/or similar look, when compared to the leading brand in a category,
- *Supplier Selection* —vendor-approval procedures with built-in checks and balances.

During the 1960s, price very often was the only bargaining chip on the table during negotiations about private label products between suppliers and the retail buyers. In the 1970s, emphasis on top product-quality, good product taste, and reliable product performance became more important for the retailers and wholesalers. In 1976, for example, Safeway Stores opened a Quality Assurance Center in Walnut Creek, CA, to oversee product research, development, and testing. This operation complemented the product testing facilities at each of the chain's manufacturing and processing plants.

For those retailers/wholesalers who did not have their own quality testing capability, the option was to farm out the work to independent commercial laboratories. Dr. Herbert Shuster of H.V. Shuster Laboratories, Quincy, MA, was one of the first to help the industry develop quality attributes and standard methods of evaluation. His company established many scoring procedures for private label products for which no formalized system existed before. Of course, other consultants in this field, in competition with Shuster, also kept the industry up to snuff in quality specifications, especially as more product categories opened to private label and more retailers/wholesalers improved and expanded their programs.

This attention to quality eventually extended to package design as well as marketing and merchandising support. Again, the retailers often would draw on outside expertise to help dress up their packages and improve on their marketing activities. Sometimes people from the branded side of the business were hired to apply their experience to private label development. Different packaging strategies also evolved, such as the so-called "copycat approach" (coming as close to the leading brand look as possible without confusing the consumer into thinking it was the brand-leader) or the family look (collecting all product categories under a single look, often using the store name identity as the logo).

Private label buyers in effect became category managers, fitting private label into designated product categories. It was less similar to today's category management strategies in which one or a few categories are assigned to an individual and in which both private label and brands are orchestrated within a category, than it was focused upon private label's role in specific categories. There also was far less marketing data available at the time. Private labels was perceived as being more like a brand within its own sphere of influence. Sometimes these methods also were applied by manufacturers serving a particular product category, such as Bordens in the dry-pasta area.

Bordens: A Pioneer in Pasta Category Management

Bordens developed first as a regional company with its Creamette brand business, supplying some private label accounts, such as Nash Finch and Roundy's. Over time, the company acquired nine other pasta firms. Its expansion into private label, however, really didn't begin until 1978-79. This was an economic decision, since its production plants had to be kept humming along at 365 days a year—three shifts per day to keep costs down. Marketing dollars also had to be generated to build pasta consumption and educate the consumer about different cuts, varieties and uses of pasta in recipes.

At this time, Bordens regarded itself like General Motors, selling Buicks and Oldsmobiles which made more money, but also selling Chevies for more business volume. So private label was regarded as another brand at Bordens. In fact, Bordens quickly learned that with private label, it could serve customers more efficiently,in terms of distribution costs, while better positioning itself within the total pasta category. The company was ahead of its time in category management, focusing on building sales in the total category and not necessarily selling its brands over private label or vice-versa. The pasta category was growing: there was room for both brands and private label. (Today, the company still applies category management, but with a difference: IRI data is used and more money is spent on consumer research; previously, the measure of sales success was to check for dust on the top of pasta boxes on the store shelf.)

Bordens become a pioneer in building the pasta category, while providing a product quality equal to its competitors. Polypropylene packaging was introduced while competitors still used polyethylene film, which was not as clear. Additionally, Bordens provided merchandising support, designed to sell more pasta in the category. Its branded lines accommodated specialty cuts of pasta and addressed certain market segments, while private label was applied in those markets that could support the volume. Private label share of this $1.3 billion business today is about 20.7% of the total market. Bordens became the market leader in private label. (Hasper 1996)

Recently, Borden Food Corp., Columbus, OH, announced that it was pulling out of the private label dry-pasta business. In 1997, Borden decided because of losses from "system over-capacity and complexity" that it would focus more on its branded business, closing or selling five of its 10 pasta facilities.

Power Returns to the Retailers: The Rise of Generics

When the name brands ruled the roost, as it were, retailers acted more like landlords renting out their store shelves to brand manufacturers. It was certainly a profitable business, especially when the retailers collected promotional allowances, rebates on products not sold, and the like from the manufacturers.

When anyone dominates market share, it is very easy to become greedy and want still more business. Many manufacturers were publicly held, answerable to stockholders who wanted to see higher profits and bigger dividends. The corporations responded by raising retail prices; by offering product extensions—almost diluting their brand equity in certain categories; by compromising on their product quality (lowering the standards for ingredients or buying cheaper); and by either subtlety down-sizing content counts (selling product at the same price) or trading up with incremental size increases that had a disproportionate price increase. Of course, not every manufacturer followed these strategies, but a great many did loosen their standards and compromise their leadership position.

With the price gap widening between private label and leading brands, consumers were encouraged to try the less expensive, but equally good private label alternatives. Retailers challenged shoppers to compare and save. Shelf signage and printed ads in newspapers, and mailed-circulars supported this strategy. Retailers, in effect, found they could become more than merchants, that is, marketers as well, by calling attention to their own store brands. What really awakened them to this marketing muscle was the debut of generics in 1977.

In its own market, Jewel Food Stores, Chicago, faced the emergence of box-store competition in a limited assortment discount outlet started by Aldi Benner. Bender, a competitor, had been acquired by the German discounter, Aldi, which since the 1940s had successfully built a chain of no-frills, limited-assortment discount stores across Europe, each store stocking 80%+ of its products under many different private labels—all sold like brands, but on the basis of price. The concept was transferred to the United States. Jewel reacted by opening its own no-frills stores, Jewel T Discount Grocery. This format, started in Florida, featured a limited line of private label and controlled label non-perishable foods.

Since Jewel had had experience in the European market during the 1960s, working with Grand Bazar department stores in Belgium and developing Supermarches G.B. supermarkets, called Super Bazars, within self-service department stores, the company was not unfamiliar with trends across Europe, when it was looking for new marketing concepts. In 1974, Jewel brought the Grand Bazaar concept to the US., combining a 66,000-square-foot food store featuring free-standing specialty shops, with a 25,000-square-foot Osco Drug store. (Jewel 1979)

A "Brand-Free Products" Orientation

Jewel, therefore, was familiar with the move by the French hypermarche store retailer, Carrefour, which in 1976 introduced 50 "brand-free products as good as the best, but less expensive." Carrefour had no private label program, so this strategy, called *produits libre* (brand free), featured simple packaging: an all-white background identified with the generic name of the product, i.e., "peas," on the label, along with a small red-and-blue band at the bottom of the package carrying the Carrefour logo.

The following year, Jewel adopted this concept but in a modified form, introducing generic label products into its U.S. stores. Its line was packaged in a plain white label with a green-and-black stripe, and covered basic items. There was no doubt that Jewel's generic program was a direct copy of the Carrefour strategy with one big difference: Carrefour offered top-quality products under a generic look and with a small store-brand logo, while Jewel with similar plain packaging had a lower-quality range without any company logo. Jane Armstrong, Jewel's vice-president of consumer affairs, identified the line in a consumer brochure as:

"Our generic (no brand name) private label family of basic bargains. These products represent real savings. When applicable, they are of standard grades as opposed to Grade 'A' or the 'top' qualities. On items that are nutritionally labeled, you can see for yourself that they are the same, or very close to the nutritional values of comparable brand name items."

Jewel had found something to complement its first-quality line of private labels. Its strategy was to carry standard-or-acceptable-quality products in dull packaging, in just one size, usually the best-selling size in a product category. Other than creating a generics-aisle in its stores with appropriate signage, Jewel offered no extensive advertising support for the program. Generics were sold at a consistently low price .

In a very short time, other supermarket chains and food wholesalers copied this strategy, the most significant being the co-op, Topco, which appeared its Valu Time generics line, a black-and-white label, in February, 1978. Federated Foods also responded quickly, first with a black-and-white label generics line, then in late 1983 with what was termed a neo-generic variation: Valu Check'd, a brand-identity with plain yellow background and black lettering on the packaging. Others also adopted variations on the generic look, adding a slight color design or identifying the line in signage and/or on the package, for example Ralphs Grocery, Los Angeles, with the Plain Wrap identity (not on the packaging itself); and both A&P and Pathmark in New Jersey, with brand identities on the packages: P&Q and No Frills, respectively. For some, such as Ralphs, it was a matter of collecting together a number of standard grade products from its old All Star packer label program, exclusive to the chain.

Within the next three years, other major food chains joined the trend: Kroger with Cost Cutter, American Stores with Econo Buy, Winn-Dixie with Price Breaker and even Safeway. The latter chain adopted a generics presentation, for its secondary private label line, called Scotch Buy, which was marketed more like a private label while addressing consumer interest in low-priced generic products. Safeway Stores, Oakland, CA, the largest supermarket chain in the country at the time (1978), opted for what it called a "second generation generics" program, which was really a lower private label quality-tier, called Scotch Buy. The packaging featured a bright green-and-white plain logo with the head of a Scotchman, designed to project an image of "good quality and thrifty prices." Safeway merely consolidated a group of its low-end standard-grade packer labels, Highway, Ovenjoy, Pack Train, Par, Piedmont, etc., under the Scotch Buy label. Throughout this period, there also were numerous packer-label generic items marketed by manufacturers.

The generics phenomenon continued up until the mid-1980s, when it lost momentum, because of inconsistent quality standards, ugly labels, and a lack of continued retailer merchandising/marketing support. Overall, it achieved a small market share—not more than 3 or 4% of total supermarket sales, according to market research data. Additionally, the U.S. economy was improving, so consumers were less interested in trading down to a price item.

Some so-called generic programs, however, endured, especially when a retailer programmed the range just like any other private label program. Ralphs Grocery, for example, did this with its No Frills program by positioning the line as a value option across different product categories, while providing consistent quality with a guaranteed-satisfaction-or-money-back policy. Signage in the store challenged the shopper to "compare any Ralphs Plain Wrap product with any similar national brand product. If you don't agree that Plain Wrap offers more value, we'll give you the national brand free." Savings up to 30% were offered in the range. Ralphs also upgraded the packaging and, where feasible, the quality over time. As a result, its program has endured.

Strategies of Differentiation

For the most successful "generics" program in North America, we turn to the Loblaw's organization in Canada. Just like Carrefour, Toronto-based Loblaw had no private label program to speak of when it introduced its version of generics, under the "no name" umbrella program in 1978. Loblaw distinguished its range with yellow packaging and black lettering, describing the generic name of the product and other label information. David Nichol, president of the Ontario chain at the time, avoided following the pack, but invented what he called a "differentiated marketing approach." His program was not strictly a private label program that sought to replicate the quality of the national brand, while offering a savings. Instead, he sought value first, "making the generic quality sometimes better than the national brands, sometimes the same quality, sometimes different, but in all cases always representing a better value." His philosophy was: "How do I change this product to produce savings which will make it the best overall value in this market, while still preserving my category percentage gross margin?" This strategy worked, and the "no name" program has continued to grow and thrive at Loblaws ever since. In 1981, Nichol said: "Generics is the most powerful weapon that retailers have developed since the introduction of the self-service supermarket." This statement, of course, must be qualified. It's true, if you look at the strategy followed by Loblaw. It's not so accurate when you look at the way generic programs developed in the United States or elsewhere in the world. Generics either disappeared, reduced to a few basic items, or they were modified into second-quality-tier private label programs at different chains.

There are arguments that generics hurt the image of private label because of their low and inconsistent quality and terrible packaging. Generics, nevertheless, gave both retailers and wholesalers full command over what products they could source, package, stock, and promote off store shelves. There were no national-brand manufacturers involved in this business. Generics had to be promoted primarily by the retailers. In fact, generics filled a vacuum created as private label quality standards improved. The consumer still wanted a bargain or trade-off buying option.

Dave Nichol Brings Brand Discipline to Controlled Labels

Nichol reasoned that even the brand manufacturers fell short of developing "meaningful product differentiation." As a speaker during a Toronto generics conference early in the 1980s, he indicated: "North American product managers are caught up in a line-extension mentality. They're spending their time on the hype instead of the product—the sizzle instead of the steak. It's easier to change a package, an ad campaign, or add a holiday contest than it is to develop a meaningfully differentiated product."

What was happening, in effect, was an erosion of brand loyalty. The advertising agency, DDB Needham Worldwide, New York, reported that consumer research showed the level of loyalty to well-known brands had decreased from 77% in 1975 to 62% in 1990. Within this period, Nichol, who championed "no name" in Canada, in 1985 moved to introduce President's Choice, a range of upscale and/or unique store brand food and beverage products—offering better quality than the leading national brands, at a lower price. He was clearly influenced in this case by the 100% own-brand retailer, Marks & Spenser, in the United Kingdom. Nichol even recruited people from that organization to help develop unique or different products. Even more important, Nichol, as president of Loblaw International Merchants, was continuing his development of a totally-integrated marketing approach to corporate brand programs, involving product package design, store signage, radio-TV, and newsletter marketing, etc. for Loblaws. As far back as 1974, Loblaw had a brand marketing system in place which was designed to raise its private labels to national brand quality standards. In 1976, Nichol introduced a category management strategy to the company, which was a pure consumer product brand management strategy. It was clearly manifested with the development of the "no name" program. The President's Choice program put it into high gear.

Interesting insights into the strategies applied by Nichol are offered in the book, "The Edible Man," by journalist Anne Kingston. In 1986, for example, Nichol had Loblaw invest $150,000 (Canadian dollars) into a "War Room," featuring eight TV screens that displayed computer-generated data about products sold in Loblaw stores. The computer program, dubbed Pierre, and created by Ray Goodman, a vice-president of information services, was used to track product sales, taken from UPC scans at Loblaw supermarkets.

Orchestrating the Store's Critical Mass

Nichol acted like the conductor of an orchestra, Kingston writes, in which each product was displayed with color-coded bands, yellow representing the No Name and President's Choice items, green for products at or above average sales, and red for weaker products: "If Nichol wanted to survey peanut butter, he would call up the department (grocery), the sub-department (dry), the category (peanut butter) and then the subcategory (smooth). In ten seconds, he could learn that No Name peanut butter claimed 31% of the category and a 37% profit margin, and compare it with Kraft, which had 59% of the category, but a margin of only 14.5%.

Nichol's strategy was to sell national brands at cost while using Loblaw's controlled brands, No Name and President's Choice, which carried higher gross margins, to generate profits. These products, Kingston explains, were sold through "a merchandising technique called bracketing," where Loblaw's own brands literally surrounded the national brand, President's Choice (PC) to the left, No Name to the right. Nichol then employed a "shielding" technique to protect against brand price wars: when the price of a brand on sale at a competitor's store was lowered, Loblaw cut the price both on that brand and the President's Choice counterpart, advertising the lower-priced brand to attract shoppers to Loblaw's store. (Kingston 1994).

Working like a brand manufacturer, Nichol introduced a new wrinkle by controlling the critical mass of the store and its product pricing. Manufacturers couldn't do that. Also, Nichol drew on all the marketing tools available, using TV and radio ads to tell the consumer to switch to Loblaws, the only place where they could purchase the unique President's Choice products. The TV spots were created in the company's own TV studio, and starred David Nichol, without hiring an expensive advertising agency and at less than $10,000 per spot—versus the average agency production costs of $150,000 in the Ontario marketplace. Nichol introduced a 16-page "Dave Nichol's Insider's Report" in newspapers across Canada—an idea he purchased in 1983 from the Trader Joe's California food chain (which itself featured more than 80% private label stock and also emphasized top quality, unique product features, and a low price). Nichol's slightly wacky format in this publication entertained consumers while promoting the new President's Choice products as well as new products introduced into the "no name" range. The flyer, which Nichol wrote, carried his own personal observations, recipe ideas, cartoons--almost like a combination of *Consumer Reports* combined with *Mad* magazine. (Kingston, 1994)

Additionally, the company ran so-called Infomercials on cable TVwhich were tied to the product line, sampling programs staged at the Canadian National Exhibition and for food service accounts, an Insider's Report Cookbook, restaurant promotions, etc. Packaging treatment changed as the corporate brand program at Loblaws evolved. Working with the Watt Design Group in Toronto, Nichol helped create bold, distinctive packaging with attractive food photography. It took several years before President's Choice took root in the United States via a strong licensing program. After that, it didn't take long for U.S. competitors like A&P, Topco and others to introduce their own upscale programs, given the success at Loblaws.

REFERENCES/CITATIONS

Gallagher, Joe 1996. Phone interview with retired private label manager at P&C Food Markets, Syracuse, NY.

Hasper, Jack 1996. Phone interview with manager at Borden's Pasta Group.

Jewel 1979. "History of Jewel Companies, Inc." Jewel Companies, Chicago, IL. September 1979 (Company background information).

Kingston, Anne, 1994. "The Edible Man: Dave Nichol, President's Choice & The Making of Popular Taste." MacFarlane Walter & Ross, Toronto, Canada, pp. 82-84.

ibid, p. 48

PLMA 1980. PLMA News, Vol. 1, No. 1. November 1980.

PART 11

Tiers of Quality in the Private Label Program

CHAPTER 13

APPRAISING PRIVATE LABEL VALUE

Within the private label program, particularly in foods, there have evolved at least four quality tiers:

- Upscale or premium quality,
- First tier, or Grade A quality on a parity with leading brands,
- Secondary or extra standard, Grade B, quality tier,
- Standard, Grade C, or acceptable quality tier.

The initial momentum and growth in private label had been with first-quality lines that comply with Standards of Identity in commodities established by the US Department of Agriculture, and in manufactured goods that match the specifications set by leading national brands.

Today, the national brand reference is no longer the final word on quality. In fact, some brand manufacturers have fluctuated in their quality standards. In building quality assurance within their private label programs, retailers and wholesalers have set their own quality goals while also working toward product consistency, purity, and stability as well as complying with all Federal Food and Drug Administration regulations or, in products not covered by the FDA, following Good Manufacturing Practices to ensure product quality.

More than any other brand in the supermarket today, private label serves consumers better, because it addresses every need in terms of its scaled quality levels, its wide range of prices, its attention to eye-appealing packaging, and its consistent built-in value when compared to the category market leaders. Replacing many secondary manufacturers' brands in the marketplace, private label now generally outperforms them by striving for year-round product availability, consistent top quality, and guaranteed value in the pricing. Unlike the manufacturer' brands, where prices fluctuate up and down, private label pricing is purposely kept consistently lower than the brand leader in a product category. Of course, occasionally, a manufacturer's brand on a special discount promotion will be priced lower than its private label counterpart.

With private label, the retailer has better control over out-of-stock situations, not being subject to a specific brand manufacturer's supply situation in which other customer orders are filled first. Retailers can purchase product under private label from different manufacturing sources, while keeping its quality specifications consistent via quality assurance back-up support. Often promoted like the name brand leaders, private label also is able to present consumers with more excitement in their shopping experience in contrast to a weaker brand which is unable to provide similar marketing or promotional support on a regular basis. Additionally, retailers who own or have exclusive rights to market private label items can cater to many different types of shoppers, with items ranging from the economically-priced up to the very best quality, including gourmet or unique products, which are still reasonably priced.

Interestingly, recent research has shown that the majority of people no longer set brand loyalty as a priority in their shopping plans. In fact, this has been a trend for the past 30 years. In 1966, for example, Leo Bushey, president of Red & White Corp., in a speech, cited a recent *Progressive Grocer*'s article about a Nielsen survey. It showed that 58% of shoppers are willing to buy substitute brands, when the brand they shop for is not stocked. A few years earlier, only 46% said they would be willing to switch. Bushey noted: "That's a 25% change in shopper receptiveness—favorable to store related private brands."

The shopper, Bushey argued, "is better informed—more self-reliant—more value-conscious, more ready to challenge yesterday's decisions and to try something else today.

"This shopper is sensitive to the direct relationship between the private brand and the supermarket sponsoring it—whether that supermarket be part of a corporate chain, voluntary chain, or cooperative group. When such a brand has a supermarket's unqualified endorsement and support, the shopper is pre-sold on it by the very fact that she has chosen that supermarket as her preferred shopping place. Furthermore, as a customer, she has ready contact with people answerable to her, if or when a product under the private brand fails to meet her expectations. It may not be going too far to suggest that the modern shopper feels that her supermarket operator owes her an obligation to make major commodities available at prices which reflect the elimination of national advertising budgets at the manufacturer level." (Bushey 1966)

Private Label Ranks Among Top Three Categories

This attitude has not changed much today. In fact, consumers are now much more value-conscious. The latest ACNielsen research shows that there are "only a handful of cases," where "a brand defines a (product) category and is itself a destination item" for the consumer. In a trade magazine article, "The Brand in a Tough Market"

(*Supermarket Business*, March 1996), Nielsen's research director Doug Handler noted that private label, measured as a single brand, takes one of the top three spots in 166 product categories—or 48%+ of the total 343 dry grocery categories measured in supermarkets. The leading brand usually collects an average of 41.6%, the second best seller 18%, and the third 10.4% of a product category's total sales.

While consumers still like name brand products sold at a discount, they also like alternative choices, especially when those products, offering comparable quality, are continually priced lower with a variety of options available. Private label pricing is established anywhere from 10% up to 25% or more below the dominant national brands in a category. It is here that private label derives its greatest strength. While it can be consistent in quality, adjusting to upgrades or improvements when necessary to keep pace with the market leaders or to technological changes in the marketplace, private label also carries its own weight. From the most superior quality available on the market, sometimes including truly unique or innovative features, through other quality tiers established in the supermarket trade, private brands address all levels: Matching or exceeding the brand leaders in product performance and/or taste, as well as being positioned a grade or two below that level, offering just standard acceptable quality, depending upon consumer preferences or needs within specific marketing areas.

Brand manufacturers, of course, can offer alternative choices such as product-line extensions, usually on a top-quality level under their brand identity, as well as at lower quality levels under another brand identity. Their first loyalty, however, is to their flagship brand. Retailers orchestrate their private label program where their first loyalty is to the consumer who shops their stores. Retailers are concerned with higher traffic counts in shoppers, not brand market share leadership in specific categories. (In fact, their store itself can become the brand leader in a market, which reflects both their private label selection and with representative name brand stock.) That's one reason why private label merchandising/marketing support can vary throughout a chain operation, emphasizing specific quality levels in different markets in order to satisfy customers who favor a certain quality level. Therefore, generics, for example, can still be viable in certain markets, while in an upscale market consumers might prefer higher-priced, best quality or gourmet-type private labels. Private label provides the retailer with this marketing flexibility.

A Difference in Philosophy: Manufacturers Vs. Retailers

There is another important point of difference between name brands and private labels. When brand manufacturers criticize or condemn private label, arguing about the superiority of their own brands, the manufacturers totally misunderstand the retailers' rationale for stocking private label. Historically, private label never was designed to steal market share away from the brand leaders. Pioneers in the retail industry offered private label to consumers, presenting the best possible quality and/or price, in order to build profits as well as to ensure and to build store patronage. Consumers could shop for their favorite brands at whatever price competition prescribed in the market, but they also were given an alternative choice—private label, representing value for their dollar. These entrepreneurs did not want to be totally subjected to the dictates of the brand manufacturers. Retailers also realized they could generate more profits from private label overall, especially when they operated aggressively in merchandising and promoting private label to build sales volume. This attitude is viable today—more so, since private label has regained its stature and recognition among consumers. Additionally, retailers know today that they are not always guaranteed high sales volume with leading brands in stock, especially when facing a large discount chain competitor which steals that business away with rock-bottom pricing. The non-discounter's option is to differentiate themselves in that market with distinctive, high-quality lines under their own store brand identities that the discount competitor cannot carry. Of course, the discounter, too, can offer its own private label alternatives. It's up to the consumer to decided which store to shop.

With the trend now toward more category management strategies, retailers find it easier and more manageable to deal with fewer brands, along with a private label range that they have fully under their control. They can orchestrate private label over its different quality tiers, allowing it to compete most effectively within each product category, i.e., an upscale private label might not sell as well against a dominant name brand in one category, while a lower quality, low-price alternative private label item would fit in better, since it does not compete on the same quality level. In addition, retailers now are becoming more focused on promoting or selling the concept of meal-solutions instead of specific brands. Options are open to the shopper on what to buy according to their budget. The retailer provides these different pricing options, which a private label program often presents to the consumer.

The First-Line Private Label Program

For retailers/wholesalers, the first-tier program represents their major effort under private label. Most often, it has formed the basis for their entry into private label, while covering the most number of products they stock under private label. Frequently, this group of products carries the store name identity or a store flagship brand(s). The chains that produce their own manufactured or processed foods, beverages, and other products, usually place them in the first-quality tier as well—not necessarily matching a brand leader in a product category but sometimes assuming market share leadership, especially in the perishables area (dairy, bakery, produce, meat, etc.). In fact, these categories now represent the biggest private label sales volume lines with commanding market share for the supermarket retailer: i.e., milk, cheese, bread, etc.

The first-tier program encompasses thousands of SKUs (Stock Keeping Units), covering a wide range of product categories—foods and non-food groceries, beverages, general merchandise, health and beauty care, etc. Over the past 30 years, most of the new entry product categories have made their debut as first-line private labels. It could be argued that private label success in one product area led to its introduction into another category. Likewise, as private label grew in other retail segments, initially in the drug store market then mass merchandising, its acceptance grew as well. In the supermarket sector, the first-tier program has evolved in recent years from a proliferation of identities, sometimes spilling into Grade B and C quality levels for foods, especially with short supplies available in a commodity item. Lately, these programs have been consolidated into one or a few distinctive identities, restricted to the top-quality level. And fewer identities have been extended throughout an organization's different chain formats under a single corporate label program.

With this move toward consolidation of labels, the retailers are better able to organize and coordinate their first tier program plus achieve stronger purchasing power. They first put the emphasis on a continuity of product quality in which identification by the consumer is reinforced through frequent packaging improvements which make the product more attractive or appealing. In the 1970s, for example, A&P dropped its Red Circle identity for a modern-style logo. Safeway upgraded its top-quality private label line with more graphic appeal, tying the range into an 'S' insignia, helping to identify first-line products. Grand Union adopted a Red Dot identity.

The trend developed around different packaging strategies: a single brand identity creating a family look; multiple brand identities limited to categories where strong brand equity was built into an identity; and a single corporate brand identity used throughout an organization's different chain formats.

Drawing on Outside Packaging Expertise

Outside packaging designers were retained to put more emphasis on package graphics appeal, design effectiveness, and mass display impact. Early in the 1980s, Ralphs Grocery, Compton, CA, hired a little-known design firm, Don Watt of Toronto, Canada, to revamp both its store decor and the Ralphs private label. The designer developed a black background for the packaging which fully accented the color photography of the product. This strategy was so effective that a supermarket chain across the country, Finast-Edwards, paid Ralphs a fee for the use of the same graphics, replacing the Ralphs logo with its own private label logos, helping both parties to realize packaging cost savings. Other chains have copied this look as well.

About this same time, United Grocers, Oakland, CA, the largest food wholesaler in Northern California, retained Landor Associates, San Francisco, to upgrade its Bonnie Hubbard identity from a controlled label into a regional brand. Retailers were discovering the value of marketing their own company name as a brand and the importance of brand equity.

Schnuck Markets, Inc., St. Louis, commissioned its own market research study in 1982 to evaluate communications practices and develop new corporate/retail identification for the supermarket chain, including a new private label packaging system. Schnucks had Landor Associates redesign the Schnucks corporate logo elements, including its Revolutionary Soldier logo and the Schnucks name. In 1983, its private label sales accounted for about 5% of total sales, covering health and beauty care items plus a few fast-moving perishables and groceries. Schnucks decided to drop out of the Staff Supermarket Associates co-op and joined as an associate of the private label buying group, Topco. Its redesigned packaging, carrying Schnucks's name and logo, appeared on 150-plus grocery items, then soon grew to 600-plus items, covering grocery items, detergents, and household products. At the time, Scott Schnuck, corporate vice-president of marketing and merchandising, explained:

"We follow extensive quality control procedures to ensure our brand quality matches our specifications of national brand comparability. We back this quality commitment up with a quality guarantee statement on the label, as well as the phone number of our consumer relations department at our headquarters. There is a greater consumer acceptance," Scott continued, "if we have our own name on the product. The image of the chain rubs off more directly on the product." (Casey 1989)

Retailers express a certain pride in the quality of their first-tier program, claiming it represents the best quality available in the marketplace. They also rely more on the equity built into their own store name appearing on the product. Chains like Kroger, for example, resisted generics at first, arguing that the Kroger brand gave consumers the same price advantage of no-name products, along with a higher, consistent quality feature. Kroger retaliated by merchandising its second line of private label, Avondale, using all the tools of the generic marketers, while competitively pricing it against generics. Eventually, Kroger relented, but followed the strategy of other retailers with its own so-called second-generation generics, which carried a private label identity, Cost Cutter, in a plain label (yellow background, black lettering and a simple graphic treatment). Kroger also resisted the move into upscale premium private labels late in the 1980s, arguing that its first-line quality is the best available. In its quality assurance laboratory, when cutting products from the Loblaw's President's Choice range, Kroger reportedly rejected becoming a President's Choice licensee on the grounds that its Kroger brand quality matched that of the Loblaws program. Kroger eventually responded by putting the word 'Premium' on some of its Kroger brand products.

Overall, the attitude toward private label has changed from a rationale of getting the lowest price on the best quality products or just treating private label as an afterthought, into full commitment from top management downward. Retailers also have received more cooperation from private label packers, who started to give more frequent allowances for promotions. The chains, voluntary groups, and cooperatives, already dedicated to private label, were joined by others making the same full commitment. It was a slow process that continued through the 1970s up until a transformation that literally shook this industry to the core. It was called "generics."

Generics: A Wake-Up Call for Retailers

It started with items like canned vegetables and fruits, beverages, baking supplies, condiments, paper goods, and household items, then spread to other categories: snacks, health and beauty care, pet supplies. The strategy at first was defensive, as in Jewel Food Stores' introduction of its low-cost, no-frills alternative to brand name products. But for many, generics evolved into an offensive strategy involving Jewel and others who followed and used generics to present a low-price image via advertising, promotions, and in-store massive displays. Through networking, word-of-mouth communications, and general copycat strategies, generics grew and spread throughout the United States. It was not a coordinated effort but a spontaneous development, fueled by a weak economy during the early 1980s.

As discussed earlier, generics as a measurable tier of acceptable, standard-grade quality products grew out of Jewel's competitive reaction to the discounter, Aldi. It is almost poetically appropriate that Aldi's predominantly private label store format (80%+ of its stock in its own brands) encouraged this wide recognition of a price brand in the U.S. supermarket trade. The debut of generics late in the 1970s definitely helped private label shed its cheap quality or price-only image, when generics took over that role. Generics filled a vacuum left by the private label programs that were being upgraded into a first-tier quality level. Retailers were left with the task of improving the quality of their private label products and enhancing the packaging with first-class, sometimes award-winning designs. They began to manage private label more like a brand which could match or exceed almost any manufacturers' brand on the market.

The impact of generics on the U.S. supermarket business created both positive and negative reactions from the trade. Since there was no control over the quality, generics unpredictably delivered both extremes—bottom-of-the barrel leftovers from a production run, or the lowest quality grade available, up to quality that matched or exceeded the national brand leader in a product category. While some retailers and wholesalers did ensure dependable quality consistency, overall, generics spun out of control, dependent on the supply-and-demand situation in the marketplace. Additionally, its packaging frequently was of poor design, sometimes smudged or torn, without any regard for aesthetics. Of course, there were exceptions, too. Even the manufacturers' packer labels, which many generic products replaced, were better looking.

With experience, retailers were able to cull the losers (including many food items). The generics program, encompassing some 200 SKUs on average, continued with the winners such as apple juice; paper products like towels, toilet tissues, plates; snack items; cigarettes; cat litter, etc. Generics, when supported through merchandising and marketing and kept consistent in quality, did work. The retailers who recognized this began to upgrade its packaging, dropping the packer-label look or black-and-white or the yellow-and-black graphic format, and adding color, vignettes, in fact creating a private label identity, i..e., Kroger's Cost Cutter, A&P's P&Q, American Stores' Econo Buy, etc.

REFERENCES/CITATIONS

Bushey, Leo J. 1966. "Private Brands Versus the Advertised Brands—What's Ahead?" Speech delivered Feb. 3, 1966 to Supermarket Advertising Club of New England, Boston, MA.

Casey, Marie 1989. "Schnucks, 1939-1989: Fifty Years of Friendliness." Schnuck Markets, Inc., St. Louis, MO, pg. 68.

Photographic Album 11

National Brand or Private Label

Who's going to "own" the grocery business in the years ahead?

In this undated ad headline atop a full page of copy, Good Housekeeping Magazine, calling itself "First in Advertising Pages," answered its own question: "We know who is going to own the grocery business in the years ahead: the manufacturer who continues to win the confidence of America's homemakers." Of course, that meant national brands, using "imaginative, effective, convincing advertising." Understandably, the magazine supported its advertisers, but its prediction was completely wrong! The retailers actually took over by taking the initiative themselves, which included using their own store brands as a catalyst--improving quality, sharpening packaging, reinforcing merchandising and marketing support, and breaking into new presentation formats--generics and upscale private labels.

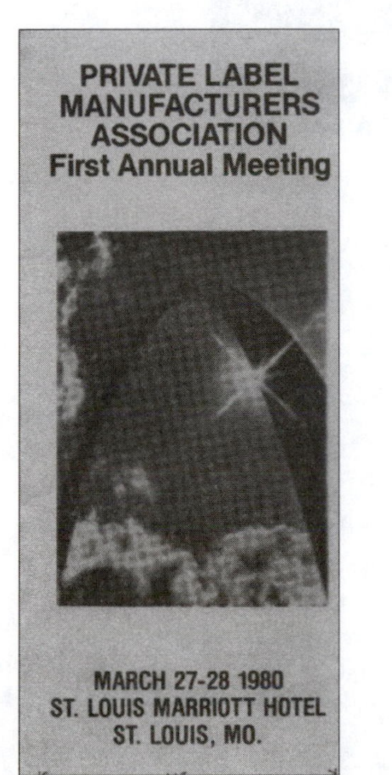

In 1979, "Private Label" magazine, the industry's first trade publication, staged an industry meeting in New York, leading to the establishment of the Private Label Manufacturers Association, New York. Its first annual meeting in 1980 drew 320 participants. Six months later, PLMA held its first Trade Show & Educational Conference, its membership exceeding 116. One primary goal: to educate the consumer about private label. Its players could not afford big ad budgets, but they did have a creative flare for merchandising and marketing at the store level.

PLMA NEWS NEWS NEWS

Published by The Private Label Manufacturers Association

Vol. 1, No. 1 May 1980

PLMA Elects 1980 Officers, Directors

PLMA started to get the word out about private label with its first house organ, "PLMA News." Its first slate of officers included a number of manufacturers who have continued to support private label growth for nearly 20 years. PLMA's first membership went to American Safety Razor Co., Staunton, VA. The group also appointed a public relations committee, and later a professional agency, to help promote the private label concept to the consumer.

Over the years, A&P developed many different private brands, identified by product categories, i.e., Ann Page in dry groceries, Jane Parker in bakery items, Sail in laundry detergents, Daily in pet food, A&P brand in a wide variety of categories, etc. Most of these exclusive brands have been consolidated under the "America's Choice" brand. Strong brand equity in the Eight O'Clock coffee line has kept that store brand alive.

The private labels on this page from Federated Foods, Inc., Des Plaines, IL and distributed by Red & White International, demonstrate a trend in identity. The top label is a simple drawing notably with the logo identified as a "brand." The middle label is more sophisticated. Besides its full ingredients statement, it also carries nutritional information with an analysis of protein, fat, fiber, moisture. Here, the logo identifies with "quality." Below, the Red & White logo becomes more stylized and distinctive, featuring a "premium quality" tag. The graphics are close-up and dramatic, including a seal certifying USDA inspection. Besides nutritional facts and ingredients, the label assures "Our guarantee--satisfaction guaranteed or your money back" and a reference to the brand's being "Famous for premium quality products since 1921."

The Stop & Shop Companies, Boston, MA, which began as the Economy Grocery Stores in 1914, developed its own ECCO private label, which is shown here through its label evolution until the company adopted its Stop & Shop identity. That also carried over to its private label identity. This leading supermarket chain in New England innovated with its private labels, including its introduction of no-salt-added to its canned vegetables and no-sugar to its canned fruits early in the 1980s--reportedly before anyone else, including the brand leaders. Today, this company is owned by Ahold of The Netherlands.

The voluntary group, IGA, Chicago, unsuccessfully tried to transplant its concept to Europe, but the first "foreign" store to take root was in Canada, and was controlled by a wholesaler, who evenutally developed into The Oshawa Group Limited, Toronto. This outlet in Ontario Province is one of its stores during the 1950s.

In this brochure (1960s or 1970s), Woolworths explains how it stocks private brands that are "equal to or better in quality and value than other private or national brands"--by dealing directly with manufacturers, mass producing large quantities, handling its own warehousing, distribution, national advertising, designing, packaging, and labelling requirements to keep the price low.

The Witco Chemical Ultra Division, Patterson, NJ, claimed strong ties with private label customers (some of them shown in its sales brochure). Note the simple package design--unchanged during the 1950s through the 1970s. Its technology equalled that of major national brand suppliers. In fact, one Witco representative, Joe Conte, became the first chairman of the PLMA.

The retailer-owned buying co-op, Certified Grocers of California, Pasadena, CA, introduced its Springfield brand in 1955. In the following decades, this brand was promoted effectively with highway billboard signs like this one in 1978.

Call it the debut of bargain brands. When the generics phenonmenon hit the U.S. market late in the 1970s, the effect was like opening the floodgates. Out poured line after line of these "no-name" products. It started with Jewel Companies, Chicago, introduced as a "no brand name" alternative. But the line was in fact branded with a specific plain white label carrying a green and black strip near the bottom of the container. This range was limited to items like canned fruits and vegetables, preserves, salt, flour, vegetable oil, spaghetti, tuna fish, dish detergent, trash bags and the like. Without fancy packaging or advertising, Jewel Food Stores stocked standard-grade products under this generic label range. The private label industry, by its nature a copycat business, jumped on the bandwagon. Everybody started to do generics, everybody, that is, except the brand manufacturers. Generics addressed a consumer need for good quality products sold at a low price. It brought a revolution in the grocery trade, and the press began to take notice. In fact, private label had never before received such attention from business and consumer publications.

"The Night Private Label Disappeared"

Federated Foods, Inc., Arlington Heights, IL, in a workshop at the 1986 Food Marketing Institute's national convention in Chicago, explored some of the trade "myths" about private label and generics disappearing from the marketplace. Federated reported on a "dramatic shift in American food retailing," where in 1985 it was reported by the Summa Group and the Majers Marketing Institute that "for the first time in this country, food wholesalers and retailers have marketing leverage over the manufacturers. This new power will grow through the remainder of this decade." Federated noted that SAMI data showed generic warehouse shipments in 1985 at $2.2 billion of the $117 billion measured.

Federated also reported that "unbranded product interest" by consumers in 1985 was strongest in specific product categories: paper towels (56%), disposable plates (43%), toilet tissue (42%), and laundry products (31%), according to Yankelovich Monitor 1985 research.

The business press, such as "Business Week" magazine (March 23, 1981), covered the "no frills" trend. Earlier, "Fortune" magazine (March 26, 1979) carried an article, "Plain Labels Challenge the Supermarket Establishment."

(Right) Reprinted from the March 23, 1981 issue of "Business Week" by special permission. © 1981 by McGraw-Hill Companies.

The generics phenon-menon evolved in the United States, where some major players were reluctant to adopt a no-name packaging strategy. The co-op Topco, Skokie, IL, kept a simple black-and-white treatment, but "branded" the package "Valu Time." Safeway Stores, Oakland, CA, felt the Scotch Buy logo would effectively respond to the generics competition. This ceiling banner offers consumers two choices: Scotch Buy or the "S" store brands. The Vons Companies, Arcadia, CA, added a red tag motif to its plain packaging, promoting its "Slim Price" generics across food and non-food categories. Some generic lines survived, but most were either upgraded to secondary-quality private labels or reduced to a select number of items, for shoppers who wanted a rock-bottom price.

In the generics saga--its strongest stage early in the 1980s--the survivors included Ralphs Grocery Co., Compton, CA, for its Plain Wrap program. This generic line looked like a no-name range, its packaging featuring only blue-and-white including a distinguishing blue strip. But Ralphs also "branded" the line with its merchandising strategy, calling it "Plain Wrap." Plain Wrap carried savings up to 30% or more. It was mass-displayed in stores and kept consistent in quality. The brokerage firm, Federated Foods, Arlington Heights, IL, offered two generic choices: a plain label (a band with stars) and Valu Check'd. Also shown: Cost Cutter from Kroger, Cincinatti.

In the 1980s, The Grand Union Co., Wayne, NJ, assigned its packaging to a design firm which updated the complete private label line, across every product category, highlighting some interesting variations. The design treatment picked up on the Grand Union logo each time, but created a family look by categories. For example, commodities featured a wide pinstripe motif and an Amish-style graphic pattern. For pasta items, a maze of tiny squares in a plaid pattern accented the plain red background with white lettering to distinguish items in the line. Condiments in glass jars carried a dark green label with tiny lighter green polka dots, on which each item's name could be accentuated with strong white lettering.

Grand Union's packaging upgrade from a plain-looking graphic treatment, often against a white background, became dramatic and eye-appealing. Examples of this are shown here. The birdseed packaging illustrates specific types of birds, here a goldfinch and a cardinal--each in bold vivid colors (yellow and red respectively), with the image commanding the package front. The design treatment in some product categories was used to create a billboard effect in mass displays of the product in Grand Union's stores. Here a cat's image is cut in half on one package, but joined together on the adjoining package. In health and beauty care items, an emphasis on colors came into play. Here the hosiery line carries light pastel-like blue and pink. Curl-shapes in a variety of colors give the package its feeling of design.

CHAPTER 14

___CURRENT STRATEGIES UNFOLD________

Upscale/Premium Programs: "The Brand-Busters"

"In 1985, Loblaw Companies introduced this new concept of what we call 'Brand-Busters' to North America with our President's Choice product program.

"To understand what a 'brand-buster' is, all you have to do is understand the President's Choice Decadent chocolate chip cookie. The national brand product is made with shortening and has 25% chocolate chips. The Decadent is made with 100% butter and 39% pure chocolate chips. And on average, the Decadent sells for less than the national brand. For the past 2 1/2 years, The Decadent has been Canada's best-selling cookie, even though it's only sold by 20% of Canadian food stores. In sharp contrast, the leading nationally-branded cookie is sold in 98% of Canadian supermarkets." (Nichol 1993)

These comments basically explain what has happened with the introduction of upscale or "premium" private labels and how this started in North America, beginning in the mid-1980s. Premium or upscale private labels were designed to "bust" the monopoly that leading brands had had in market share by adopting better quality products at a lower price —offering value to the consumer. Questions remain: Why did this first happen at Loblaw in Canada? Also, how did this development influence U.S. retailers and wholesalers, encouraging them to move from a strictly gourmet target market for upscale or premium private label into high-sales-volume product areas, and then into sub-branding strategies with their own exclusive brand identities?

Part of the answer is found in the merchandising and marketing strategies adopted by Loblaw Companies going as far back as 1974, when its International Merchants subsidiary began pioneering with a category management strategy—focusing on consumer needs, rather than what the manufacturers of brands dictated to the retail trade. Loblaw ,by then Canada's largest retail and wholesale food distributor, began to impose this strategy on the manufacturers. Its positioning was reinforced by the fact that George Weston Ltd., (a majority shareholder of Loblaw and also a leading brand manufacturer in Canada) stayed an arm's length away from supplying products to Loblaw's corporate brands program. Weston still will only do this when such a role is geared to its economic needs, as in chocolate products, where a synergy exists with its custom packaging business.

Retailer/wholesaler control over category management (CM) in North America really has been in an evolutionary stage ever since, developing out of a number of trends in the retail food trade. Traces of CM were formed in the Direct Product Profitability (DPP) system for tracking direct transportation, warehousing and retailing costs, leading into Efficient Consumer Response (ECR), which began in the 1980s in the United States. ECR involved key areas: product replenishment, store assortment, promotions, and new product introductions. It offered solutions to overcome obstacles within specific functions carried out between the retailers (buying and logistics) and manufacturers (sales and production). Category management better coordinated the retailer's buying with the manufacturer's selling activities, changing that relationship into a partnership. Its focus was not so much on either of those players as on the consumer. This partnership has been critical to the development of upscale/premium private labels, manifested in brand-new identities and/or in first-tier private label lines.

Loblaw Embraces a Corporate Label Strategy

In 1979, the CM strategy appeared in the "no name" program launched by Loblaw in Canada. At that time, Loblaw had different regional private labels under its various store identities but no consolidated banner. It prescience was not so much in joining the generics phenomenon taking root in North America, but in adopting a corporate label strategy for its diversified operations across Canada, similar to European retail organizations. This strategy addressed different product categories and patterned itself after a first-tier private label program, available throughout all its divisions across Canada. Lobaw, in effect, was creating a national brand with the "no name" program.

Dave Nichol began building a team of professionals within the company with the mandate of unifying Loblaw's corporate brand strategy. In fact, Loblaw's continues to be one of the few retail food companies in North America, in which the responsibility for the development of corporate brand strategies is not integrated into store operations and/or merchandising. Instead its strategy is patterned after the European model, where a group within the retail division dedicates itself to meeting the business needs of Loblaw's divisions. This group, maintaining checks and balances, was forced to become more business-oriented and to adopt a category-management approach years before anybody was even using this term. The group had to make its presentations to the divisions and then sell them products that made economic and merchandising sense. The group also had to do its homework, producing products that made sense for the business, and helped the different divisions differentiate themselves from the competition. This strategy also gave the group a national perspective.

Started as Loblaws Corporate Brands division, Nichol soon changed the name to Loblaw International Merchants, charged with product development, quality assurance, package design, and U.S. sales. Nichol became president, while Rob Chenaux was brought in as president of the new Intersave Division, charged with sourcing, procurement, and management of all costing. Overall, Nichol's role was as the "taste buds" for Intersave. Loblaw had centralized its private label purchasing into Intersave Canada, which handled all products including national brands. Four product category managers shared responsibilities for broad categories.

Basically, the "no name" range of products offered quality as good as the leading national brands but at a significant savings to the consumer. Shoppers got a tasty product, a product that performed well at a significant savings. It was exactly what Carrefour in France had done with its *produits libre* (brand-free) range of products, which had inspired the whole generics movement in the United States and subsequently worldwide. Figuratively speaking, Nichol understood French. That is, he understood exactly what Carrefour said in its advertising: "Brand free products as good as the best, but less expensive... no amount of fancy wrapping and free offers will make it taste any better... Simple packs. No giveaways. No sendaways. That is why they can afford to be as good as any of your favorite brands."

Nichol retained The Watt Group in Toronto to design the "no name" packaging as well as store formats, using the "no name" yellow motif in the decor and on some store identities. The "no name" no-frills program was positioned as a first-tier private label program, matching the quality of branded product leaders in each category. Proof of the soundness of this strategy is the fact that today, "no name" is Loblaw's leading corporate brand program, encompassing 4,000-plus products while representing sales in excess of $500 million.

(In the United States, Jewel copied Carrefour's concept with generic label products, taking a diametrically-opposed strategy: "When applicable, they are of standard grades as opposed to Grade 'A' or the 'top' qualities.")

Upscale And Unique "President's Choice" Products Debut

Nichol again was ahead of the pack in 1985, when, inspired by his visits to European retailers, he launched the upscale, premium-quality President's Choice program, including unique or one-of-a-kind products. Overall, this range of products offered better quality than the national brand leaders, but at a lower price. Don Watt was commissioned to design upscale packaging with stunning photography to illustrate a product's benefits. As that brand matured, a "PC" signature was introduced onto the packaging, serving as a brand seal to convey the guarantee of premium quality and savings.

Working through Loblaw, President's Choice expanded into the United States, and was additionally picked up by non-competitors on a licensing arrangement, although it took three to four years before President's Choice took root here. Today, there are some 18 accounts in the United States, selling this line, as well as licensees in Bermuda and the Caribbean.

On the other hand, Loblaw did not attempt to market its "no name" program in the United States, because it looked like a generic product with its bold yellow packaging and plain black type, which in the U.S. carried a negative perception of quality. President's Choice, however, was a different story. No supermarket retailer offered a comparable range of upscale private label products. However, when Loblaw attempted to market the President's Choice concept in the U.S., through its wholesale and retail operations, it achieved only scattered success. A licensing effort was also at first slow in development.

From the 'no name' launch forward, Dave Nichol has figuratively put himself in front of consumers, promoting "no name" then President's Choice on TV, radio, the print media, as well as on posters and promotional material in the Canadian market. The strategy was kept cost-effective because Nichol served as spokesman. As marketer-extraordinaire, Nichol helped build a fanaticism around the President's Choice brand while building consumer awareness and demand. It became almost like a cult or a religion, in which consumers felt they could not do without the 20 or more products in the program.

Indeed, Dave Nichol worked better than Michael Jackson or Madonna might have as spokesperson and was a lot cheaper: TV commercials were shot in Loblaw's own studio. He also appeared in the *Insider's Report*, a humorous, entertaining, quarterly corporate-brands newspaper insert.

Wearing his marketer hat, Nichol then began a sub-branding strategy with President's Choice, bringing out other Decadent-branded products, after the smashing success of the Decadent chocolate chip cookie, plus an environmentally-friendly G.R.E.E.N. range of products, Memories sauces, Splendido Italian foods, Quick Cuisine, Too Good To Be True health-oriented foods, all under the President's Choice brand, were marketed to different consumer needs.

The success of President's Choice did not go unnoticed by Wal-Mart , Bentonville, AR, which had already commissioned Don Watt to design its Equate line of health and beauty care line—equivalent to national brand quality, but at a better price—and then its Spring Valley lines of vitamins and dietary supplements. Wal-Mart had secured an exclusive license to market the Equate label from L. Perrigo Co., Allegan, MI, a private label manufacturer. Interestingly, in both programs Wal-Mart departed from the traditional use of its name or the mention of its own distribution operation on the package distribution statement. Instead, the actual manufacturer of the product had its name carried in the distribution clause on the label. This meant actually including a number of different manufacturers. By 1992, Wal-Mart called on Loblaw and Don Watt for help again in the launch of Wal-Mart's Sam's American Choice premium line of food and beverage products, followed the next year by the Great Value mid-tier private label grocery products line. Within six months of the launch of Sam's American Choice, that line become Wal-Mart's highest velocity SKU in the chain. Altogether, Watt designed more than 5,000 SKUs (Stock Keeping Units) of Sam's American Choice and Great Value products. The design firm followed up with another Wal-Mart private label program, Better Homes and Gardens, covering more than 1,000 SKUs of gardening supplies and equipment for the consumer. If Wal-Mart by itself could have done it cheaper or equally as well they would have.

Attacking the National Brand Mentality

In 1989, Loblaw dispatched Nichol's right hand man, Tom Stephens, director of unique product development, to the Food Marketing Institute Supermarket Convention in Chicago to publicly announce President's Choice and to punch holes in the U.S. food trade national brand mentality itself. Stephens condemned all the expensive market research as "inaccurate, incomplete," adding that it "does not cater to the consumers." He indicated that President's Choice "is designed for the consumer by someone who thinks like a consumer, not an accountant or a research analyst." Further, Stephens dismissed the "supermarket style" in the U.S. as catering to "the cheapest price image." In Europe (and by association, Loblaws in Canada), retailers are "product- and consumer-led rather than letting the food manufacturers play roulette on their store shelves with thousands of new products for which they tried, at enormous expense, to create a demand."

Since then, these themes have been publicized more by Nichol in numerous press interviews and speeches at trade shows, where he has lashed out at different accepted practices in the trade, such as retailers imitating Tide with "cheap & nasty" private labels. A new generation of private label manufacturers are killing that practice, he explained.

In a 1993 speech, Nichol described the "samurai consumer," who facing the struggle "to salvage as much as possible of the standard of living acquired during the booming 1980s. . . (is) willing to slash away at all of their traditional shopping habits to get better value for their money."

In a *Supermarket News* interview, Nichol also predicted the emergence of the "samurai store." He explained:

"Picture an 80-wash Tide for club stores, which sells at something like $14. Now if a club chain developed a product that could test equal to Tide, under the club's own label, it could sell for about $7 or $8. They could make more profit and they could sell it for half of the price of Tide." Within the next few years, he said, "there will arise a new form of club store, with no sales history, in which the primary emphasis will be superpremium brands. They will be able to undercut the Sam's and Price/Costco clubs by 30% to 40% and earn more money." The Aldi box store form comes closest to this concept, but without the "high-quality component," he added. (Supermarket News 1994)

Loblaw, in effect, had molded the category-management concept to fit its supermarket formats, so that brand manufacturers were forced to fight for shelf space while Loblaw controlled the critical mass in the store as well as its product pricing. Nichol knew his corporate brands could match almost any brand-leader in the market-place. In 1985, corporate brands accounted for 20% of total sales in its 250 corporate stores. By 1992, "ACNielsen data indicated that the brands controlled by Loblaw accounted for 32% of its Canadian dollar sales and 37% of its unit sales.

At the 1993 PLMA conference, quoted above, Nichol added:

"At the present time, we have eight corporately-owned retail divisions in Canada with multi-billion dollar sales, which have retail controlled brand unit penetrations in excess of 40%, and the top two divisions averaged over 48% in 1992... It is my contention that a retailer-controlled brand unit penetration in excess of 40% is inevitable in the USA and that traditional food retailers who do not achieve these levels in the next 10 years will not survive."

By 1997, four years into that prediction, several major supermarket chains in the U.S. had publicly announced their intentions of pushing private label penetration of total sales upward to the mid-20% range.

In 1994, Nichol had a falling out with top management at Loblaw. He left that company and soon became president of Cott Corp., Toronto, a leading supplier of premium quality retailer-branded beverages. He was regarded by Cott's chairman Gerald Pincer as a "retailer brand guru," who had warned that "consumers no longer have to or want to pay a brand tax." Pincer picked up on some telling remarks in Cott's 1994 annual report, especially regarding collaboration between retailer and manufacturer: "More and more, retailers are coming to realize that relationships with manufacturers need not be confrontational, but rather can be in the spirit of true partnership. In fact, collaboration is essential, if consumers are to be provided with 'better for less.'" He added: "...we are hearing (from retailers) about their desire to respond more effectively to consumers' needs, to merchandise more intelligently, and to improve both consumer loyalty and store profitability. The result is an enormous focus on product innovation, quality, price, and profitability." (Pincer 1994)

The Category Management Strategy

This observation, of course, ties directly into the growing trend toward category management. Category managment is also perhaps the most important element in "Efficient Consumer Response" (ECR) today.

According to a major dedicated private label food manufacturer in the United Kingdom, CM is now being practiced by the major retailers to one degree or another. "It really has taken shape over the past three to four years," he continues, "based on five industry developments:

"1. The use of bar scanning, which allows more information for the retailers and becomes a subject of discussion between manufacturer and retailer,
2. Shelf management skills improved,
3. EDI (Electronic Data Interchange), where there is direct computer-to-computer exchange of information with an almost immediate reac tion time,
4. Certain brand manufacturers come equipped with direct consumer contact studies,
5. The introduction of ideas like the store's proprietary membership club card, which gives regular customers a discount based on what they spend plus extra benefits, while the retailer collects a consumer profile on its shoppers." (Anonymous by request 1996)

The same manufacturer reports that it now focuses its efforts on more narrow category activities, where it can become a big player, while supporting the retailer's own brand with respect to pricing differentials and promotional activities. He indicates that brand manufacturers are more apt to "keep information up their sleeves and to be less forthcoming with the retailer. After all, the brand manufacturers impose their own strategy on the retailer. We see some hardening of this feeling."

As a preferred supplier, this manufacturer works with major retailers in frequent board-to-board reviews, which break out into large category studies, but also include individual categories focused on business target analysis, target sets, and strategy development, all done in conjunction with the trade customer. This works in the United Kingdom, where there is strong own-brand commitment to top-quality products.

Since Loblaw has been strongly influenced by European retail developments, its strategies tie into this idea as well.

Gourmet Evolves into High-Volume Premium Store Brands

At the 1989 Food Marketing Institute meeting, mentioned above, Peter O'Gorman, A&P's senior vice-president of development and marketing (and the chief architect of its upscale Master Choice brand) spoke about the interesting development of "retailer-inspired, high-quality own brands." O'Gorman outlined the roll-out of Master Choice, products offering the finest quality with a more affordable price than gourmet foods—meeting or beating the national brand on both price and quality.

A&P, which first began testing Master Choice in 1987, did not follow the strategy adopted by Nichol with President's Choice. A&P's line included about eight SKUs of preserves, all priced higher than the national brands, but less expensive than gourmet imports. The packaging, however, was unique: hexagonal jars with distinctive graphics. Consumers were introduced to "the affordable gourmet. . . It only tastes expensive."

With its launch of the upscale Royal Classics line about the same time, Federated Foods also focused more on a gourmet-orientation, an idea shared by others in the trade. President's Choice was really a direct assault on leading brands in the traditional, high-volume product categories. Initially, the U.S. retailers, looking at possibly entering upscale private label, stayed focused more on gourmet foods—condiments, preserves, teas, candies, etc. They felt that their first-line private label, targeted toward an equal footing with major brand leaders, filled the need for premium quality. O'Gorman indicated that the growth of specialty food sales in the United States had triggered A&P's interest in a line of better quality, more attractively packaged foods.

Grand Union, Wayne, NY, for example, had introduced its Laurent label in 1984 as a proprietary brand—inspired by the chairman of Grand Union's parent company at the time, Generale Occidentale in France. This executive owned Le Laurent restaurant in Paris. When the concept of gourmet private label lines emerged in the trade, it was logical for Grand Union to begin adding to its Laurent range, which was focused on imported foods: crackers, mustard, olive oils, preserves, vinegar, and so on.

Beginning in 1987, through its food manufacturing operations, Kroger developed the International Bazaar brand, an upscale range which was started with whole bean gourmet coffees and dry soups. This was short-lived, because Kroger later working to side-step a buyout attempt by outsiders was forced to sell off some of its properties, including this brand which was purchased by a regional manufacturer. In the prior year,

First National Supermarkets, Cleveland/Windsor Locks, CT, had introduced its Finast Classics spaghetti sauce. That chain also looked to expand into other categories, particularly orange juice, frozen entrees, ice cream, and butter sauce vegetables. Its strategy, however, was focused less on gourmet than on value-added items targeted more toward brand leaders in a variety of high-traffic product categories.

Crumbling Brand Loyalty

The conditions of the food trade at this time were ideal for the development of upscale private label lines, which offered value to consumers, because their brand loyalty continued to ebb. DDB Needham Worldwide found in a 1990 study that 62% of packaged-goods shoppers purchased only well-known brands. Fifteen years earlier, that ratio was closer to 77%. *Forbes* magazine pointed this out in its September 1991 cover story, "Hell no—we won't pay! Why consumers are no longer faithful to their favorite brands."

Some of the reasons for this loss of loyalty are cited in that article. Most significantly, brand-manufacturers were putting more marketing dollars into retailers' rebates and cents-off coupons, which *Forbes* called "a thinly disguised form of price-cutting." The article noted that the brand-manufacturers had enjoyed phenomenal growth through the 1980s, a period which saw "some of the costliest takeovers." That cost was paid for by consumers in higher product prices at retail; additionally, instead of spending thousands or millions of dollars in new product development, brand manufacturers opted to emphasize less costly line extensions, riding on the coattails of their brand name equity.

"Marketing Intelligence Services Ltd.," the article stated, "a marketing research firm, reports that since 1987, almost 70% of the 24,000 new products introduced were line extensions. The problem here is that this can cause a blurring of brand identity and a confusing proliferation of brands."

This argument is supported by an earlier trade magazine article, referring to data collected by Mediamark Research, Inc., New York, showing that for 30% of those categories, "time stood still...(with) no change (in sales coverage)" while for the remaining 70% of categories, "twice as many (47.0%) saw top-three (brand) coverage decrease as saw it increase (23.0%). And many of the decreases were more than marginal, with half of them exceeding 15%." (Supermarket Business 1991). *Supermarket Business* pointed to prominent category losers, such as spaghetti sauce, household cleaners, and frozen desserts, in contrast to the substantial gains for top-three brands were found in denture adhesive, men's hair sprays, stuffing mixes, and canned ham.

Consumers were becoming more disenchanted with name brands for a number of reasons:

"The big brands had become greedy. An eighteen-ounce box of Quaker Oats, for example, cost 73 cents (U.S.) in 1980. In 1991, that same box cost $1.73; its price had increased an average of 9% each year. Yet during that time, the wholesale price of oats had declined by one-third. The product price was 3,000% higher than the value of the raw material. Despite flat demand and falling commodity prices, manufacturers kept revenues growing by hiking prices. . ." Consumers also were smarter, recognizing all packaged staples as containing only a single ingredient, such as salt, baking soda or whatever, made with a single ingredient. The brand manufacturers reacted, continues author Kingston, by reducing their advertising and switching more to premium rebate and coupon offers: "This strategy, too, served only to erode brand loyalty, encouraging shoppers to switch brands solely on the basis of price." (Kingston, 1994)

Interestingly, in looking at specific product categories, in which premium private label programs had established their beachhead, the Mediamark report showed the sales of ready-to-eat cookies—a staple item in upscale lines— down by 15.8% for the top three brands' percentage of sales in the previous five years. In a similar comparison, the top three brands lost market share significantly in other target premium private label categories: spaghetti sauce was down 43.6%, salad dressings down 26.8%, corn/tortilla chips & cheese snacks down 18.4%, barbecue/seasoning/misc. sauces (bottled) down 17%, popcorn snacks/popping corn down 16.7%, nuts down 10.2%, regular & non-diet cola drinks down 7.9%, and fruit juices/drinks, misc. down 5.5%.

Indeed, a near-panic developed on April 2, 1993, when Philip Morris announced price cuts up to 20% in its major cigarette brand, Marlboro, in response to the market-share growth of generic and value-priced, or private label, cigarettes. Wall Street interpreted this move, called "Marlboro Friday" as an indication of lower profits for Philip Morris. As investors began selling their Philip Morris stock, a rippling effect occurred, spreading to other name brand products. The brand manufacturers reacted by cutting their prices. This practice has continued, serving the brand leaders as a marketing tool, which they can promote to consumers. Such price-cutting is in fact a step in the direction of value-added products, which private label generally and upscale/premium private label in particular offer to consumers.

REFERENCES/CITATIONS

Kingston, Anne, 1994. "The Edible Man: Dave Nichol, President's Choice & The Making of Popular Taste. MacFarlane Walter & Ross, Toronto, Canada, pg. 292.

Nichol, David A. 1993. Keynote address at Private Label Manufacturers Association Conference in Miami, FL, March 1993.

Pincer, Gerald 1994. Chairman & CEO's comments in Cott Corp.'s 1993-94 Annual Report.

Supermarket Business 1991. "Brand Power: How Top Brands Compete for Share of Market in 350 Categories, Today and Five Years Ago." March 1991.

CHAPTER 15

THE IMITATION FACTOR

The Copycat Syndrome

Imitation has always been the lifeblood of the private label industry, just as in any competitive situation. If a competitor's success is left unchecked, that is, its lead not followed and copied, that competitor will monopolize the market. Anyone should have the right to try to dominate the marketplace, but they also must face copycat competitors, who can be expected to follow a success in their own fashion, without confusing the consumer. That consumer needs to know that this offers an alternative choice and not be misled into thinking this is the first or original product or service.

Imitation not only flatters the originator; it also keeps that competitor on his or her toes: they want to be in a number-one position, over their competition, by improving their product and giving it aggressive marketing support.

Major brand name manufacturers are no exception to this rule of business. No one has a monopoly on market creativity. Good ideas develop anywhere and they will be copied, so that the end-user, the consumer, benefits by having these alternative choices. Of course, this is exactly what has happened with the premium or upscale private label phenomenon. The opportunity was there, initiated by Loblaw's President's Choice, so retailers and wholesalers in the food trade seized it. The word about President's Choice began spreading, as Loblaw worked the program into its U.S. operations: Peter J. Schmidt Co., Buffalo, NY; The National Tea Co., Rosemont, IL; and its St. Louis and New Orleans divisions. Early in 1987, Loblaw signed Cullum Companies, Inc., Dallas, as the first U.S. licensee for President's Choice. The range began appearing in Tom Thumb-Page supermarkets. The next year, D'Agostino's Supermarkets, New York, signed on as a licensee. Perhaps because it was premature, perhaps because it did not give the program enough support, Cullum dropped President's Choice but later returned again as a licensee. D'Agostino's has stayed on course, joined by upwards of 18 accounts in the U.S., operating as licensees, including major companies, such as American Stores (Jewel, Acme, Lucky, etc.), and Fred Meyer.

For different reasons, premium private label fits into the competitive strategies of these retailers. Mainly, they are interested in differentiating themselves from competitors. The President's Choice licensee, for example, has exclusive rights to the President's Choice line within their marketing area. The upscale program also complements their first tier private label and secondary-tier program, because it completes the selection for consumers: quality at or above leading brands; quality matching the market leaders; and a price brand.

U.S. Retailers Move From Gourmet Into Select Categories

While President's Choice was positioned in the market to compete against the top brands in numerous product categories, the United States strategy has been much more selective with respect to upscale private label development. It began with a gourmet reference product. A&P's Master Choice, the largest U.S.-based premium program, evolved into "superbly-crafted food products gathered, literally, from the best sources around the world," to quote an A&P Master Choice full-page ad (November 3, 1993) in *The New York Times*. The copy added: "Each product is developed with one goal, to bring together extraordinary quality, taste and authenticity with surprisingly affordable prices."

The company has supported its marketing effort with a slick consumer magazine, *Master Choice Magazine*, introduced in October 1992, which is "dedicated to excellence," featuring some articles that tie into the Master Choice product line, while carrying only Master Choice advertising, with coupon savings on Master Choice products. A&P followed a corporate brand strategy, similar to the Loblaw system, distributing Master Choice throughout its many supermarket chains—A&P, Waldbaum's, Kohl's, etc. This strategy later was picked up by A&P when it consolidated its first-tier private labels under the America's Choice corporate brand. In its Canadian operations, A&P developed a very strong Master Choice program, competing against Loblaw's President's Choice; its consolidation of other private labels, however, was designed around a new brand identity, Equality. (America's Choice was viewed an inappropriate brand name for Canadian shoppers, proud of their own heritage.)

Federated Foods Arlington Heights, IL, introduced Royal Classics, an upscale gourmet line, in 1988, which was made available to its retailer/wholesaler customers,althought they initially did not show that much interest in the program. About the same year, the co-op, Topco, debuted World Classics, which at first was aimed at imports. By 1992, Topco changed its strategy to high-tonnage products, which provided more profits—items like ready-to-eat cereals, coffee beans, and so forth.

In the 1990s, the floodgates were opened as almost every major retail chain and a number of wholesalers introduced their version of an upscale private label: Safeway's Safeway Select, Fleming's Marquee Premium, SUPERVALU's Preferred Selection, Shurfine Central's Award Winner Collection, Western Family's Excellence,

Pathmark Supermarkets' Pathmark Preferred, etc. This happened primarily in the food trade, but eventually spilled over into the drug store segment as well.

These upscale or premium private label programs were designed to be selective in their range of product offering—no more than a few hundred SKUs per program. A&P's Master Choice led the pack with upwards of 500 SKUs; most other programs kept within a range of 100 to 300 SKUs, targeting specific brand leaders. None of the U.S.-based programs came near Loblaw's President's Choice program in Canada, totaling 1,900 items at last count. While President's Choice trails behind the "no name" range of more than 4,000 SKUs, the President's Choice program is growing at a faster rate. Loblaw estimates some 40% of its grocery sales are now in control label, that is, private label, while Loblaw captures 35% of the total control label market in Canada. The growth continues: Loblaw Companies Limited reported that in calendar year 1995, its President's Choice, "no name," and Club Pack (larger size President's Choice or no name products), increased about 17% versus total company Canadian sales which were up 8%.

Program Support Equals Success

The reason for the success of President's Choice traces back to the support given the program. It is truly handled like a brand buster. Nichol stated emphatically at a Wall Street Store Brand Conference, held in 1993 in New York, that "just like national brands, brand busters must be actively promoted and marketed on a year-round basis." He stockpiled a veritable arsenal of marketing tools to support President's Choice, including TV and radio advertising; the 16-page-plus *Insider's Report* inserted in newspapers across Canada; recipe videos played in the stores; "Infotainment Shows" on cable TV featuring President's Choice items; Toronto's top restaurant chefs creating recipes with PC unique products; sampling at trade shows; a cookbook, and more.

With few exceptions, U.S. retailers and wholesalers have not been that aggressive in marketing upscale private label, because their programs are smaller than the one at Loblaw. They also face a stronger adversary: leading manufacturer's brands in the U.S. have built strong brand equity over the years with multi-million-dollar advertising and promotions. Nevertheless, there have been small victories for upscale private label. It really has depended upon the marketing support behind each program. Topco, for example has mounted an impressive effort for World Classics, including billboards, TV-radio ads, and point-of-purchase materials; Safeway, too, has given its Select program ad support plus strong in-store merchandising efforts, such as mass displays of product, end-aisle display, and signage.

Marketing is expensive, something that private label owners have gingerly approached in the past. Advertising costs, in fact, inflate the price of name brands, while private label circumvents that cost by emphasizing in-store merchandising efforts.

With upscale private label, the marketing focus has been on quality and packaging upgrades. When Fleming introduced its Marquee line of health and beauty care products late in the 1980s, the emphasis was on its packaging, merchandising and marketing support, because Marquee was truly positioned as a true brand in the marketplace— "a money-saving brand with the top quality guaranteed." The Marquee identity, therefore, served as a logical launchpad for Fleming's move into a branded, upscale product line, Marquee Premium, in 1994. In this case, Fleming has put more emphasis on value-added features such as more product per package, special formulations (combining different fruit spreads or tortilla chip blends, for example) and/or fancy packaging. It's basically a move toward offering more value instead of just trying to build brand loyalty.

Sub-Branding & Category Management

When retailers target a consumer group with a specific line of products within a product category under their own special brand identity, this strategy could be called "category management." In fact, such a strategy is exactly what has been employed in the upscale/premium private label business. Loblaw's President's Choice brand first began to target groups, adopting a sub-branding strategy. Others since have followed this pattern. Additionally, first-tier private label identities more recently have extended their reach by adding sub-brands to address certain consumer needs, such as healthier foods, ethnic food preferences, an upscale health and beauty care line.

Don Watt, head of The Watt Design Group Inc., Toronto, which helped Loblaw design the packaging for its corporate brands, "no name" and President's Choice, observes that the President's Choice program in particular "has evolved into a sub-branding strategy, featuring signature products with unique added-value features, such as more ingredients in the Decadent line (cookies, ice cream), environment-friendly G.R.E.E.N. products, Too Good To be True health-oriented foods, and Club Packs (multi-packs and economy-size products), Free & Clear (low calorie beverages)."

Now owned by Cott Corp., Toronto, the Watt Design Group also has worked with Safeway, Oakland, CA, in the package design of its Select premium quality products, in each case exceeding the national brand package design in terms of quality perception. In this development, Watt notes in a company brochure: "As an integral part of the strategy to exceed the customers' needs, Safeway targeted various consumer groups with the development of sub-brands. Each of the sub-brands has established an identity for a specific category of products. The 'Enlighten' sub-brand was created as a response to the consumer trend towards healthier foods, and included products such as light salad dressings that are free of oil and fat. Alternatively, the 'Indulgence' sub-brand includes absolutely decadent treats and desserts. Safeway's latest sub-brand, 'Gourmet Club' offers consumers frozen restaurant-quality meal solutions."

Sub-branding, of course, is not new to the private label business. A&P, for example, had been doing this for decades with its A&P Eight O'Clock bean coffee. (With the licensing program started in 1979, however, A&P has been marketing Eight O'Clock brand without the A&P identity.) IGA's Tablerite fresh meat program is another example, dating back to the late 1940s. Even the idea of distinguishing certain product categories within a first-tier private label range, by using emblems or banners is old hat. In 1979, Walgreens drug stores introduced an embossed Gold Seal, imprinted with the Walgreens "W" logo inside a blue ribbon for its vitamin line. Over the years, Walgreens also has sub-branded different products, i.e., Super Aytinal vitamin and mineral formula, Dalai musk, Jeri cologne, and so on. In health and beauty care products particularly, retailers have sometimes picked up on a part of the brand leader's name, using it as their brand, i.e. Revco's Tussin, a reference to Robitussin cough syrup expectorant. The idea of selling to a target group, however, has been a more recent development, for example addressing ethnic interests—Mexican or Hispanic foods—with sub-branded lines, under their first-tier private label program. Fleming's TV brand, sub-branded with La Comida; Certified Grocers of California's Corona brand; and IGA's brand, sub-branded with Celebración are good examples.

Ralphs Grocery Tightens Management Control over Private Label

In 1988, Ralphs Grocery Co., Compton, CA, established a Merchandising Division, which took over management of the private label function from the Grocery Division. This brought together all the private label program activities—buying, packaging, and merchandising, assigning Terry Peets, senior vice-president of merchandising, sole control over all perishable and non-perishable products in the Ralphs private label program. Every manager involved reported to Peets, who, in turn, met monthly with Ralphs marketing people and the representatives of the brokerage firm, Daymon, which served as the sales rep for private label. They would set private-label sales goals and create new packaging concepts, helping to better coordinate the whole effort. The following year, a private label administrator was appointed as well.

This coordinated effort moved Ralphs private label into new product areas in the store, via a sub-branding strategy. Ralphs did not want to give up the strong equity built into its name, which had appeared on first-tier grocery and perishable products. And so in 1990, Ralphs Private Stock liquors appeared—a line of whisky, bourbon, dry gin, etc., each package carrying a label with a glass filled with the product against the familiar black background of Ralphs' first-tier program.

The following year, Ralphs Private Selection identity was put on fresh meats and poultry, which featured a value-added highlight: hand-selected cuts of quality fresh beef, pork and poultry (stuffed, seasoned or fully cooked). The line carried, for example, stuffed pork chops with herbs, apples and cinnamon, Cajun wild rice or wild rice and mushrooms. The Private Selection name also was extended to a select number of grocery items, each also reflecting value-added features. This range grew into an upscale program, going "a step beyond brand quality... in terms of quality and/or value-added packaging." (Fitzell 1992)

The 1990s really marked the start-up of different sub-brand strategies in private label, either extending a store logo on its first-tier quality range into new upscale areas (for example, Pathmark Supermarkets' Preferred Selection or Kroger Select), opening a separate private label identity, positioned as a brand (Sensational at Edwards Super Food Stores), or adopting both strategies (the Western Family Smart Bites and the Excellence brand at Western Family Foods).

However, with the spread of upscale or premium private label programs, the trend toward sub-branding has accelerated with many variations appearing on these labels. American Stores, for example, besides being a licensee of the President's Choice program, introduced the American Premier upscale range, which recently was expanded into wine and distilled spirits, then further sub-branded with the identity Daily Rituals, covering premium health and beauty care items.

Similarly, CVS drug stores has established its Gold Emblem premium private label line of beverages and snack foods, which since has been sub-branded with Absolutely Divine cookies. In the drug-store segment, CVS has taken a leadership role in private label through its different sub-branding strategies which have been extended to other product categories: snacks, soft drinks, and other convenience items. Wegmans, which started with The Ultimate cookie line, following the lead of President's Choice Decadent chocolate chip cookie, in 1991 introduced Wegmans Food You Feel Good About range, linking different foods with "great taste, no artificial colors, flavors, or preservatives, and containing low fat or lean," all related by a yellow banner on the package, working more like a slogan. Rounding out the range is Wegmans Italian Classics pasta.

Another strategy has been that of co-branding, which for private label perhaps started with the use of trademark names like NutraSweet on soft drinks, for example. Weis Markets, Inc., Sunbury, PA, has picked up the key ingredient in its Weis Choice cookies line, advertising that brand on the package as well, such as Sunmaid raisins or Peter Pan peanut butter.

REFERENCES/CITATIONS

Fitzell, Philip 1992. "Private Label Marketing in the 1990s." Global Book Productions, New York, NY.

PART 111

Structure of the Marketplace in North America

CHAPTER 16

__THE SIZE OF THE U.S. PRIVATE LABEL MARKETPLACE__

There really is no accurate way to determine the total size of the retail private label marketplace in the United States. Private label, in fact, is sometimes just too difficult to identify. The diversity of label owners alone clouds this perspective. Its market spread throughout small independent retail outlets found in remote rural areas defies measurement. Some retailers fail to recognize a product line as being their own brand. Until recently, brand equity development, while practiced in private label programs, has not been a top priority for most retailers, who have very often managed an entire stable of private label identities. Lately, however, this emphasis has changed, as larger companies develop a corporate brand strategy, consolidating their label identities.

In the multiplicity of marketing and merchandising strategies, varying from category to category, private label parameters can best be tracked within certain product categories in the business. Private labels are too diverse in terms of their direct or indirect, i.e. licensed, ownership, resulting in uncountable different label identities, different levels of quality, and diverse packaging strategies, plus a wide range of products across nearly every product category. In fact, each retail market segment presents a different set of product mix variables.

In the supermarket segment, for example, some products are cut and wrapped, or prepared in-store, often without too much concern for package identity. A store sticker on freshly-cut meat may be the only way to identify the producer or owner of that item. Often, fresh fruits and vegetables are piled high on a display ready to be picked by the consumer, who puts them in a plastic bag imprinted without any reference to a brand identity. Freshly-baked items, too, are frequently presented in a lighted display and boxed or bagged into containers that may or may not contain a store name/department identity. In-store food service operations also skip the branding stage. While private label branding does sometimes occur in every one of these areas, in the majority of cases it is basically a no-brand strategy. In the trend toward more perishable foods and convenient, quick-solution prepared meals, brand identity loses its impact, replaced by the store itself becoming the brand.

In chain drug store operations, prescription drugs can carry a brand name, a private label identity, or the generic name of the drug. Often the consumer relies on the pharmacist, who has the license to fill out a prescription with any one of these options.

Unless a doctor specifically prescribes a brand name drug, or allows for a generic substitute drug, the pharmacist will determine the formulation. Consumers, of course, can request a brand name or generic drug. Private label's role in this area is nebulous at best; although it is an important part of this business. Its presence in the front of the drug store, however, is easily noted. This is the area where private label growth continues.

Similarly, in any mass merchandise store, many soft goods (clothing, intimate apparel, and accessories) and hard goods (pots, pans, nails, tools, and the like) do not carry any label identity. If a label is affixed, it may not be a recognizable brand name. The store, in fact, may own that label identity, or have exclusive rights to distribute it, but it is not always distinguishable from a manufacturer's brand. Market leaders in this segment, such as Wal-Mart, Kmart, Target, etc., have developed more of their own private brands in recent years.

Of course, there are overlapping areas, where, for example, the supermarket stocks many health and beauty care products that are also found in a drug store; the drug store features food and beverage items usually carried by supermarkets; and the mass merchant sells both food store and drug-store merchandise. In these areas, private label crops in as a strategy for the retailer which is sometimes picked up as a completely different store brand identity taken from a related chain store operation, i.e., Osco Drug Store's Osco-brand items sold in Jewel Supermarkets and other American Stores supermarket chains.

United States Profile of Supermarkets

The United States represents the largest private label market in North America in terms of sales volume by virtue of its sheer size and population. In private label market share, however, the United States ranks somewhere between fifth and eighth place among the top private label countries in the world. The United States trails in this respect because of its dominance of manufacturers' name brands in the marketplace. By contrast, in some European countries, there is a high concentration of trade, that is, a few leading retailers dominate market share. They have developed a stronger commitment to private label than retailers in the United States. In Canada, brand names are not as strong, and private label sales held in the number-three position, according to ACNielsen global 1995 market research data.

1995 Store Brand Dollar Market Share By Country

1. Switzerland	41%
2. Great Britain	29%
3. Canada	24%
4. Belgium	22%
5. France	16%
6. The Netherlands	16%
7. United States	16%
8. Denmark	13%
9. Germany	11%
10. Spain	10%

SOURCE: ACNielsen 1996 (Exclusive Brands Sourcebook '97)

Private label sales in the United States are measured within each market segment—supermarket, drug chain, and mass merchandiser—at the retail level, focused specifically on product categories that carry store brand identities. The principal market research firms taking this measure are Information Resources Inc. (IRI), Chicago, using its InfoScan data, and ACNielsen, Schaumburg, IL., using its ScanTrack data, both reporting on food and non-food dollar and unit sales.

Using scanning data compiled from the stores' cash registers, these market researchers track private label sales from a product-by-product category perspective. Their focus is on food and beverage, health and beauty care, household chemical products, and general merchandise. The research studies segment the market, beginning with a focus on supermarkets, followed by drug stores and more recently mass merchandise store. Basically, they take a sampling of the retail stores in major markets who subscribe to their research efforts, and include some retailers in peripheral markets, then project that data onto a national picture.

IRI has compiled 1996 store brand data for more than 450 product categories, reporting on dollar and unit sales in supermarkets, drug stores, and mass merchandisers. Its report, compiled in "PLMA's 1997 Private Label Yearbook," published by the Private Label Manufacturers Association, New York, shows total store brand sales in these three market segments at $39.6 billion for 1996. Supermarkets claim the biggest chunk of this business for the 450 product categories under study, representing $33.9 billion in private label sales. Mass merchandisers ($3.3 billion) and drug store chains ($2.4 billion) share the balance. Interestingly, IRI, in tracking these sales in supermarkets from 1993 through 1995, shows private label outpacing the manufacturers' brands in 10 of the 12 quarters represented.

In the biggest segment, IRI shows private label with a 15.9% market share of the $214.4 billion overall supermarket business for 1996. Since IRI began tracking private label sales, its market share has unevenly edged upward from an 11.6% dollar market share in 1988. As a result, dominant name brand share has steadily been eroded.

U.S. Private Label* Dollar (Millions) Sales 1990-96
(Market Share in %)

Year	Supermarket	Name Brand	Private Label
1996	$214.4	$180.2 (84.1%)	$34.2 (15.9%)
1995	209.3	177.7 (84.9%)	31.5 (15.1%)
1994	204.6	174.1 (85.1%)	30.5 (14.9%)
1993	201.6	170.9 (84.8%)	30.7 (15.2%)
1992	200.8	170.6 (85%)	30.2 (15%)
1991	189.3	162.6 (85.9%)	26.7 (14.1%)
1990	185.3	159.0 (85.8 %)	26.3 (14.2%)

*Private label sales include both regular private label and generics .
SOURCE: IRI —PLMA'S PRIVATE LABEL YEARBOOK (1992-97)

When you closely examine the United States supermarket trade, most of the private label volume belongs to the major chains. It's estimated that the top three supermarket chains together represent more than one-third of these tracked sales or $10-plus billion in private label sales (see Chart 1 in Chapter 19).

By virtue of their decades-long private label involvement (including manufacturing/processing operations), the leading supermarket chains have the strongest commitment to private label, carrying multi-billion programs today. The top 10 U.S. supermarket chains together command an estimated $23 billion in private label sales—not counting their store-made private label products. Using the private label volume projected by IRI, this represents some 75% of that total $30-plus billion private label volume for U.S. supermarkets.

Kroger, operator of the largest private label program of all the U.S. supermarket chains, posted 1996 food store sales of $23.5 billion. More than an estimated 20% or $4.7 billion of those sales—not counting its store-made private labels—are in private label. If Kroger's total private label food store sales are estimated at 33% (really a conservative guess), its total private label volume is closer to $7.7 billion. More than half of its stocked private label products are manufactured by Kroger's 36 food processing facilities.

Each of these leading U.S. grocery chains operates on a regional basis, but commands leading market share in their respective markets. The independent food retailers, working through different organizations, also have a significant private label commitment, picking up on programs offered by the voluntary groups, cooperatives, or food wholesalers. In recent years, in fact, food wholesalers have aggressively expanded their private label programs, offering different label identities to their owned retail chains, as well as to the independents and chain store operators they serve. Food wholesalers, however, have been consolidated through acquisitions and mergers, resulting in fewer but larger companies. Retailer- and wholesaler-owned cooperatives have remained viable as well, serving independent retailers. Additionally, the independents and chain store operators are served by account-specific brokers, such as Federated Foods or Marketing Management, who also provide them with private label programs. These sales may or may not be picked up by major research studies, because the operations can be spread throughout many secondary markets or into rural areas, not included in the researchers' tallies of major markets. Some of these labels may not even be recognized by the researchers and/or the retailers as private labels. Top food wholesalers and co-ops are outlined in Charts 2 & 3 (Chapter 19).

In its 1996 survey, IGA Inc., the country's leading voluntary group, which is owned by leading food wholesalers, on a worldwide basis described itself as an "Alliance" of 3,600 licensed, independently-owned supermarkets that generate annual sales of $18.6 billion. In the U.S., there are 2,200 IGA supermarkets, followed by 240 in Australia, 140 in Japan, and 240 in 18 other countries. Additionally, there are some 707 "sister IGA stores" in Canada. In this mix, there are some single-store operators and multi-store operators (10 or more stores owned). The biggest share of IGA retail sales are in the U.S., representing $10.3 billion. In other countries, including Canada, IGA accounts for $8.3 billion. The U.S. stores are served by more than 60 U.S. distribution centers. These IGA retailers also have the strongest commitment to private label in the IGA system, representing about 10% of their total sales ($1.5-plus billion). This covers more than 3,000 products, sold as IGA Brand, TableRite Meats, and IGA TableFresh Produce. IGA Brand development is in its infancy worldwide, including the separate Canadian IGA system, especially those where this system is only now being introduced. IGA has estimated total global IGA Brand sales at more than $3 billion.

Drug Store Developments

Because of the nature of the drug-store business—smaller stores with an emphasis on prescription drug sales, private label has had a limited growth record. It has been only within the past 20 years that private label has taken root and started to spread, thanks in part to the growth of private label health-and-beauty-care products, starting in the 1980s. Also these retailers have come to realize the potential profits of private label in front-of-the-store merchandise (i.e., non-prescription items). More drugs switched from a prescription-only formulation into Over-The-Counter (OTC) drugs have buttressed this growth. Recent drug chain mergers and consolidations have accelerated this growth as well, helping retailers build a larger private label SKU base, backed by their increased volume purchasing power. The trend has been toward more upscale convenience foods and a range of bath and body items in private label, in addition to branded merchandise.

In recent years, druggists have focused increasingly on building their prescription drug sales, too. This is what truly differentiates them in the marketplace. However, prescription drugs derive from branded or generic pharmaceutical manufacturers, so there is little if any private label activity in this area of the business. On the other hand, medical accessories, such as wheel chairs, walkers, and the like can carry a private label. Within the drug store, private label finds its niche primarily away from the pharmacy, up front, specifically in non-prescription OTC drugs, health and beauty care products, vitamins and minerals, general merchandise (film, batteries, adhesive tape, women's hosiery, and the like), household cleaning chemicals and paper products, specialty bath-and-body products, and the newest entry, upscale foods (soft drinks, snacks, cookies, and so forth) . Restricted to these areas, private label share of total sales in each drug chain segment rarely amounts to more than 10%, and frequently to less than 10% of total chain store sales.

Indeed, the recent 1996 market research data shows private label share in drug chains remains at a modest $2.4 billion or 9.7% of a total measured market of $24.6 billion as tracked by Information Resources Inc. (IRI), Chicago, and reported in the *PLMA Yearbook*. IRI estimates that there has been steady growth for private label, up from an 8% dollar market share in 1992.

It appears likely that this perspective is understated, when examined in the context of the rash of mergers and acquisitions since 1997 in the drug store market. Out of a multitude of small regional chains, the industry has spawned giants. While the market leader, Walgreen, remains on top, its lead has been dramatically cut as the result of the ownership changes by its competitors.

Of the leading drug store chains, it is still Walgreen, Deerfield, IL, that is number one with a sales volume at $13.6 billion. Its private label share is estimated at about 10% of that amount or $1.3 billion. In the recent past, other chains have trailed by a significant margin—the closest rival, Rite Aid, Shiremanstown, PA, registering just over half Walgreen's volume. This market segment has dramatically changed since 1997. In terms of sales volume, the second, third and fourth largest chains are now close behind Walgreens. Together, the top five chains—Walgreens, CVS, Rite Aid, Eckerd, and Osco/Sav-on— alone represent sales of $50 billion. Their private label commitments are as strong or stronger than Walgreens. If you conservatively estimated their private label share of sales at 10% average, private label volume is close to $5 billion in the chain business alone.

Add to this the independent retail pharmacies, which number well over 20,000 stores in the U.S, and that volume rises considerably. There are, for example, voluntary cooperatives formed by leading drug distributors. The market leader, McKesson Corp., San Francisco, which started its Valu-Rite program more than 20 years ago, now serves approximately 5,200 Valu-Rite pharmacies in the U.S. These independent operators average over $1 million in annual sales per store. Additionally, McKesson operates a franchise pharmacy program, called Health Mart, for some 650 franchisees. Both programs feature private labels just like the chains stores.

Drug Store Retailers as Manufacturers

As market leader in the chain store segment, Walgreen has the longest track record with private label, dating back to 1910 when Charles R. Walgreen, Sr. began manufacturing his own line of drug products, then moved into ice cream. From a handful of products, produced with siphons, funnels and cooking pots, this operation grew into a modern mnufacturing laboratory. By 1975, Walgreen's private label sales exceeded $40 million—up by 50% from 1970. The chain, in fact, was one of the largest private label manufacturers in the world at that time, operating two plants and producing more than 500 different Walgreen products: bubble bath, shampoo, shaving creams, vitamins, etc.

In 1988, as competition intensified, Walgreen decided to concentrate exclusively on the drug-store business, selling off its Xcel Labs operation to private investors. Xcel Labs at that time generated sales of some $30 million.

There's no question that Walgreen has established its market leadership with the help of its private label program. The same could be said for Rexall Drug Stores, except that its fate was totally different. Early in this century, Rexall developed a strong franchise in the drug-store business, but jumped tracks in 1977 to build its name as a brand, rather than a private label. The Rexall story began in 1902, when Louis K. Liggett introduced his first drug store, selling codliver extract preparations under the name "Vinol," as well as other products. Soon the store name was adopted as a private label, covering packaged medicines and a few toiletries.

Rexall Drug Stores began as a cooperative of drugstores in 1902, then evolved into United Drug Co., which extended the Rexall private label line, spreading through a full range of items: rubber goods, brushes, pharmaceuticals. By 1920, the Rexall drug store became a fully-stocked outlet. Over the decades, Liggett promoted his products aggressively, starting with his famous one-cent bargain sales in 1914, later adding the "2 for 1 Sale." This idea was so novel that it failed until the ad copy was changed to read: "See what one cent will buy!" Customers paid a penny more for a second item. In 1974, the company reintroduced its Two-For Sale concept. But three years later, the firm decided to cut its ties with the Rexall franchise stores, promoting Rexall as a brand. Today, Rexall brand is owned by Rexall Sundown, Inc., Boca Raton, FL, which is a manufacturer of branded and private label vitamins, nutritional supplements and OTC drugs.

Other drug store chains have followed the manufacturing route with little success. Revco Drug Stores, Winesburg, OH, started in 1956 as a discount drug chain, emphasizing a discount image, in which its Revco brand later blended in in terms of the low-pricing strategy. The Revco label appeared in 1960; 10 years later, there were still only 100 items in the program. By 1980, however, the range exceeded 400 different items, helped by Revco's move through acquisition into manufacturing operations: Private Formulations for vitamins and food supplements, Barre National for liquid generic drugs, Carter-Clogan labs for human and veterinary injectibles, etc.

In 1995, Revco completed the largest chain drug store acquisition in industry history, taking over the 1,100-unit Hook-SupeRX, Inc. chain, based in Ohio. In turn, Revco itself was courted the following year by Rite Aid Corp. The Federal Trade Commission and State Department, however, pulled the plug on that acquisition, because of antitrust regulations. Rite Aid already had purchased the Perry Drug chain, Pontiac, MI. At that time, Rite Aid called itself the country's largest drug chain in terms of number of stores. Its business, which had started in 1962 as a discount drug chain, took on private label business starting slowly at about 2% of store sales. In recent years, private label at Rite Aid has developed into the largest commitment in the drug chain business in terms of percent of non-prescription store sales: 14%.

Drug chains traditionally have been either sluggish or aggressive in their development of private label, depending on store policy. Most of this development has occurred since the 1980s. For example, Jack Eckerd Corp., Clearwater, FL, traces its roots back to 1898, when J. Milton Eckerd opened his first drug store as a new concept in affordable medicine. Now positioned as the country's third largest drug store chain, Eckerd really didn't commit to private label until early in the 1980s.

Drug Store Industry Consolidates

Developments since late in 1996, however, have completely restructured this market segment. While the Walgreen chain continues its leadership role, its competitors have redefined their market position. Each has become regional through a rash of acquisitions and mergers. The biggest surprise came at the end of 1996. Department store leader, JC Penney, Dallas, and its Thrift Drug operation, based in Pittsburgh, PA, had acquired a small regional chain, 97 Kerr drug stores in 1995; this was followed by the 1996 by the takeover of Fay's, Inc., Liverpool, NY, a 270-drug store chain. Then at 1996 year's end, JC Penney decided to purchase Eckerd Corp., Largo, FL, comprised of 1,748 drug stores. That put its total drug-store sales at $10 billion, generated from 2,699 drug stores in 23 states.

Ordinarily, this action would have made JC Penney number two in this market segment. Not so! In the meantime, Rite Aid, discouraged by its failure to buy Revco, turned to the country's fourth largest drug store chain, Thrifty Payless, Inc., Wilsonville, OR. That takeover plus the subsequent acquisition of the 13 largest drug store chain, K&B, Inc., New Orleans, LA (186 stores) and the 17th largest chain, Harco, Inc., Tuscalosa, AL (146 drug stores), repositioned Rite Aid into the number three spot with sales of $11 billion and a store count of 3,963 outlets.

Remarkably, Rite Aid had dropped a position because CVS Corp., Woonsocket, RI, previously ranked number five or six, had successfully acquired Revco in May 1997, emerging with close to 4,000 drug stores and sales approaching $13 billion. This action earned CVS the number two position. (Revco previously had acquired Big B, Inc., Bessemer, AL and its 382 drug stores.)

Clearly, the trend is toward ever-increasing consolidation in this market segment, where CVS, Rite Aid, and Eckerd appear to be emerging as the surviving top chains along with Walgreen. They all remain regional in scope: Walgreen in 34 states, CVS in 24 states, Rite Aid in 27 states, and Eckerd in 23 states. Nevertheless, they continue their growth, which may lead to more acquisitions. The recent industry consolidation means the demise of some very viable private label programs: Revco, Fay's, Thrifty PayLess, and Treasury (Thrift Drug). It also means stronger private label commitments by each chain, as a result of stronger purchasing power. In fact, some of these chains now are working synergies within their operations. JC Penney, for example, is tapping into its department store merchandising strength with private label home accessories, bath-and-body items, and certain apparel merchandise, which also is carried by Eckerd. The company can create more value in these lines by combining procurement.

Rite Aid looks to its increased buying power; a greater strength in managed care plans, opening up options and more benefits for its customer members; and more new product introduction, using ideas at Thrifty PayLess, which Rite Aid stores had not capitalized on before, such as green goods and extra large seasonal displays. For details on market segment leaders, see drug chains outline in Chart 4 (Chapter 19).

The drug-store industry, of course, is still comprised of many other smaller chains. The trade publication, *Chain Drug Review*, estimates total drug store sales at $121.4 billion in 1996. Chain drugs take 67% of that volume or $81.3 billion. (Some $57 billion comes from the top 10 chains in North America.) In the magazine's "State of the Industry" report (April 28, 1997), of 100 top drug chains, only eight U.S. chains show sales in excess of $1 billion: the four mentioned above plus American Stores' drug store business (Osco and Sav-on), Salt Lake City, UT; Longs Drug Stores, Walnut Creek, CA; Phar-Mor, Youngstown, OH; and Medicine Shoppe International, St. Louis, MO. Some 22 more chains in the U.S. show sales of between $100 million and $855 million. The balance of the United States chains fall below $100 million. (There also are 10 chains listed from Canada and one from Puerto Rico in the top-100 tally.)

There has been impressive double-digit private label growth in the mass merchandiser segment in the recent past, where total private label sales of $2.9 billion represent an 8.9% share of the total $29.8 billion market. Of course, here the measure taken by IRI, as reported in the *PLMA's 1996 Private Label Yearbook,* is based upon only 450 product categories, common to the other market segments. Mass merchandisers also carry many soft goods and hard goods that are private label as well.

This segment recently has been redirected, too, as the market leaders move into more profitable supercenter formats. Here the product mix is divided between general merchandise (60%) and a supermarket selection (40%). Interest by players like Wal-Mart and Kmart, in particular, has resulted in stronger private label commitments. Some of their strategies are discussed later.

Photographic Album 111

A new aggressiveness emerged in the 1980s, buttressing private label with more creative merchandising and marketing activities at the store level. Above, Wakefern Food Corp., Elizabeth, NJ, capitalizes on its Can Can Sale (1987), which includes name brands and the ShopRite brand. That store brand also is effectively cross-merchandised with Coke in this end-aisle display (right) that same year.

(Left) Jewel Foods places its brand of bleach in the aisle.

(Right) Ralphs Grocery helps with barbecue plans--all Ralphs brand oriented.

Retailers from every business segment picked up on the "compare & save" shelf-talker. Here Kmart, Troy, MI, promotes its Kmart saline solution versus the brand, Bausch & Lomb. Private label was entering new product categories throughout the 1980s.

Retailers have adopted different ways to compare private label with a name brand.
(**Left**) Winn-Dixie, Jacksonville, FL, matches its Thrifty Maid microwave popcorn against Orville Redenbacher's product--at a 30-cents savings. Both products originally sold at 20 cents more than the "everyday low price" discount advertised here.
(**Right**) Albertson's, Boise, ID, uses a hand-printed sign to accent an eight-cent price difference between its Janet Lee pork & beans and the Van Camp's brand.

Publix Super Markets, Lakeland, FL, makes an interesting price comparison here (left), matching its Publix brand soft drinks at seven cents less than Albertson brand soft drinks. This shelf talker appeared early in the 1990s in a Florida market.

Safeway Stores, Oakland, CA, extended its Cragmont soft drink sales outside the store via vending machines—meeting the giants, Coke and Pepsi, right on their own turf. Private label in the vending area has kept pace with the more sophisticated vendors such as that used by Rochester, NY-based Wegman (right).

During the 1990s, the 100-store Kash n' Karry chain, Tampa, FL, which more recently was acquired by Food Lion, Salisbury, NC, developed an effective private label program that addressed all the latest trends in the business. For example, the chain merchandised its dip-style chips with shelf-talkers, offering free tickets to the local hockey team games. The chain also addressed the latest product innovations offered by the brands, such as its own brand of Crunchy Cubs graham snacks, while making a price comparison (Kash n' Karry brand at $1.49 versus Nabisco at $2.19. The chain also addressed consumer interest in the environoment with paper towels featuring 100% recycled paper. The chain catered to bargain shoppers with its Kash Saver secondary line in the diapers area as well as in other product categories.

Food wholesaler Fleming Companies, Oklahoma City, OK, proudly described its controlled brands that are "Guaranteed Finest Quality" in a brochure. Shown here is the firm's Consumer Services Department, which addresses customer questions and problems, while also publishing recipes and nutritional information. Flemings' full quality-assurance lab offers follow-up analysis for product taste, color, and consistency.

CVS Pharmacy, Woonsocket, RI, frequently promotes the CVS brand. This recent flyer shows the extension of that brand into categories that are not usually stocked under private label in drug stores, i.e. floor and rug /carpet cleaners, detergents and other household chemical items.

Brand loyalty takes a beating

Gannett News Service

LOOKALIKES: Private-label packaging gives appearance of brand names.

Source: USA TODAY research

Brand-name stocks fall

After Philip Morris said Friday that it is cutting the price of Marlboro cigarettes, a move likely to hurt profits, investors in other consumer-product stocks began selling.

	Thur.	Tue.	52-week high/low
Coca-Cola	$42 7/8	$40	45 3/8 / 36 1/8
Procter & Gamble	$49 7/8	$46 3/4	55 3/4 / 45 1/2
PepsiCo	$42 3/4	$40	43 5/8 / 33 3/8
Colgate-Palmolive	$65 7/8	$60	67 1/4 / 45 5/8
Philip Morris	$64 1/8	$49 1/8	86 5/8 / 48
Quaker Oats	$67 1/4	$63 3/8	71 / 50 1/4
Kellogg	$60 7/8	$56	75 3/8 / 54 5/8

By Marty Baumann, USA TODAY

Big Blue begins new search

By Leslie Cauley
USA TODAY

IBM again is breaking with tradition and looking beyond its own ranks for senior management talent.

The computer giant hired two headhunters to find a CEO. Now IBM has another search firm looking for a chief financial officer.

Russell, Reynolds Associates of New York has been looking at candidates worldwide, says Peter Crist, a managing partner. Candidates reportedly include a few superstars outside the computer industry.

IBM CEO Louis Gerstner, lured away from RJR Nabisco on March 26, is expected to begin meeting with CFO candidates soon.

IBM declined to comment.

The company also has asked Russell, Reynolds and other firms to find presidents for several IBM business units. IBM has nine units that specialize in items from mainframe computers to software.

Some IBM executives are

COVER STORY

Consumers go private to save money

Thousands of store brands compete for cost-conscious shoppers

By Gary Strauss
and David Craig
USA TODAY

Brand loyalty isn't dead. But to some brand-name consumer-product marketers and the Wall Street types who closely follow them, brand loyalty is looking mighty sickly.

For years, brand-name marketers such as Philip Morris and Procter & Gamble routinely could boost prices on consumer products ranging from cigarettes to pet foods. Consumers would grumble, but what could they do? Their choices were limited due to a lack of high-quality, low-priced alternatives.

But escalating prices on brand-name goods, the reces-

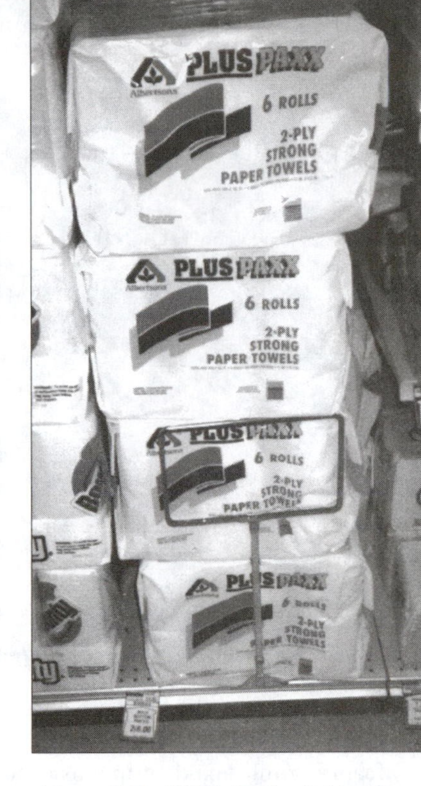

Above left: "USA Today" (April 7, 1993) reports brand loyalty as being "mighty sick."
Above right: Albertson's address savings issue with Plus Pax 6-pack of paper towels .
Below: Private label enters a new product category, showing the sophistication of the industry and the willingness of consumers to buy sensitive personal-care products.

Left: There's probably no person alive today who has had more of an impact on the private label marketplace in North America than Dave Nichol, shown here late in the 1980s, at the time Loblaw Companies (Toronto) was launching its President's Choice G.R.E.E.N. environment-friendly products. Other pictures on this two-page spread show the packaging development, product expansion and promotional support given to both "no name" and President's Choice controlled labels in Canada.

Right: Some of the early products introduced under President's Choice, featuring full-text descriptions about these products on the front panels.
Below: In 1983, Dave Nichol introduced the "Insider's Report." This 1984 issue illustrates the chatty format, including a picture of Georgie Girl, his bulldog who also helps to promote a give-away.

Dave Nichol's Insider's Report

Vol. IV, Sept., 1984

back-to-school issue

PRICES EFF. MON. SEPT. 10, 1984

A Great Canadian Tradition Since November, 1983 © 1984 Loblaws Limited

Dave Nichol and Loblaws' back-to-school bulldog, Georgie Girl

Putting together an Insider's Report is a tremendous amount of work. Why do we do it? BECAUSE FOOD IS IMPORTANT! As my mother used to say, "If you're going to prepare food three times a day for the rest of your life, it's worth learning to do it well."

Let's be honest: in the great capitalist tradition, one of our primary reasons for assembling these reports is to encourage you to shop at our stores where the Insider's Report products are available. However, there really are other reasons: For one thing, Jim White and I write the Insider's Report because the process of compiling one — sourcing the products, discovering new foods, getting background (or Insider's) gossip, finding new recipes — IS AN INCREDIBLE AMOUNT OF FUN. And we hope, in some small way, to transmit to our readers the sheer joy that cooking can bring to your life.

Everyone has a deep-seated need to be creative, a need that cooking can go a long way to satisfy. Yet, I constantly meet people who feel that cooking well is too complicated, beyond their abilities. NONSENSE! Look at the simplicity of the world's best recipe for Scalloped (Dauphinois) Potatoes on page 11 and see how simple good cooking really is.

Jim and I hope that The Insider's Report encourages you to discover the simplicity and satisfaction of trying to cook well. And as Soei Yoneda suggests in *Good Food From A Japanese Temple* "trying" may be the most important element of all: "A MEAL REFLECTS THE GENTLE NATURE AND WARM HEART OF THE COOK. OF COURSE, SOME OF US ARE MORE CLEVER WITH OUR HANDS THAN OTHERS. BUT, IF ONE DOES THE BEST HE CAN, A FINE MEAL RESULTS, ALMOST AS IF BY DIVINE GRACE." Amen!!

484 free Cabbage Patch Dolls see back page

HOW DID YOUR COFFEE DO? 6 LEADING ONTARIO COFFEES RANKED BY TOP COFFEE EXPERTS. PRIDE OF ARABIA 454g $2.99

Above left: President's Choice Decadent chocolate chip cookie eventually was extended into other cookie "delights," as shown here.
Above right: Loblaw's "no name" yellow packaging is upgraded with colorful drawings while being promoted here on an end-aisle display.

Above left: Wegman Food Markets (Rochester, NY) has adopted sub branding strategies for its Wegmans line, including "The Ultimate" upscale cookies, "The Ultimate Coffee Alternative," bean coffees, "Food You Feel Good About" (no artificial colors, flavors or preservatives), "Fisherman's Wharf" seafood, etc.
Above right: Tops Markets (owned by Ahold USA), Buffalo, NY, uses its Tops brand cereal box as a merchandising vehicle, offering 55-cents off as part of a tie-in promotion with NutraSweet.

The two "private label" packages shown on this page represent outstanding premium quality products from A&P (Canada) in its Master Choice range and Safeway Stores, Pleasanton, CA, in its Safeway Select Gourmet Club range. Both epitomize the status of private label today—offering the best quality available, presented with tasteful graphics (sometimes in award-winning packaging), and representing true value for the consumer in terms of quality and price.

The CVS Pharmacy "Gold Emblem," appearing on select premium-quality CVS brand products, is backed with a statement from the chain's president & CEO. This strategy often is adopted in private label programs, connoting a pride of ownership and a desire to build brand equity into the logo.

Canada

CHAPTER 17

____FEWER BUT LARGER PLAYERS IN CANADA____

In the recent past, the Canadian grocery and drug store retail/wholesale business has been marked by dramatic changes across the board, including a significant restructuring of operations within each of the major players' organizations. Also acquisitions and an amalgamation of different chains and/or companies have resulted in the survival of fewer players who command a greater concentration of market power. All these factors together with a depressed economy have helped foster the aggressive growth of private label in the 1990s.

Canadians distinguish between private label and generics, which together are called "control label." The business of control label in Canada is now the largest growing segment of the grocery business. Recent ACNielsen MarketTrack data (1996), based on annual consumer sales in grocery supermarkets (covering 255 categories) shows control label dollar share in Canada at 21.7% for the year ending February 5, 1994. That share climbed by 11% to a 22.9% share for the 52-week period ending February 4, 1996, then repeated another 11% jump to a 23.8% share for the period ending February 3, 1996. In unit sales, store brands started at a 26.4% share, climbed to 27% (up 9%), then to 27.2% (up 2%) over the same period. The slower unit sales growth rate is attributed to a trend toward larger-size packs (club packs) as well as the growing importance of premium private label products (versus more commodity-oriented product categories).

Canadian Private Label Dollar Market Share (1993-96)

Year	National Brand	Store Brand
2/5/94	78.3%	21.7%
2/4/95	77.1%	22.9%
2/3/96	76.2%	23.8%

Note:: Based on annual consumer sales across 255 product categories sold in grocery supermarkets.
SOURCE: ACNielsen 1996

In the recent past, Canadian retailers and wholesalers have turned away from their historic growth-strategies of diversification, including both new businesses and new geographic markets, after experiencing some heavy losses. A number of retailers/wholesalers faced with economic uncertainties early in the 1990s, underscored by "a combination of high labor costs, decreasing productivity, and onerous taxation," as reported by one major food wholesaler, have looked to relocate and/or expand across the United States border. Some have tried to circumvent failure by selling out. For the most part, their ventures into the United States have proven to be financial disasters, resulting in a pull back to their own turf, with a renewed effort on developing business within a Canadian province, or country-wide. Market leaders like Loblaw Companies Limited, Toronto; Provigo Distribution Inc., Montréal; and Shoppers Drug Mart /Pharmaprix, Toronto, each have taken this plunge and pulled back.

One exception is The Jean Coutu Group (PJC) Inc., Longueuil, Quebec, operator of the second largest network of retail pharmaceutical and parapharmaceutical product franchises in Canada. In November 1994, this company expanded across the border and acquired the Brooks Drug Stores, Pawtucket, RI, the second largest drug-store chain in New England. That chain now operates 237 Brooks Pharmacy outlets in five states, while representing nearly half of The Jean Coutu Group's total sales volume of $1.1 billion. In Canada, the company operates as a franchisor of approximately 228 units under the PJC Jean Coutu name or Maxi Drug banner.

In the meantime, major food retailers like Dominion and Steinberg as well as the United Kingdom-based Boots The Chemist's Canadian drug stores, all have been absorbed by other Canadian companies. Likewise, food wholesalers have experienced significant consolidation, tracing back to the 1960s.

Non-Canadian-based retailers/wholesalers have had mixed success in Canada. Boots The Chemist and Marks & Spencer, both from the UK, have struggled to maintain market share in Canada. In 1988, Boots sold its 109-store chain to The Oshawa Group Limited, Etobicoke, Ontario, which converted those stores to its new banner, Pharma Plus Drugmarts, creating the second largest group of drug stores in Ontario. Long-time U.S. supermarket chains, such as Safeway and A&P have endured in Canada since the late 1920s. In fact, The Great Atlantic & Pacific Tea Company of Canada was incorporated in 1919, although its first A&P store did not open until 1927 in Montreal, Quebec. An important step in its evolution came in 1985, when the A&P Canadian Company acquired 93 Dominion Stores (mostly around Toronto), which had been a major player in eastern Canada for decades. Safeway had similarly established its Canadian roots about 1928 in western Canada. Recently, Wal-Mart also has established a presence in Canada, having purchased Woolco stores from Kmart, but these operations are in the mass merchandising sector. Additionally, PriceCostco, a chain of cash-and-carry warehouse stores, has established a presence as well: 52 units (also see Mexico section, Chapter 18).

In addition, there is the newcomer Shurfine International, a U.S.-based cooperative that has strengthened its membership of wholesalers in Canada, adding Itwal, Ltd., Mississauga-Ontario; Sobey Inc., Stellarton-Nova Scotia; Surrey, British Columbia; Lakeside, Nova Scotia, etc. Shurfine finds Canada especially compatible because of the common interests between U.S. and Canadian consumers, as well as the ease of access, since most of their customers are near the United States border. To date, the company has set up 195 suppliers, serving the Canadian customers with private label goods, as well as some goods shipped into the United States. Canada has become the co-op's strongest foreign market, second only to Kuwait, where Shurfine does a significant business.

Refocused on the Home Front

For most Canadian food and drug store retailers/wholesalers, however, a greater focus has developed on business nearer to home, fostering a national pride in which Canadians have melded the different trade styles of European and the United States into their own modus operandi. Not too long ago, Canadian retailing was more like a mirror, reflecting trends set in Europe and the United States.

Market-leader Loblaw, as already noted, had adopted a European-style management strategy with a stronger emphasis on private label, and has also carried out a distinctive and creative control label program, which emanates from Canada. This started late in the 1970s with its "no name" program that looked like generics packaging, but was positioned as first-quality private label. In the mid-1980s, Loblaw introduced an upscale President's Choice program which put the emphasis on choice or specially-selected and/or formulated products, including products that often were unique, different, or superior in quality to leading brands in a product category. These strategies have had a significant impact on competitors throughout North America and more recently on competitors in Europe and the Pacific Rim countries.

In Canada, recent private label growth can be traced to the consolidation of major retail/wholesale players. It's already been proven in Europe, where private label is dominant in many countries, that such an environment is particularly suitable to aggressive private label marketing. A similarity in the marketplaces of Canada and the United States in terms of their consumers has contributed to private label development to a lesser extent.

Generally speaking, private label tends to achieve its highest market penetration in countries where there is more concentration of power in one or a few dominant chain store operations. When grocery retailing is concentrated this way, as in Switzerland, Migros, a consumer cooperative, takes a dominant role in that country. Its private label commitment exceeds 95% of its total retail sales. The impact of its private label market share is felt nationally, where its "M" brand is a national brand. Also, Coop Schweiz and Denner, the second and third largest consumer cooperatives in Switzerland, each have 50% commitment to private label in their flagship stores. So private label penetration in Switzerland is the strongest in the world— estimated at 40-plus %. A similar concentration of retailer power exists in the United Kingdom, where five top retailers (called "multiples") dominate UK grocery retailing (60-plus % share). There is a slightly smaller dominance in countries like France and Germany, where the independents-sector offers competition that results in a more fragmented market. It depends on the quality of the commitment made by the retailers/wholesalers. In the late 1970s, Loblaw made its commitment to private label. Today, private label commands more than 30% of its total sales. In the United States, there is no national grocery chain but rather strong regional dominance by different chains. The trend there, however, is toward greater consolidation and therefore fewer dominant players.

Canada in Profile

Canada, composed of 10 geographic provinces, has most of its population clustered in major metropolitan centers. The most densely-populated cities are Toronto (4.1 million); Montreal (3.3 million); Vancouver (1.7 million); Ottawa-Hull (980,000); Edmonton (897,000); Calgary (814,000); Quebec City (679,000); Winnipeg (662,000); and Hamilton (618,000). Other metro areas have fewer than 500,000 people. Some 90% of the country's total population is found within 100 miles of the U.S. northern boundary, in areas where agricultural and industrial activities support such a concentration of people. This proximity has had a profound effect on Canadian food retailing in particular, because in many cases, the U.S. food stores compete directly with their Canadian counterparts for the same consumer dollar. When U.S. chains emphasis private label, Canadians to stay competitive must do likewise. It works the other way as well.

Not surprisingly, Canadian food-store volume—covering supermarkets, grocery and convenience stores and totaling $52.4 billion, has nearly one-third or 32.2% of its total sales concentrated in Ontario province, where you find Toronto and Ottawa. The next biggest share (28.2%) is centered in Quebec province, the location of Montreal and Quebec City. Most of the major retailers/wholesalers are based in these two provinces— Loblaw, Oshawa and A&P Canada, all in Ontario; and Provigo and Metro Richelieu, both in Quebec. In the drugstore sector, Shoppers Drug Mart is based in Ontario and Jean Couteau in Quebec. Outside those areas, food store volume tends to thin out, ranging from only a 13.9% share in British Columbia, the home of Vancouver, to Alberta Province, the location of Calgary, taking a 10.9% share of that volume; the other provinces share the balance, each taking 3.8% or less share of food-store volume.

An independent research project by Marketing Advantage, Kanata, Ontario, found the total Canadian grocery market for 1995 to be $51.4 billion (Canadian dollars), where private label share accounted for 23.9% of the total or $12.3 billion. The breakdown by Canadian provinces showed Ontario taking $4 billion in private label sales, followed by Quebec with $2.5 billion; British Columbia with $2.1 billion; Alberta with $1.4 billion; the Maritimes (Prince Edward Island, Nova Scotia, Newfoundland, and New Brunswick) with $1 billion; Manitoba with $800,000; and Saskatachwan with $300,000. Within each province, private label share of sales was definitely strong: 30% of $1.5 billion in Saskatachwan; 28% of $7.4 billion in British Columbia; 27% of $2.9 billion in Manitoba; 25% of $15.9 billion in Ontario; 15% of $5.5 billion in Alberta; 23% of $4.1 billion in the Maritimes; and 19% of $13.3 billion in Quebec.

Canadian food retailers and wholesalers have been strongly influenced by their counterparts in the United States, making them virtual competitors because of geographic proximity. The Canadian retail/wholesale trade also has made forays into the U.S. market, setting up subsidiaries and/or through acquisitions in the past. Lately, however, this trend has contracted sharply, as most major Canadian companies have pulled out of the U.S. market, concentrating on their own turf.

An Historical Perspective on Canada

As the grocery business developed in the United States early in this century, a similar evolution was underway in Canada. Early in the 1920s, for example, as S. M. Flickinger formed the Red & White voluntary group, the same voluntary group concept took root north of Buffalo, New York. T. Kinnear & Co., Toronto, launched the "Service" store banner for independent grocers. This was followed by other pioneering efforts under the "Leader" and "Adanac" store groups, then followed by the "Superior" stores .

Frank Grimes, an accountant based in New York state, had strong ties in Canada. Early in the 1920s, Grimes helped promote the merger of 25 wholesalers and their branches in the Ontario province. This joint effort become the National Grocers Co., Limited. In 1932, Grimes also helped bring 50 independent druggists in Ontario together in another voluntary group, the Drug Trading Company, a buying group which developed a merchandising and advertising plan, called the Independent Druggist Alliance(IDA). They developed the IDA private label program. It is very likely that Grimes heard about, or met people at John Sloan & Co., which was one of the first wholesale houses to bring the Red & White stores voluntary group to Toronto, beginning as Serv-us stores. Grimes, of course, took that idea back to the United States, where he worked to form the Independent Grocers' Alliance (IGA) in 1926.

Other Canadian grocery wholesalers also formed Red & White store groups, such as H. E. Guppy Co. and Western Grocery Limited. By 1927, Red & White Chain Stores Limited was incorporated by Guppy, Western Grocery, and John Sloan. Two years later, National Grocers had purchased John Sloan and the Guppy Company. National Grocers' T. H. Kinnear then recruited J. O. Elton to open up a Red & White office for all of Canada in 1929. The group at that time had four affiliates: Western Grocers Ltd. for the Prairie provinces and Northwest Ontario; Kelly, Douglas & Co., Limited for British Columbia; National Grocers Co., Limited for Ontario; and J. B. Renaud & Cie. for Quebec City.

In his personal recollections, Elton reports that these wholesalers financially helped many small retailers throughout the years. The Red & White group in Canada grew to some 900 stores, many of which later were converted to the larger Foodmaster format. After World War II, the voluntary store movement gathered impetus with Red & White in the vanguard in many parts of the country. But just as in the U.S., a number of its affiliated wholesale houses were acquired by larger wholesalers, having other store banner priorities: both Western Grocers and Kelly, Douglas & Co. were acquired by George Weston Ltd. and its Loblaw Companies. The Red & White Corp. name itself was changed in 1963 to FOODWIDE of Canada Limited, because of the different group stores affiliated with the company. (Elton, 1960s)

IGA Succeeds in Canada

Similarly, IGA in Canada followed the development pattern of IGA's fate in the U.S. IGA founder J. Frank Grimes filed for incorporation in Canada in 1927. This organization became the largest food store group in the Dominion in 1954 with 400-plus stores and five wholesalers with sales exceeding $100 million. In 1948, Ray Wolfe of Ontario Produce, a supplier of fresh produce to food retailers, visited Don Grimes, president of IGA Inc., Chicago, requesting an IGA franchise in Canada. Wolfe was declined, because he did not operate a full-scale grocery wholesale house. He returned to IGA in 1950, having acquired Bakers Food Supply Co., which allowed his company, Oshawa Wholesale, to became the first Canadian IGA franchise. Almost immediately, some 25 independent grocers joined the group and, in 1951, the first IGA store was opened in Ontario. That same year, another wholesaler, M. Loeb, joined the group, followed the next year by G. T. Armstrong & Sons. The IGA group spread throughout Quebec and into the Atlantic provinces and Manitoba. In 1955, Tong Louie, a wholesaler in British Columbia, also agreed to join the IGA group. The other Canadian provinces picked up with IGA stores, when Loeb, already affiliated, acquired Horne & Pitfield in Alberta. In 1960, Quebec and Saskatchewan province wholesalers completed the national coverage of Canada by IGA.

While the Red & White group was not tied to the U.S. group, IGA Canada operated as its franchisee up until 1964 when the Canadian wholesalers negotiated a "share swap" with IGA Inc., exchanging all the shares they held in the U.S. company for all the shares owned by IGA Inc. in the Canadian company. That made IGA Canada a wholly-owned business of the Canadian wholesalers—completely independent from the U.S. operation. The Canadian group, however, still maintained a "fraternal relationship" with their U.S. counterparts, sharing distribution ideas, different resources and, of course, the same store and private label identity.

Over subsequent years, IGA Canada changed dramatically through a series of acquisitions and mergers, from 1959 to 1973, after which only three shareholders remained: The Oshawa Group and M. Loeb, both operating in Ontario province, and H.Y. Louie out of British Columbia. In 1992, IGA Canada was further consolidated when Oshawa, owning 46.5% of the stock, bought out Horne & Pitfield in Alberta from Provigo and the IGA franchising rights from Loeb as well as its interest in IGA Canada—a 46.5% share. This gave Oshawa 93% ownership, leaving H. Y Louie with 7%.

From the 1940s onward, supermarket chains, such as Loblaws, Dominion and others, were also growing in strength. Loblaw's became the market leader, its evolution described earlier in this book. A&P Canada, established in Canada since the 1930s, acquired Dominion stores in the late 1980s, and then Miracle Food Mart and Ultra Mart food stores from Steinberg Inc. in late 1990. This led to a consolidation of its private labels within three Canadian divisions—A&P, Dominion, and Miracle Food Mart. The company canceled out two of these private label programs, focusing on a single store brand program systemwide. A new corporate brands strategy for all 256 stores in the operation was launched. Master Choice (introduced into Canada in 1992) was targeted as high quality products; Jane Parker covered bakery items and snacks; and Marvel addressed non-foods and health and beauty care. Some other private labels which were strong in certain product categories, i.e., Daily in pet foods, Yukon in beverages, were retained. The company also created its Equality brand, which was designed to be carried by all its store banners: Dominion, Miracle Mart, foodBasics, Ultramart, and Superfresh. A&P in the U.S., began its consolidation of corporate brands strategy, under America's Choice label in 1993. A similar strategy was adopted in Canada for A&P stores, but with the Equality corporate brand.

As the chain operations strengthened, Oshawa, too, emerged as a major player in Canada. Traditionally, Oshawa had been a national brands house. The country's deepening recession since 1990, hit Ontario hardest and brought new emphasis to Oshawa's control label program. Its strength in the IGA organization prompted a complete integration of its operations in August 1994, when IGA Canada was joined with its Horizon International Division, which had been responsible for control label products, market development, and national IGA banner marketing. This paired Horizon's brand marketing and product development expertise with IGA's procurement experience. The reorganization also allowed Horizon to coordinate national consumer promotions throughout Canada while programming its control labels in a true category management fashion.

The IGA brand became the wholesaler's first-tier control label, matching mainstream national-brand quality; its Our Compliments upscale foods range (introduced in 1994) addressed the premium sector (following a pattern established by Loblaw's President's Choice), while its economy/generic value range, Smart Choice, introduced in 1992, was targeted to the price-conscious consumer.

New initiatives at Oshawa include the establishment of a national buying office to consolidate purchasing activity for its entire division. The company addresses an estimated $48 billion (Canadian dollar) food-store market, shared by corporate chains and independent retailers. The company reports that between 1980 and 1992, the market share of supermarket chains has declined from 60% to 52%, recovering to 55% in 1996. Independent grocers, in turn, have grown primarily from the franchise area, moving their share from 27% in 1980 to 37% in 1996. In the meantime, unaffiliated grocers continue to lose market share. It's not surprising to see this company converting all of its Food City supermarkets to IGA stores—giving this banner a stronger presence in its major markets. This move, of course, also enhances the presence of the IGA Brand. (Oshawa also is converting its Dutch Boy stores to IGA.) While the company has fewer IGA stores today (655 of which 67 are company-owned), the trend is toward larger IGA stores, featuring fresh food departments.

REFERENCES/CITATIONS

Elton, J.O., late 1960s. "Sixty Years with Food." (From Flickinger Archives)

Mexico

CHAPTER 18

MEXICO'S ECONOMY IN A CRISIS

There is very little documentation available on the private label business in Mexico. This may be because of the modest growth of this activity, as defined in this book, in the country. Mexican retailers and wholesalers only recently have been drawn into private label, beginning in the 1980s. But they entered this business on the wrong foot, as it were. That is, private label generally was introduced as the cheapest product available, rather than presenting itself as being of good quality to customer perception. Consequently, shoppers thought of themselves as second-class citizens when they purchased private label. This attitude is beginning to change in the 1990s, thanks to two factors in particular. One has been the growing interest of U.S. retailers, wholesalers, and cooperatives, both in establishing joint ventures with Mexican players, and also in having private label stock shipped south of the border to trade customers willing to stock popular U.S.-made products that consumers want. The other factor has been the critical economic situation in Mexico, which has forced many consumers to budget their income. Retailers are beginning to capitalize on this new attitude by providing their customers with the best option possible in terms of a lower price and good quality products, under private label.

In reporting on "Mexico's Largest Companies," the magazine, *Mexico Business* (July/August 1997), pinpoints only four retailers out of a total of 27 publicly-traded companies that show 1996 sales in excess of $1 billion: Cifra at $3.1 billion, Grupo Gigante at $1.9 billion, Controladora Comercial Mexicana at $1.8 billion, and Organización Soriana at $1.1 billion. At the same time, the first three showed sales declines of minus-9.7%, minus-6.5%, and minus-4.5%, respectively, while the fourth showed only a 5.7% sales gain. While the sales picture does not reflect a rosy economic picture, these companies reported more promising net profits, all except Controladorado Comercial Mexicana (minus-13.8%) showing gains——that is, Cifra up 2.4%, Grupo Gigante up 16.7%, and Organización Soriana up 1%.

The economic crisis faced by Mexico has had a dramatic impact on consumers there. The Mexican magazine, *Expansión*, recently calculated that the minimum salary of Mexican now buys 63% less than it did a decade ago. Mexico continues to be a troubled country, politically unsettled, where the average exchange rate from pesos to dollars has escalated from 3.09 in 1992 up to 7.60 in 1996. At the end of 1994, when the peso was devalued, the repercussions on the retail-wholesale sector penetrated deep into bottom-line profits.

Grupo Gigante Copes

One of Mexico's leading supermarket retailers, Grupo Gigante, S.A. de C.V., Mexico City, called 1995 "one of the most difficult in (our) history with critical economic conditions in Mexico further complicating the already difficult situation we have faced in previous years. In 1995," the company continued in its annual report for that year, "the main adversities we faced at the macroeconomics level were: a 52% general inflation, a 61% inflation of the basket of staple products, a 62% rise in the prices of food and beverages (which account for approximately 65% of our sales), as well as a GDP drop of approximately 7%, and increases in financing costs from minimum levels of 12% in 1994 to maximum levels of 10% in 1995. In addition, the Mexican peso lost 53.8% of its value against the U.S. dollar (dropping from 5 pesos per dollar to 7.69)." This sharp devaluation of the peso pushed inflation upwards by 52%, while household purchasing power dropped by some 20%, and even more in non-food products.

Grupo Gigante operates 195 self-service stores: 117 Gigante stores (groceries, perishables, clothing and general merchandise), 35 Bodega G stores (no frills, discount warehouse stores), 26 Super G supermarkets , 13 Carrefour Hipermercados hypermarkets (joint venture with Carrefour of France), and 4 Supermarts (a joint venture with Fleming Companies, Inc. of the U.S.). In addition, Gigante operates 30 Toks restaurants, 47 Radio Shacks (a joint venture with U.S.-based Tandy International Corp.), and 7 Office Depots (a joint venture with Office Depot, Inc. in the United States).

The company's total 1996 net sales were approximately $1.8 billion (14.2 million pesos), off by 6% from 1995. Needless to say, the company, operating under stringent cost control measures, is down-sizing, reformatting its store concepts and working out operating efficiencies to turn around its 29% drop in operating income for 1995. In fact, operating profits, rose by 72% in 1996. Part of this strategy involves avoiding new store openings for Gigante, Bodega Gigante and Super G formats as well as reducing the number of products and number of lines of the same product sold in its stores. Private label, of course, plays a major role in this strategy. Consumers have less money to spend and now look harder for cheaper products, including private label items.

Grupo Gigante started into private label about five years ago; but this business has not grown exactly by leaps and bounds, according to the company. Private label share of total sales is now between 6 to 8%. Last year, the company closed its books with a high residual inventory of private label products because of the weak economy.

Efforts have been underway to improve private label sales and expand the range of products, but consumer interest is still low. Three years ago, the company attempted to expand into private label clothing, but the effort failed. Yet, the company continues to try hard to sell these products.

This position is clearly stated in its 1996 annual report: "We are convinced that the sale of private-label products with our own trademark, 'Productos Selección Gigante,' offers great potential for growth and for increasing our operating margin, so every day we dedicate more resources and creativity to incorporating new products with the same quality as leading brand articles, but at a lower price. We are currently handling an assortment of almost 500 articles in all store areas under the name 'Productos Selección Gigante,' now representing more than 6% of total sales."

In Mexico, another opportunity for private label development comes to retailers through joint-venture activities with companies outside of the country. Grupo Gigante started such a venture with wholesaler Fleming Companies Inc., Oklahoma City, OK, in February 1991. Because of the recent depressed economic picture, however, there are now only three supermarkets operated under Gigante-Fleming, S.A. de C.V. For a number of years, Fleming has shown a good deal of interest in exporting its private label into Mexico. On another front, in France, the Mexican firm has had a similar venture with Carrefour for the past four years and now operates 13 hypermarkets under the Carrefour banner, handled through Grandes Superficies de México, S.A de C.V. While Carrefour's strategy had previously been to introduce its exclusive brands into different foreign markets where it operates stores, its efforts in Mexico have not been impressive. Private label has not caught on. Some Carrefour-brand grocery products have been imported, such as foods, paper items, champagne, wines and the like. Estimates are that they amount to no more than 1 or 2% of Carrefour store sales there. By contrast, in Argentina, Carrefour's brand "tex" textiles, shoes, and Firstline consumer electronic products are already firmly established.

While Mexico's population exceeds 95 million people, the majority (60-plus %) are lower-class in terms of income (under $10,000 per year), while less than one-third of the population makes between $l0,000 to $40,000 per year. Besides Gigante, two other retail chains dominate the country: Commercial Mexicana, the parent company of Comercial Mexicana, Bodega Comercial Mexicana, and Sumese stores; and Cifra, parent of the Aurrera, Bodega Aurrera, Gran Bazar, and Superama stores. Those companies and others, too, operate diversified businesses (i.e., restaurants, clothing stores, etc.) and also have joint ventures with U.S. companies.

Controladora Comercial Mexicana (CCM), Mexico City, operates 144 stores: 85 Comercial Mexicana, 4 Bodegas, 17 Sumesa, 4 Mega, and a Hipermercado as well as a joint venture 13 Price Club de México stores. In addition the firm has 29 restaurants. CMM reported sales off by 4.5% in 1996, at $1.7 billion (13.7 million pesos)—still victimized by Mexico's economic situation. This company has curbed its losses via operational and financial consolidation. Part of this strategy includes development of its own private label program, encompassing more than 30 product categories.

Private label grocery products at CCM started about the mid-1980s. The low estimate placed on these goods by consumers did not help sales. Only recently, CCM has begun to work more diligently toward changing that perception of low-quality because of the economic crisis in the country. The company now has a team working on developing vendor relationships, while searching for better quality products. In its stores, CCM conducts sampling of its own Comercial Mexicana brand products. Each product is now given its own personality in terms of colors and label design. Attention also is focused on its different store brand clothing lines.

CCM maintains 50% ownership in its joint venture with PriceCostco, Issaquah, WA, a chain of cash-and-carry membership warehouse stores. CMM, which also had an association with retailer Auchan of France to build hypermarkets in Mexico, has ended that agreement. (PriceCostco has a much larger stake in Canada in nine provinces—its biggest foreign commitment, operating 52 warehouse stores, which join its U.S. store count of 193 units.) The PriceCostco warehouse outlet carries about 32% of sales in food, 32% in sundries (candy, snacks, health and beauty care, tobacco, beverages including alcoholic, and cleaning and institutional supplies), and the balance in hardlines (appliances, equipment, etc.) and softlines (apparel, jewelry, etc.). Many of these categories include the Kirkland Signature line of private label products, representing almost 100 different items.

Cifra, S.A. de C.V., which claims to be Mexico's largest retailer, reported sales of $2.9 billion in 1996 (off by 10% from the previous calendar year). This company operates a diverse portfolio of chains: 35 Aurrera self-service stores, 60 Bodega Aurrera discount stores, 36 Superama supermarkets, 18 Wal-Mart Supercenter hypermarkets, 28 Sam's Club membership wholesale outlets, 36 Suburbia apparel department stores, and 156 Vips restaurants.

Cifra Marries Wal-Mart

In 1992, Cifra teamed up with the world's largest retailer, Wal-Mart Stores, Inc., Bentonville, AR, in a joint venture, where each partner shared fifty-fifty in the startup of new stores. It marked Wal-Mart's first venture outside the United States. With Wal-Mart's help, Cifra has been able to more than double the size it had attained in the 33 years prior to that association. In other words, in 1991, Cifra operated 130 units; it closed in 1996 with 213 units. The partners, who together invested equally $1.5 billion since the beginning of their relationship, now share in 141 units, including 28 members-only wholesale outlets, 18 hypermarkets, 25 discount warehouses, 4 combo self-service stores, 3 supermarkets, 7 apparel stores, and 56 restaurants. In 1997, Wal-Mart bought a majority of the shares of Cifra, thus giving it control over all of Cifra's operations.

Cifra over the years has built an impressive private label program. Its relationship with Wal-Mart has increased its private label stock, since the latter company has brought in selected items from its Sam's America's Choice and Great Value lines. Most of the merchandise sold in the Mexican stores, however, is branded goods, both Mexican and United States. Opportunities for private labels growth in this operation are very real in the near future.

It's likely that both Wal-Mart and PriceCostco will move their growing private label stock into this market. United States-based co-operative, Shurfine International, Northlake, IL, already has a head-start in this area. The co-op added Calamax as a member about four-plus years ago. This supermarket chain of 40 stores has expanded its selection of Savers Choice second quality products from Shurfine. The program has been highly successful, representing up to 15% of total store sales. In some cases, Shurfine has put first quality products under the Savers Choice brand, because that's the brand Calamax promotes—and the brand consumers want.

Shurfine, in fact, is as optimistic about the future of Mexico as are the giants Wal-Mart and PriceCostco. Shurfine's former CEO and president Tuck Jasper reports having just started another expansion effort with its Western Empire associate, involving seven other regional supermarket chains. In all of its efforts, the company put bi-lingual labels on its private label stock. Jasper feels that the peso is on the way back up, having hit bottom. Also the labor situation has improved while productivity is quite good. In fact, Shurfine has begun cost-effective sourcing of private label product from a diaper manufacturer; a feminine protection products producer; and frozen vegetable processor in Mexico, exporting back into the U.S. and elsewhere. NAFTA (North Atlantic Fair Trade Agreement), he believes, has created an improved atmosphere, reducing some of the duties and regulations, and created a more positive outlook.

Another important U.S. player in this market is Safeway Inc., Pleasanton, CA. Safeway, which maintains a 49% interest in Casa Ley, S.A. de c.V., a privately-held firm that operates 71 food and general merchandise stores in western Mexico, has recently reported increasing sales from this operation. The company is optimistic about the future prospects of this venture.

In Mexico, the majority of stores remain as small traditional outlets, operated by one person, followed by kiosks, and then by larger traditional stores with self-service check-out. The distribution system overall is still very poor. Larger size supermarkets and hypermarkets, however, while in the minority, are a growing part of the retailing trend in this country.

Wholesale Grocer's Perspective

Beginning in 1996, significant economic recovery has been felt, following the crisis that started with the devaluation of the peso, at the end of 1994. Retailing is one of the slowest sectors to recover from such actions, since it is so dependent on employment levels, real wages, and the availability of credit. Despite this, Grupo Corvi closed 1996 with a 3.4% sales gain in real terms, showing consolidated sales of $600 million+. Positioned as Mexico's largest wholesale grocery distribution company, as well as one of its leading producers of chocolate and candies nationwide (Empresas La Corona), Grupo Corvi now serves some 46,000 clients, including wholesalers, middle wholesalers, and retailers. Its Organización Sahuayo (grocery distribution) operates through a network that includes 22 distribution centers, six over-the-counter sales centers, and four Superpack self-service stores.

Just like its counterparts in retailing, Grupo Corvi has begun expanding its own brand selection. In 1996, for example, the company began distributing canned tuna and sardine under its Marinero brand name and hot sauce with the Torito brand name. These products join its Hidrovit spring water brand, marketed since 1995.

The potential for private label growth in Mexico is anyone's guess. Private label sales are still small when compared to other parts of North America, but are definitely growing, especially from the influence of foreign retailers and wholesalers, looking to tap into this market.

The best evidence for potential private label or generic brand growth in Mexico is found in recent ACNielsen data, profiling Mexico's 369,747 food shops. Nielsen, taking a tally of 30 product categories, shows double- and even triple-digit sales gains for generic brands in 1996. This data, presented in the Autumn 1997 issue of *Exclusive Brands* magazine, shows disposable diapers, the biggest category, registering a 90% gain, pushing its share of sales in the category from 7.1% in 1995 to 10.4% in 1996. Other big gains in foods include generic brand milk modifiers, up 163%, consomme shells up 122%, Ready-To-Eat cereals and processed beans, each up 133%, and biscuits an crackers up 108%.

Mexico's food retail sales come mostly from supermarkets and traditional food stores, taking 74.9% of total sales. Other outlets include: pharmacies with 10.2%, government-owned shops with 7.4%, small corner shops with 4.1%, and liquor stores with 3.4% of sales.

CHAPTER 19

____CHARTING THE MARKETPLACE________

Chart 1

Top U.S. Supermarket Chains

Rank	Chain	Total Sales (billions)	Private Label Sales (billions)	Stores*	States
1.	Kroger (12/28/96)	$23.5	$4.7 (20%)	1,356	24
2.	Safeway (12/28/96)	$17.3	$3.5 (20%)	1,052	18**
3.	American Stores (2/1/97)	$13.4***	$2.5 (19%)	813	12
4.	Albertson(1/30/97)	$13.8	$1.9 (>14%)	826	20
5.	Winn-Dixie(6/25/97)	$13.2	$2.6 (20%)	1,174	14****
6.	Ahold USA(12/29/96)	$11.2	$2.0 (18%)	800	14
7.	A&P (2/2/97)	$10.1	$2.3 (23%)	973	20*****
8.	Publix (12/28/96)	$10 (E)	$1.7 (18%)	500+	3
9.	Food Lion (12/28/96)	$ 9.0	$1.1 (12%)	1,112	14
10.	Ralphs Grocery (2/2/97)	$ 5.5	$1.0 (15%)	405	3

*Food stores only. ** Also operates in Canada, see Chart 5 . *** Food store sales only, excludes Osco Drug, see Chart 4. **** Also operates stores in the Bahamas under City Meat Markets name. *****Also operates in Canada, see Chart 5.

Notes to Chart 1:

1. Kroger, Cincinnati, OH, is a $25.2 billion company which also operates 831 convenience stores in 15 states, under such names as Quik Stop, Turkey Hill, Kwik Shop, Mini Mart, Tom Thumb, Loaf 'N Jug. This business accounts for $948 million in sales. Kroger's supermarket business encompasses 1,105 Kroger supermarkets in 16 states; Dillon Companies, a subsidiary operating 251 supermarkets in nine states (under Dillon Food Stores, King Soopers, Fry's Food Stores, Gerbes Supermarkets, City Market, and Sav-Mor identities). Additionally, the company operates 36 processing facilities Its Dillon Foods subsidiary also operates convenience stores, totaling $850 million in sales, which are not included here.
2. Safeway, Pleasanton, CA, also maintains minority interests in two other chains: The Vons Companies and Casa Ley, S.A. de C.V. in Mexico. Its 34% interest in Vons, the second largest supermarket chain in southern California, based on sales, was increased to 100%, effective April 1997, thus bringing Safeway's total store count to 1,370 with sales exceeding $22 billion—neck-and-neck with the segment leader, Kroger. Safeway continues to hold 49% interest in Casa Ley, a chain of 71 food and general-merchandise stores in western Mexico. Safeway also operates 26 manufacturing/processing plants in the U.S. and an additional 14 facilities in Canada. In terms of sales, half its private label stock is obtained from these facilities.
3. American Stores, Salt Lake City, UT, operates as a food and a drug store retailer, its total sales at $18.7 billion. Its food chains include: Acme Markets, Jewel Food Stores (including Jewel Osco combination stores), and Lucky Stores.
4. Albertson's, Boise, ID, operates mostly combination grocery/drugstores, a few conventional stores, plus its Max Stores no-frills outlets. The company also operates 11 distribution centers.
5. Winn-Dixie Stores, Jacksonville, FL, also operates 13 stores, called City Meat markets in the Bahamas. Additionally, the company operates 22 manufacturing facilities and 17 warehouse and distribution centers.
6. A&P, Montvale, NJ, operates a number of regional supermarket chains: A&P, Waldbaum's, Food Emporium, Super Fresh, Farmer Jack, Kohl's, Sav-A-Center, Dominion, and Food Basics.
7. Publix Super Markets, Lakeland, FL, is an employee-owned supermarket chain.
8. Ahold USA, Parsippany, NJ,, is the U.S. Division of Royal Ahold, Zaandam, The Netherlands, an international retailing organization that has sales of $18.5 billion. Its U.S. operations include: BI-LO, Giant Food Stores, Finast, Edwards, and Tops. After its fiscal year, the company signed a merger agreement with Stop & Shop Supermarkets, operator of 128 stores in 4 states. Its U.S. sales, now exceeding $13.8 billion, will move Ahold up in this ranking.
9. Food Lion, Salisbury, NC, is owned by Delhaize Freres et Cie "Le Lion" S.A., Brussels, Belgium, an international supermarket retailer with sales of $12 billion. In December 1996, Food Lion acquired the 100-store Kash n' Karry chain based in Tampa, FL.
10. Yucaipa merged with Ralphs Grocery, Compton, CA in 1994, bringing in its Food 4 Less supermarket chain, creating the largest supermarket operator in southern California. Later, Yucaipa acquired Dominicks Finer Foods, Northlake, IL. This brought the following chains under its control: Ralphs Grocery, Food 4 Less, Alpha Beta, Boys, Viva, and Dominick's. Recent developments (at press time for this book) promise to push this Yucaipa-owned business up to a $14.2 billion multi-regional company (800+ stores in 14 states). In November 1997, a strategic merger agreement was announced, which could bring together Ralphs, the

$3.7 billion Fred Meyer, Inc., Portland, OR, an operator of 109 Fred Meyer multi-department stores in six states and 110 specialty stores in 17 states; and the $2.1 billion Quality Food Centers, Inc., the second-largest supermarket chain in the Puget Sound region of Washington State (90 stores as well as 57-store Hughes Family Markets, Irwindale, CA). In terms of food or supermarket sales, this merger, if completed in the first quarter of 1998, will position the combined Ralphs, Fred Meyer, and QFC with supermarket sales exceeding $12 billion. In 1997, Fred Meyer acquired the $2.9 billion Smith's Food & Drug Centers, Salt Lake City, UT, thus boosting its commitment to the supermarket business, adding 150 stores in seven states and pushing its sales to $7 billion.

Chart 2

Top U.S. Food Wholesalers
($ Billions)

Rank	Company	Food Distribution Sales	Retail Sales	Total Sales	Estimated Private Label Sales*
1.	SUPERVALU (2/22/97)	$ 14.5	$ 4.7	$ 16.6	$1.5 (10%)
2.	Fleming (12/28/96)	$ 12.8	$ 3.7	$ 16.5	$ 2.0 (16%)
3.	Nash Finch (12/28/96)	$ 2.5	$ 0.9	$ 3.4	$ 0.5 (15%)
4.	C&S Wholesale Grocers (9/28/96)	$ 0.0	$ 0.0	$ 3.4	$ 0.3 (10%)
5.	Richfood (5/3/97)	$ 0.3	$ 3.3	$ 3.4	$ 0.4 (13%)

*Private label share estimated here as a percentage of wholesale food distribution sales.

Notes to Chart 2:

1. SUPERVALU, an Eden Prairie, MN-based food wholesaler and retailer serves 4,300 retail grocery and general merchandise stores (including 611 Save-A-Lot limited assortment stores), most of them independently-owned in 48 states. Its 322 company-owned stores include; Cub Foods, Shop 'n Save, bigg's, Save-A-Lot, Scott's Foods, laneco, Foodland, Ultra IGA, Price Slasher, County Market, SUPERVALU, IGA, and Foodland. SUPERVALU also owns Hazelwood Farms Bakers, one of the largest frozen bakery manufacturers in the U.S. The company operates 37 distribution centers.
2. Fleming, Oklahoma City, OK, is a food wholesaler and retailer, serving 3,100 supermarkets in 42 states and D.C. as well as international markets. Additionally, the company operates 35 distribution centers. Fleming owns 270 food stores, including 12 regional grocery chains:

Bakers in Nebraska, SuPeRSaVeR and Sentry Foods in Wisconsin, Hyde Park Markets in Florida, and ABCO Foods in Arizona. Its multi-state chains: Rainbow Foods, Market Basket, Jubilee Foods, Festival Foods, Thompson Food Basket, Boogaarts Food Stores, and Consumers Food & Drug in eastern and Midwestern states. Additionally, the company franchises or licenses registered trade names to some 2,000 food stores, under such names as IGA, Piggly Wiggly, Food 4 Less, Big Star, Big T, Buy-for-Less, Buy Ways, Country Pride, Checkers, Festival Foods, Jubilee Foods, Jamboree Foods, MEGA Market, Minimax, Sentry, Shop 'N Bag, Shop 'N Kart, Super 1 Foods, Super Save, Super Thrift, Super Duper, American Family, BestYet, Thriftway, and Value King. The firm is consolidating its private labels from 13 to 5 brands: BestYet, Piggly Wiggly, Rainbow, IGA, Marquee Premium.

3. Nash Finch, Minneapolis, MN, is a food wholesaler and retailer that serves nearly 2,350 affiliated and other independent supermarkets, military bases, convenience stores and others in 30 states. Nash Finch also owns and operates 108 retail stores 74 supermarkets, 30 warehouse stores and four combination general merchandise/food stores) in 14 states, principally under such names as Econofoods, Food Bonanza, Sun Mart, Family Thrift Center, Food Folks, and Easter Foods. Additionally, the firm owns Nash DeCamp, a produce marketing subsidiary. Its distribution is handled through 20 centers. In calendar 1996, Nash Finch acquired the Ohio-based grocery wholesaler, Super Food Services, Inc., representing fiscal 1996 sales of about $1.2 billion.
4. Privately-held C&S Wholesale Grocers, based in Brattleboro, VT, which has recently taken over grocery and perishable distribution for the retail chain, Grand Union Co., Wayne NJ, operates with private label stock under the National brand as well as controlled brands supplied by the cooperative, Topco (see Chart 3).
5. Richmond, VA-based food wholesaler, Richfood , the largest in the Mid-Atlantic states, operates through four business units—Richfood/Virginia, Richfood/Pennsylvania, METRO/-BASICS Retail Div. (Metro superstores and Basics supermarkets), and the Richfood Dairy. Its strong private label program (1,600 items)covers brands such as Richfood, Econ, IGA, and Frosty Acres. The firm serves 1,500 + retail grocery stores in its marketing area.

Chart 3

Top U.S. Food Retailer/Wholesalers Co-Ops (1995-96)

Rank	Company	Total Sales (billions)	Total Stores	Total Est. Members	Private Label Sales* (billions)
1.	Topco	$ 4.0	3,500	50	$ 2.4 (60%)
2.	Wakefern / ShopRite	$ 4.0 (E)	185	—	1.4 (35%)
3.	Assoc. Wholesale Grocers(12/31/96)	$ 3.2	800	—	0.4 (20%)
4.	Roundy's(12/30/95)	$ 2.5	2,000+	—	0.2 (10%)
5.	Spartan	$ 2.5	500+	450	0.5 (20%)

*Private label share of total group sales estimated here.

Notes to Chart 3:

1. Topco Associates, Skokie, IL, is a retailer-owned cooperative that works as a marketing /procurement organization on behalf of its members as well as its associate members (who take only partial service), made up primarily of U.S. food chains. Altogether, its membership comprises more than 3,500 stores. Its exclusive brand identities, which total more than 18,000 SKUs, include: Food Club, Kingston, Top Crest, TopCare (health and beauty care), TC Color Shop (cosmetics), World Classics (upscale foods), Topco, GreenMark (environmental line), and economy lines like Mega, Maxi, and ValuTime.

2. Wakefern Corp., Edison, NJ, oversees the ShopRite co-op, which it claims is the country's largest food wholesaling collective, operating in five states and serving more than 190 supermarkets, 100 pharmacies, plus liquor stores. The firm controls more than 3,500 private label products, under such exclusive brand identities as: ShopRite, Farm Flavor, Flavor King, Very Best, Value Pak, and Chef's Express.

3. Associated Wholesale Grocers, Inc., Kansas City, KS, claims to be the oldest grocery cooperative and the second largest co-op and sixth largest grocery wholesaler in the U.S., serving more than 800 member stores in a 10-state market (Kansas, Missouri, Arkansas, Oklahoma, Illinois, Iowa, Nebraska, Texas, Tennessee and Kentucky).The AWB corporate brand arsenal includes more than 1,500 items, covering such brands as: Best Choice and the Always Save value brand (500+ items)

4. Roundy's, Inc., Pewaukee, WI, is a food and non-foods distributor owned by retail supermarkets which operate in more than a dozen Midwest states. Its private labels include Roundy's and the Super Choice range.

5. Based in Grand Rapids, MI, Spartan Stores is a retailer-owned co-op that serves 500+ independently-owned grocery stores in Michigan, Indiana, and Ohio. Spartan also operates convenience store distribution business, cash 'n carry wholesaling, and other services. Its private label lines include more than 1,800 Spartan and Spartan Supreme brand products and 285 SAVE RITE value brand items

Chart 4

Top U.S. Drug Store Chains

Rank	Chain	Stores	States	Total Sales (billions)	PL Sales (Share) (billions)
1.	Walgreen (8/31/97)	2,193	34 *	$ 13.4	$ 1.3 (10%)
2.	CVS (12/31/96)	4,000	24 +D.C.	$ 13	$ 1.3 (10%)
3.	Rite-Aid(3/1/97)	3,963	27 +D.C.	$ 11	$ 0.9 (8%)
4.	Eckerd (2/97)	2,699	23	$ 10	$ 1.0 (10%)
5.	Osco/Sav-on (2/3/96)	882	21	$ 5.2	$ 0.490 (10%)
6.	Long's Drug (1/30/97)	337	4	$ 2.8	$ 0.140 (5%)
7.	Drug Emporium (3/2/96)	226	27	$ 1.3	$ 0.039 (3%)

*Also in Puerto Rico.

Notes to Chart 4:

1. Walgreen Co., Deerfield, IL, is the leading U.S. chain drugstore. Its pharmacy sales are45% of total store sales. In the year 2000, Walgreens expects to be operating 3,000 drug stores.
2. CVS (Consumer Value Stores), Woonsocket, RI, has grown through acquisition, beginning with its 1990 takeover of Peoples Drug Stores (490 stores) from Imasco Limited, the Canadian firm that owns Shoppers Drug Mart. Recently, CVS has taken over Big B Inc. and Revco D.S., pushing the company into the number-two spot. (Revco D.S., Inc., Twinsburg, OH, had already acquired 801 Hook-SupeRx, Inc., Cincinnati drugstore chain operator--Hook Drugs, SupeRx Drugs, Brooks Drugs--in July 1994, adding substantially to its store base and nearly doubling its sales volume. Its prescription sales are 56.3% of its net sales.)
3. Rite Aid Corp., Camp Hill, PA, after acquiring Perry Drug, more recently has added Thrifty PayLess, K&B, and Harco, Inc., building itself into one of the top three chains in the country. Its pharmacy sales are 54% of total Rite Aid sales.
4. Eckerd Corp., Clearwater, FL, has been absorbed by JC Penney Co., Dallas, the giant department store retailer. The latter already owned Thrift Drug, Pittsburgh, and more recently acquired Kerr drug stores and Fay's Inc. Altogether, with the Eckerd business, JC Penney is now a major player in the drug store sector—all its stores are being converted to the Eckerd format. Some 53.7% of Eckerd's total sales are in prescription items.
5. American Stores Co., Salt Lake City, UT, operates 551 Osco Drug stores in 20 states and 281 Sav-on drugstores in two states. The Osco Drug count includes 153 jointly-operated Jewel Osco combination food-drug stores, counted in both the Jewel Food Stores (see Chart 1) and Osco Drug totals. Besides the Osco & Sav-on private label programs, the chain also sells an American Premier premium brand plus a Value Wise budget brand at these stores.
6. Longs Drugs, Walnut Creek, CA, reported 33% of its total sales in pharmacy items. Its product selection covers a broad assortment of products.
7. Drug Emporium, Inc., Powell, OH, operates 136 corporate stores, and also serves as franchisor to 90 additional Drug Emporium outlets. Positioned as a deep-discount chain, the firm acquired 26 F&M deep-discount HBA stores in 1995.

Chart 5

Top Canadian Food Retailers/Wholesalers ($ U.S. Billion)

# Company	Retail/-Wholesale %	Total Sales	Store Count Owned/Wholesale	Private Label Sales (%)
1. Loblaw(1/3/98)	72.7/26.3	$ 7.9	360/547	$ 1.2 (15%)
2. Oshawa (1/25/97)	_____	$ 4.6	105/1,433	—
3. Provigo (1/27/96)	75/25	$ 5.7	162/962	—
4. Safeway (12/30/95)	——	$ 3.5*	—	—
5. Metro-Richelieu(9/27/97)	24.4/75.6**	$ 2.4	30+/1,000**	$0.3 (14%)
6. A&P (2/22/97)	----	$ 1.8*	176/49	--

* Only Canadian Sales **Company also serves 2,750 customers in food service plus convenience stores.

Notes to Chart 5:

1. Loblaw Companies Limited, Toronto, Canada, is Canada's largest retail and wholesale food distributor. The company's majority shareholder is George Weston Limited, Toronto, a major food manufacturer. Loblaw operates numerous store banners across Canada: 64 Loblaws stores, 46 zehrs markets, 18 save-easy stores, 7 the super centre stores, 14 SuperValu stores, 11 zehrs food plus stores, 10 the real atlantic Superstore stores, and 15 Dominion stores, all in the east. Loblaw also operates 34 the real Canadian Superstore stores, 10 The Real Canadian Wholesale stores, 39 OK! economy stores, and 15 Extra Foods stores in the west. Additionally, the company serves many wholesale customers: no frills, Fortinos, your independent grocer, valu-mart, Atlantic Grocer, save-easy, mr. grocer, Shop Easy Foods, Lucky Dollar Foods, Super Valu, and Extra Foods. In 1995, the company sold its National Tea business in the U.S., while continuing to license its President's Choice product line to select supermarket chains in 36 states plus Bermuda and Barbados. Its other corporate brand products include; "no name," TOO GOOD TO BE TRUE!, G.R.E.E.N, as well as other controlled labels that are unique to each operational segment.
2. The Oshawa Group Limited, Etobicoke, Ontario, Canada, is Canada's largest retail food franchiser, overseeing 655 IGA food stores (588 of them franchised, 67 company-owned) and 902 other food stores (845 of them franchised). Its franchised associates trade under such banners as IGA, Food Town, Knechtel, Bonichoix, etc. Its company-owned stores operate under the IGA, Price Chopper, and Dutch Boy banners. Additionally, the company has company-owned or franchised convenience stores (Boni-Soir, Smartcart, and Dutch Girl) as well as cash and carry outlets. Its food operations, divided into three regions, Eastern, Central, and Western, represent 83.7% of Oshawa's total fiscal 1997 sales. Oshawa also operates SERCA Food Service Inc, which generates sales of $357.3 million.
3. Provigo Inc., Montréal, Québec, is a leading retailer and food distributor in Canada, operating Provigo Distribution Inc. in Québec (57 corporate and 98 affiliated/franchised Provigo Supermarkets and 69 maxi stores) and LOEB Inc. (36 corporate and 75 affiliated/franchised LOEB stores) in Ontario and western and northwestern Québec. In the wholesale/convenience stores area, the company supplies 800 smaller independent stores (L'Intermarché, Axep, Jovi, proprio, and atout-prix banners, as well as operating 42 Presto and Linc cash and carry warehouses, and five L'Economie corporate stores). The company's Dellixo operation handles 1,600 food service customers, while its C Corp. serves as a network of franchised convenience stores (Provi-Soir, Winks and Red Rooster banners). Its own corporate brands include Experiences, Zel, and Generation Zel.
4. Canada Safeway Limited, owned by Safeway Inc., Pleasanton, CA, operates stores principally in British Columbia, Alberta, and Manitoba/Saskatchewan. This subsidiary also operates a wholesaling business, distributing national brands and private label items to independent grocery stores and institutional customers. Some 17 of the company's total 43 manufacturing and processing facilities are located in Canada as well.
5. Métro-Richelieu Inc., Montreal, Quebec, celebrating its 50th anniversary, is a leader in the Quebec food distribution industry, maintaining a dominant position in the supermarket segment with its 295 Metro supermarkets, as well as 192 Marché Richelieu stores, 33 Super C stores, Les 5 Saisons, Ami, and Gem stores. The company through its Econogros, Pecheries Atlantiques and Distagro divisions serves institutional and food service accounts of more than 2,750 customers plus a wide network of convenience stores. Additionally, its McMahon-Essiam Inc. pharmaceutical distribution subsidiary operates as the franchisor of the Brunet chain of 65 drug stores. Its private labels include Selection Merit and Econochoice, Metro-The Obvious Choice, Marche Richelieu, and Super C brands, totaling more than 2,000 items.
6. A&P Canada, owned by A&P, Montvale, NJ, operates 114 A&P/ Super Fresh stores outside the Toronto area; 55 Dominion supermarkets in metropolitan Toronto, and 56 Food Basics Canada (49 of them franchised), the latter chain a new limited-assortment format, all basically in the Ontario market.

Chart 6
Top Canadian Drug Store Chains/Franchisors

Rank	Company	Retail/ Licensed Sales(%)	Total Sales (billions)	Stores Owned/- Franchised	PL Sales(Share) (billions)
1.	Shoppers Drug Mart/ Pharmaprix (12/31/96)	0/100	$ 2.8	0/819	$ 0.2 (6%)
2.	The Jean Coutu Group (5/31/97)	50.6/49.4	$ 1.7	232/251	$ 0.1 (6.5%)
3	Pharma Plus Drugmarts (1/25/97)	100/0	$ 0.3	137/0	——

All sales in U.S. dollars.

Notes to Chart 6:

1. Shoppers Drug Mart /Pharmaprix, Toronto, owned by Imasco Limited, Montréal, a leading consumer products and services company with sales totalling $12.1 billion (Imperial Tobacco, CT Financial Services, Hardee's Food Systems, Genstar Development Co.), is Canada's leading drug-store group. The company recently acquired 24 Bi-Rite Drug Stores in Saskatchewan and then 135 Big V drugstores in southwestern Ontario, all of which are being converted to Shoppers Drug Mart. Some 11% of SDM's sales, excluding prescriptions and tobacco, are in corporate brands—Life Brand and Rialto brand. Its prescription sales are 34% of total sales. The Big V stores, owned by the company after the acquisition, will be licensed in 1998 to associate-pharmacists (as are other stores in its system). The Shoppers Drug Mart/Pharmaprix revenues for the year totalled $820 million for the year.
2. The Jean Coutu Group (PJC) Inc., Longueuil, Quebec, carries on a franchising network of PJC Jean Coutu and Maxi Drug stores in Canada, totalling 251 units. The company also owns 232 Brooks Pharmacy (Smithfield, RI) drug stores in five Northeast states in the U.S. Its takeover of the Brooks chain from Revco (from its buyout of Hook SupeRx), resulted in a conversion of its Douglas and maxi stores in the U.S. to the Brooks banner. The U.S. operations represents 48.9% of the company's total sales. In Canada, the company markets its Personnelle private label products (some 950 items), while in the U.S., its Brooks brand program totals 800+ items.
3. Pharma Plus Drugmarts Ltd., Toronto, Ontario, represents just 6.1% of its parent company's sales: The Oshawa Group Limited, Canada's largest retail food franchiser, has total sales exceeding $4.6 billion. This division has 137 Pharma Plus drugstores in Ontario province.

CHAPTER 20

PRIVATE LABEL CATEGORY-BY-CATEGORY

In the supermarket segment, private label dollar-share is largest within the dairy department, claiming $9.7 billion for three top categories or 38.5% share in the total dairy category. This is because three of the top five private label categories overall are dairy items—milk ranks No. 1, followed by cheese at No. 3 and fresh eggs at No. 4. Each of the top four categories represents private label sales exceeding $1 billion. (Ice cream, No. 5, could be considered a dairy product, except that it is classified as "frozen foods.")

Comparing reports over the past five years in the *PLMA Private Label Yearbook,* beginning with its first issue in 1992 (for the calendar year 1991), the data prepared by Information Resources, Inc. for the Private Label Manufacturers Association, there has been virtually no change in the ranking of these top categories. Further down the list, however, certain product categories have jockeyed for higher dollar volume, notably refrigerated juices from a number 11 to a number 10 ranking), cold cereal (from a number 16 to 11), and cookies (from a number 18 to 14). On a sales gains basis, since 1991 (see Chart 7) the big winners are the top three categories, by virtue of their huge sales volume—milk up by $800 million, fresh bread and rolls up $400 million, and cheese up $500 million. Other big gains: carbonated beverages up $236 million; cold cereal up $213 million; and cookies up $168 million. The big losers are frozen juices down $151 million; frozen plain vegetables down $75 million; and canned & bottled fruit, down $69 million.

On a unit volume basis, private label sales (including generics) since 1990 have fluctuated, yet steadily have increased overall. The 1992 *Yearbook* showed 1991 sales of 23.6 billion units. In 1992, that volume climbed to 26.3 billion units, followed by another increase, to 26.5 billion units in 1993. For the 1994 period, the volume dipped to 25.4 billion units and to 25.3 billion units in 1995. The following year, private label edged up again to 25.7 billion units--still ahead of the 1991 sales. (Generics over this period have steadily eroded from 0.9 billion units in 1991 to 0.1 billion units in 1996.) Obviously, private label share has been taken from national brand unit sales. Tracing their tally from 1991, these sales also fluctuated: 102.6 billion, to 106.4 billion, to 105.5 billion, to 104 billion, to 103.1 billion, and to 100.7 billion for 1996.

Chart 7

Top 20 Private Label Categories Dollar Volume (1991-96)

Ranking 1991	Ranking 1996	Category	Sales (Millions) 1991	Sales (Millions) 1996
1	1	Milk	$5,400	$6,200
2	2	Fresh Bread/ Rolls	1,500	1,900
3	3	Cheese	1,300	1,800
*	4	Fresh Eggs	——	1,600
4	5	Ice Cream	911	976
6	6	Carbonated Beverages	620	856
5	7	Frozen Plain Vegetables	815	740
8	8	Sugar	603	689
7	9	Vegetables	604	645
11	10	Juices Refrigerated	518	643
16	11	Cold Cereal	318	531
10	12	Bottled Juices Shelf Stable	540	480
12	13	Canned/Bottled Fruit	449	471
18	14	Cookies	276	444
9	15	Frozen Juices	570	419
14	16	Chips and Snacks	350	397
13	17	Deli Luncheon Meats	374	395
15	18	Food & Trash Bags	345	392
*	19	Cups and Plates	——	379
20	20	Diapers	272	351

*These categories not included among the top 20 in 1991. Breakfast Meat was ranked No. 17 ($284 Million) and Cottage Cheese No. 19 ($273 million) in 1991.

Editor's Note: This comparison is made only to reflect the strength of different product categories in private label. The 1991 figures, compiled by IRI, may very well have been revised in subsequent reports.

SOURCE: PLMA's Private Label Yearbook 1992, 1997/Information Resources Inc.

Chart 8

Supermarket Private Label Sales by Department (Dollar Share 1991 Versus 1996)

Department	1991 Sales (%)	1996 Sales (%)	Change (Points)
Dairy	35.6	38.5	+2.9
Bakery	23.7	26.2	+2.5
Frozen Foods	15.4	15.3	-0.1
Deli	12.4	12.2	-0.2
Edible Groceries	9.4	10.6	+1.2
Non-Edible Groceries	7.6	10.5	+2.9
Health & Beauty Care	6.4	9.7	+3.3
General Merchandise	13.2	10.1	-3.6
Total Dollar Share	13.7	15.8	+2.1

Editor's Note: This comparison is made only to reflect the growing strength of private label in product departments. The 1991 figures, compiled by IRI, may very well have been revised in subsequent reports.

SOURCE: PLMA's Private Label Yearbook 1992; /Information Resources Inc. 1997.

Some observers believe that unit volume provides a more accurate measure of private label growth. In the IRI data, private label market share in supermarkets is now estimated at 25.7 billion units or 20.3% of total unit sales for 1996. Its recent performance, in fact, has been stronger than brand name unit sales growth: Private label climbed by 1.4% in units sales from 19.5% in 1995, while name brands dropped by 2.4% to 100.7 billion units in that same period (IRI/PLMA).

Early IRI reports for 1997 show private label dollar sales share at 20.6%, while private label unit sales climbed by 0.7% and name brand sales dipped by 2%.

There's no question that private label dollar-and-unit-sales-share continues to grow in the supermarket segment. It's worth looking at this change from the perspective of major categories. ACNielsen, Chicago, has tracked this market, based on $2-plus million supermarkets. Its findings:

Chart 9

Private Label Market Share in Supermarkets (1993-96)
Volume Review Report (52-weeks ending 12/7/96)

(For Food Stores of $2 million+)

Department	Private Label Share				1996	
	1993	1994	1995	1996	Total Volume ($ Billions)	Private Label Volume ($ Billions)
Dry Grocery	10.7%	11.3%	12%	12.5%	$110.7	$ 13.5
Non-Foods	8.5	9.6	10.3	10.7	27.8	2.9
Dairy	39.2	39.4	40.2	41.7	25.3	10.5
Frozen Foods	15	14.8	15	15.2	21.5	3.2
Health & Beauty Care	7.1	8.2	8.9	9.4	11.9	1.1
Alcoholic Beverages	0.1	0.1	0.1	0.0	8.1	0.002
Packaged Meats	10.6	10.6	10.7	11.3	7.5	0.8
General Merchandise	2.9	3.6	4.6	5.2	3.7	0.2
Deli	5.2	5.4	5	7.5	2.9	0.2
TOTALS	**12.9%**	**13.6%**	**14.4%**	**14.9%**	**$219.4**	**$32.6**

ACNielsen SCANTRACK 1997

CHAPTER 21

THE FUTURE: EXPLOSIVE GROWTH OF EXCLUSIVE BRANDS

"Our stores offer approximately 1,700 different Albertson's Brands items. These account for about half of our stores' top 100 selling grocery items... We have concentrated on redesigning our Albertson's Brands packaging and have reviewed the quality of every product and every supplier. We want our private label program to do more than offer lower-priced products. It should be a brand identification program that promotes the Albertson's name. Our new Albertson's packaging and in-store signs emphasize the product quality and the Albertson's name. Our bakery items have a new 'Fresh Baked' quality seal, and all meat and produce labels highlight our 'Quality Guaranteed' pledge." — Albertsons 1995 Annual Report

The private label revolution in North America now heads toward the 21st century, promising accelerated growth as private label truly stands on its own as a brand—an exclusive brand—uniquely positioned in the marketplace via a variety of quality-options and specialty line offshoots. Private label, in fact, is now getting its biggest push and the most support ever provided in the history of this phenomenon:

(1) Consumers are more value-conscious: They want the best quality at the lowest possible price and, being better educated, they are not easily misled anymore.
(2) Retailers and wholesalers, through mergers and acquisitions, are consolidating their operations, which allows them to achieve greater and more efficient purchasing power to support their exclusive brand business.

The premise for private label success for decades has been more value for the money spent. Lately, retailers and wholesalers have put more emphasis on tightening their operations and exploring ways to generate more profits. Private label offers them one of the most viable solutions, because that's where they realize their greatest profits. Category management has enlightened them about the role and fit of private label in their business on a market-by-market basis. In 1994, for example, Cub Foods, Stillwater, MN, a subsidiary of Minnesota-based SUPERVALU, Minneapolis, MN, launched a category management policy. It started with a director overseeing up to eight in-house brokers. The strategy has evolved into a separate manager of private label, working with an entire staff: an in-house broker, a field sales coordinator, a fund/label coordinator, and an administrative assistant. Beginning in March 1996, the private label program focused on launching a Cub Foods brand, at first with five SKUs. The program has grown to some 400 SKUs—all top sellers in different product categories, covering all store departments. The goal is to push private label penetration to 15% by the year 2000, stocking upwards of 1,500 Cub Foods Brand items. Incidentally, Cub Foods has been no small influence in convincing its parent company to adopt a category-management strategy as well. (Exclusive Brands 1997)

The second largest supermarket retailer in the United States, American Stores Company, announced in its 1994 annual report that it has "set a goal to increase its private label market share in the next five years to 25% of total sales from a range of 16 to 18%." By the end of 1996, private label represented 19% of its total grocery sales. Another example: The country's largest supermarket retailer, Kroger, recently reported that its current Kroger-brand product sales have outpaced the company's total corporate revenues growth. This is not uncommon for other major chains as well; accelerated private label sales growth clearly constitutes a trend of the 1990s.

The rationale behind current private label growth strategies is explained in the quote at the beginning of this chapter. Albertsons recognizes the strength of private label in its overall organization. Recently, this chain has put more emphasis on solving its customers' needs with specific programs designed to build sales: its Quick Fixin' meal ideas and information; and its "expanded destination categories, such as baby care, pet care, Albertson's Better Care pharmacies, and snack and beverage centers." Additionally, Albertsons has introduced new, gourmet-quality bakery items and expanded its product selection with organically-grown produce as well as organic grocery items. Its Albertson brand—if not now, eventually—fits into each of these areas. Attitudes about private label are changing, moving away from the traditional, low-cost, copycat approach of the past and towards increasingly innovative and creative brand-positioning in the marketplace.

The strategy of business positioning is perhaps explained most effectively in a new book, "The New Positioning" by Jack Trout with Steve Rivkin. In many of his recommendations to brand-name manufacturers, Trout reiterates his disapproval of brand-line extensions.

"To gain cost efficiencies and trade acceptance, (companies) are quite willing to turn a highly focused brand, one that stands for a certain type of product or idea, into an unfocused brand that represents two or three or more types of products or ideas. . . The more variations you attach to the brand, the more the mind loses focus." (Trout 1996)

Unless, Mr. Trout, unless that brand happens to be a store brand, where many different products fall under its identity. The consumer doesn't lose focus, because their orientation is directed toward a trusted store-name, that same name identifying the store's own store brand products. If consumers find fault with any of those products, they know the store will guarantee a complete refund—with no questions asked. Retailers now regard their store name as a brand, Its equity reflects throughout the brands owned by the retailers.

Latest Trends Support Private Label Growth

Change should never be avoided, especially in the highly-competitive business of food and drug store retailing/wholesaling. With respect to private label, this principle is now in the forefront of management thinking. It's manifested in new product development and product innovation, initiated no longer by just the brand manufacturers but by the distributors of those products—the retailers and wholesalers—within their own private label programs. Today, a number of industry trends reinforce the proliferation of private label activity :

- Product line extensions
- Multiple quality tier programs
- Sub-branding strategies
- Co-branding with famous name brand products used as an important ingredient in the private label item
- New product category ventures
- Ethnic ranges, i.e., catering to Italian, Hispanic/Mexican, or Asian tastes
- Upscale or premium food and health-and-beauty-care lines
- Corporate brands marketed throughout different chains owned by an organization.
- Continued industry consolidation, producing greater purchasing power.

Today's retail, wholesale, and manufacturing managers link their business strategies for product distribution in the food and drug store trade directly to consumer purchasing patterns. It's a discipline called Efficient Consumer Response (ECR), which involves distribution logistics, information technology, pricing strategies, marketing support, etc. Its effects are seen in changing store formats, changing product assortments, and changing in-store services provided to shoppers.

Nearly every retailer and wholesaler in the trade is now focused on building private label sales, because private label is where they realize their biggest profit margins. In private label development, they are not burdened by high R&D costs, or by the inflated marketing expenses sustained by the name-brand manufacturers. The private label owners tend to know where to cut corners, how to foster cost-efficient, quality-enhancing synergies within their organization, and how to market both creatively and inexpensively within their own marketing retail sphere. Private label serves as the platform where the store brand owners can provide more value to the consumer, in the form of lower-priced products that address exactly what that store's consumers can afford and/or what they want in terms of product quality or performance and packaging aesthetics. Ownership is exclusive to the retailers/wholesalers themselves, even though the range of products can also be under a licensing agreement. The base line is that they directly control that store brand, corporate brand, retailer brand, controlled brand, private brand, or whatever term is used to describe this range of products. It is theirs exclusively. The store's own exclusive brands can appear within different presentations, ranging from the basic, low-cost, standard grade product; to first-tier products that match or exceed the name brand leader in each product category; to premium or uniquely-different products that attract the gourmet, the discerning shopper, or the adventuresome consumer; to specialty premium, ethnic, or healthy lines of product that please different tastes or interests.

Trade awareness of consumer interest, in fact, is tied directly to the category-management strategies that are now being adopted industry-wide. Secondary or weaker manufacturers' brands, or even a retailer's or wholesaler's neglected control brand, long established in different product categories, have been discontinued or squeezed off the store shelves in favor of an expanded, diversified and more focused private label sales mix. This is not a theory; it's observable fact. You now see more emphasis on private label growth no matter what size the program in all forms of the retail chains—from a few hundred private label SKUs up to the array of a mass merchandise chain like Meijer's, selling some 22,000 private label SKUs across its grocery and general merchandise categories. The range today is truly amazing.

Revco D.S., Inc. previously had indicated that it stocks more than 18,000 different items in a typical Revco drug store. Less than 5% of that stock, or slightly more than 800 Revco private label items ranging from vitamins to soft drinks, "offer the quality of the national brands at a substantial savings—an average of 50%. Revco is always seeking new items to add to its private label line, which combine superior quality and value for the customer and excellent profit for the company," according to the company's 1995 financial report. This strategy also is part and parcel of the program at CVS, Revco's new owner as of May 1997.

A sense of pride has developed in the corporate chain name, which often carries over to the company's private label program with the same identity. This was dramatically illustrated recently when Smart & Final, Los Angeles, CA, operator of 158 Smart & Final non-membership warehouse stores, decided to downplay its Iris private brand, which has been marketed since 1895. Instead, this company, the oldest warehouse grocery chain in the United States (founded in 1871 as Hellman-Haas Grocery Co.)

wants to capitalize on its Smart & Final logo, not only to build its brand equity; but, also to reduce the expense and effort necessary to promote two separate names. Its corporate brands include Smart & Final, Smart & Final Premium (top quality), La Romanella (Italian food service line), and Montecito (Hispanic products). All have been energized recently with new packaging and promotional support. The attention paid to its corporate brands is understandable, when you consider that, while its private labels make up just 10% of its 11,000-item assortment, they contribute nearly 25% of sales and almost one-third of gross profits for the company, according to results reported in 1993.

Another example of a store trying out an increased brand identity is that of American Stores which is now reportedly converting its Lady Lee brand to the Lucky brand in its Lucky Stores. Similarly, the major food wholesaler SUPERVALU has agreed to drop its first-line Flavorite controlled brand in Cub Stores, and replace it with the Cub Food brand, thus reinforcing its store name equity.

In an effort to eliminate "redundant corporate overhead," after Thrifty Drug Stores acquired Payless Drug Stores (renaming itself Thrifty Payless, Inc. in April 1994) the company began to integrate both operations, including the combination of a Thrifty Payless brand identity with a TPI icon logo, serving as an acronym for Thrifty Payless Inc. Thrifty Payless, of course, now is part of Rite Aid, which has made its store brand the corporate-wide exclusive brand of all its operations.

Wal-Mart Supercenters Open Private Label Opportunities

Private label interest has captured the attention of the world's largest retailer, the $100-plus billion Wal-Mart, Bentonville, AR, a general merchandise retailer, which in recent years has put increased emphasis on its Supercenter concept, i.e., merging general merchandise stock with groceries. These stores feature a 60,000-square-foot supermarket within the total 130,000-square-foot mass merchandising environment. There are now more than 250 Wal-Mart Supercenters in operation with more than 100 planned for opening in fiscal 1997. Overall, Wal-Mart operates some 2,400 Wal-Mart stores and 470 Sam's Clubs membership warehouse stores. While Wal-Mart traditionally has been a national brand retailer, its interest in private label has grown in the 1990s. Its Equate range of health and beauty care products and Spring Valley vitamins and dietary supplements form the base for this expansion. More recently, Wal-Mart has introduced Sam's American Choice premium foods and beverages, followed by Great Value first-line grocery products—two exclusive brand programs that account for more than 5,000 SKUs. This tally does not include its private label stock in health and beauty care, paint, apparel, hardgoods, and other product categories. In fact, Wal-Mart owns a HomeTrends brand for home furnishings, a 1,000+ SKU Better Homes and Gardens brand (under exclusive license with the magazine with that name) for gardening supplies and equipment; a House Beautiful brand for paint and a Popular Mechanics brand for hunting apparel (both also licensing-rights with publishers), as well as a number of other exclusive brands in clothing (Bobbie Brooks and other brands). Recently, the company also began a sub-branding strategy, adding Healthy 4 You food items under its Great Value range. Arguably, Wal-Mart's total private label count may be approaching, if not exceeding that of Meijer's. Wal-Mart, however, will not disclose this information. What is now obvious is the fact that its exclusive brand commitment is growing, especially with the strong move into Supercenters.

Based on Wal-Mart's total sales—now exceeding $100 billion, its exclusive brand share of total sales, if estimated at 10%, would top $10 billion. That would make this retailer the largest private label/exclusive brand merchant in North America. (On a global basis, there are some European retailer/wholesalers, such as Aldi in Germany and Sainsbury's in the United Kingdom, who have a larger exclusive-brand sales volume.)

The multi-department store chain, Fred Meyer, Portland, OR, carries an overall stock of about 225,000 food and non-food products. Within that mix, private label sales in food items alone has nearly doubled from about 12% in 1991 to over 20% at the end of 1995. Its private brands in groceries include: Fred Meyer first-tier products, the licensed, upscale President's Choice selection, and FMV (Fred Meyer Value) economy brand. This $3.4 billion retailing giant has put more emphasis on food over the past four years, going from about 36% to 41% of its total corporate sales in food. Some 94 of its total 102 stores now carry both food and non-food departments. Nevertheless, non-foods still represent nearly 60% of its total sales. In that area, Fred Meyer also has stepped up private label expansion, where its share of total sales, now at between 12% to 13%, is expected to climb to between 15% to 20%. The home department features appliances, sporting goods, housewares, auto supplies, etc. The apparel department includes not only clothing and sportswear, but cosmetics, accessories, and shoes. In 1995, Fred Meyer introduced its Personal Choice brand of toiletries and personal care products. The line now is replacing certain Fred Meyer brand items in order to expand into more fashionable private label basics in the cosmetics section of the store. Recently, this company acquired Smith's Food & Drug Centers, Salt Lake City, UT. At presstime for this book, the company entered a merger agreement with Ralphs Grocery, Compton, CA, and Quality Food Centers, Bellevue, WA, which, when consummated sometime in early 1998, will create a $15 billion multi-regional supermarket company.

Europeans Gain Control & Influence

While it's still unlikely that private label sales will overtake name brand sales in the United States in the near future, the disparity of market share between dominant name brands and private label is decreasing—in some cases, quite dramatically.

Shaw's Supermarkets, Inc., East Bridgewater, MA, drew the interest of the United Kingdom's largest grocery multiple, J Sainsbury, London, which in 1983, purchased 21% of Shaw's stock, and then five years later made that small New England chain its wholly-owned subsidiary, increasing its U.S. holdings. Sainsbury's, which has some 65% of its supermarket sales in its own brand in the United Kingdom, has tilted Shaw's into a similar strategy. In the 1990s, Shaw's own brand strength has climbed to more than 4,000 lines, representing 40% of its total sales ($2.3 billion for fiscal 1996, covering 96 stores). That's far ahead of all the other large supermarket chains in the U.S., where private label commitment ranges from the high teens into the low 20% range. (Even Loblaws in Canada trails behind this commitment!) These are indeed trends to watch, for they are bound to change name brand dominance in the marketplace.

European influence in the U.S. is also evident from Royal Ahold, a Dutch retail organization that operates Ahold USA , Atlanta, GA, representing $14.3 billion in sales (1996) from such regional chains as Giant, Finast, Edwards, Bi-Lo, Tops, and Mayfair, located east of the Mississippi River. In March 1996, the Dutch firm acquired The Stop & Shop Companies, Inc., Boston, a chain of 128 supermarkets ($3.8 billion+ in sales). The Ahold USA chains average from 15 to 20% of their chain sales in private label. There is now an integration process underway, in which the company is seeking to centralize its purchasing efforts, while also working synergies with a corporate brand strategy, i.e., selling Finast brand under health and beauty care and general merchandise products through all its chain operations in the U.S. Additionally, the Finast brand is now the first-tier private label program at its Finast, Edwards, and Giant chains. It's expected that exclusive brand commitment in this operation will grow as well.

Synergies also have been developed by Dave Nichol, formerly of Loblaw and then more recently president of Cott Corp., Toronto, the leading supplier of premium quality retail-branded beverages and fourth largest manufacturer of carbonated soft drinks in the world. Nichol until recently headed up a Cott subsidiary, Destination Products International (DPI), which is positioned as a developer of retailer-brand products. DPI already has developed 15 food products for retailers like Safeway, Vons, and Stop & Shop. Its plans call for an additional 15 items. The company strategy basically is to tap into the airline catering-business, which in recent years has suffered major losses as a result of airlines cutting back on food service. DPI leverages their strength for product development at the retail level. So far, products have appeared under the Safeway Select, Vons Select, and Stop & Shop Select premium private label programs. The same packaging can be used, changing only the exclusive brand identity for each chain.

Here the trend is obvious. If anyone doubts the explosive growth of exclusive brand identities, one need only turn to Trader Joe's, Pasadena, CA. This small West Coast food chain with under 100 stores has spread its wings beyond California into

Arizona, Oregon, and Washington State. Recently, the chain established roots in Boston, MA, and now plans a major East Coast expansion, opening up some 100 stores there by the year 2000. This innovative and exciting store features upscale and quality foods that appeal to the discerning shopper seeking sound value at remarkably lower prices. This 30-year-old chain positions itself as similar to a fancy, upscale gourmet shop, but which caters to a broad customer base. Most interesting, some 80-plus % of its food stock is in exclusive brands that Trader Joe's has developed over the years, with exciting graphics and food packaging that actually rivals or surpasses that of the famous name brands.

The country's largest chain of natural food supermarkets (40+ stores), Whole Foods Markets, Austin, TX, also has made a major capital investment in its Whole Foods Market brand. The company reports: "As more and more premium quality products are sourced under the Whole Foods Market label, our customers begin to make a greater commitment to our brand. Each successful product encourages our customers to try other products under our label. Since these products can only be found in our stores, they help build customer loyalty to our company." Talk about a winning strategy. Again the emphasis is on quality, purity of content, but with a tilt toward the upscale consumer.

The recognition of exclusive brands as a critical component to bottom line profits within an organization appears to guarantee future growth in this business. It is difficult to predict just how fast, or how far, this development will carry. But it is obviously a trend that is shaping the future of retailing.

The major players betting against the private label/exclusive brands business are the big name brand manufacturers, who are obviously invested in and want to protect their own brand equity and market share.

The 21st Century: A New Focus

There is a plethora of business books now being churned out by researchers at leading brand manufacturers, ad agencies, and universities, all advancing ways and means of protecting "brand equity," which really means an emphasis on the brand's net worth to the manufacturer. From the viewpoint of this author, this is a losing philosophy, representing a narrow focus—protecting market share and net worth. They need to focus on the needs of the consumer as much as their own needs. In the process of achieving this end, manufacturers must address issues that will make their product attractive to and worthwhile for consumers. They can do this by delivering the best quality, via R&D efforts, put into very attractive packaging, and supported by strong broadcast and print consumer advertising all at an affordable price. The marketing analysts call the end result: "premium brands."

It is surprising that there is not more focus on the private label element in the marketplace in the business press. Private label is probably the most neglected brand now in distribution in terms of analysts attention. (It is true that in recent years, the trade press has been increasingly attentive to this important marketing sector. Additionally, Wall Street analysts also have issued special reports on private label.) The power of private label, i.e., exclusive brands, slowly is being recognized as a significant economic force. Lynn Upshaw, formerly of Ketchum Advertising, San Francisco, in his new book, notes this clearly. . .

"Retail chains used to be simply the conduit for the sale of packaged brands; now they are iron-willed gatekeepers, armed to the teeth with state-of-the-art information technology, as determined to sell their own higher-margin private label brands as they are in stocking the nationals." (Upshaw 1995)

Private Labels Dominate Product Categories

Interestingly, Upshaw paints a picture of the typical supermarket in the year 2020, where

"Private labels—a class of top-notch products now commonly called 'best brands'—dominate the majority of categories. One-third of all brands are rotated off the shelves every 90 days, replaced immediately by new items that turn more quickly based on daily scanner projections. Only the number 1 and 2 brands in each category are allowed to remain on the shelf on a semipermanent basis." (Upshaw 1995)

While this may seem overly optimistic, it is, in fact, already becoming a reality today. There are food retailers who are very close to following this type of strategy at different stages of development, and to different degrees. When Wal-Mart, for example, introduced its Sam's American Choice in June 1992, it reportedly became the highest velocity SKU in the chain within six months. As part of its expansion of Supercenters, Wal-Mart now has more than 5,000 SKUs in its two major exclusive brand food programs, Sam's American Choice and Great Value. It's also important to remember that Wal-Mart was among the first U.S. retailers to adopt category management strategies in its operation. This perspective has led Wal-Mart into more exclusive brands.

Shaw's Supermarkets, Inc., the Sainsbury U.S. chain operating in New England, added 560 exclusive brand products in 1995, bringing the total count to more than 2,500 lines, representing some 25% of total sales. In 1996, that commitment shot upwards to 40% of total sales, with the addition of 750 more Shaw's brand products, representing 4,000 lines total.

Whole Foods Market, Austin TX, the country's largest chain of natural food supermarkets, is a textbook example of Upshaw's retailer. In 1955, it introduced more than a dozen new products, as well as updating its Wellspring jams, reintroduced everything under the Whole Foods Label, and re-released its Whole Foods line of herbs and spices. As a result, there are now exclusive brand products in 22 different categories, totaling 500 products with ongoing expansion on the drawing board.

This trend punctuates the direction retailers are now taking in replacing name brand stock with their own exclusive brands.

There are many other examples, some more dramatic than others. Also, the trend in sub-branding continues. Albertsons Food & Drug stores, for example, now stock "Albertsons Mighty" premium towels and "Albertsons Baby Basics" diapers. The companies lagging behind have also received their wake-up call. Associated Wholesale Grocers, Inc., Kansas City, KS, for example, as the second largest retailer-owned cooperative wholesaler in the United States, had just about 15% of its total $2.9 billion sales by 1995 in AWG brands. On a case basis, those exclusive brands accounted for 20% of sales. AWG plans to push that share to 30% for both dollar sales and case sales by the year 2005. (Lancaster 1996)

The new century will see accelerated growth in exclusive brands, because of the trend toward marketing the store as a brand. McDonald's Restaurants is a classic case. Many brand-oriented marketing people, in fact, view McDonald's as a brand. It is really a private label retail business, where almost 100% of its stock is sold—even within licensing agreement in other types of businesses— under its own exclusive brands.

While famous-name brands will never completely disappear, it seems fair to predict that there will be fewer and fewer of them left. Their Achilles heel may be their own manifest self-interest. Against their hegemony, private label has positioned itself as an attractive alternative choice, offered by an independent store distributor with an already loyal customer base. As such, its primary interest has always been its responsiveness to, and built-in value for, this customer. With today's consumers becoming more value-conscious and more selective, the words of Lynn Upshaw should be fair warning for any brand producer:

"Branding is the art of trust creation; with trust on the run, brands cannot be far behind." (Upshaw 1995)

While market data can be construed as showing only incremental growth in the aggregate private label category, it is the success of individual players in this business that tells the true story. Many of them have been involved in private label for decades, others are brand new to the idea. They all have their sights set on building more "exclusive" brands, where they can realize their best profits, while giving consumers exactly what they shop for: value for their dollar. They are, to quote, "armed to the teeth" with category-management savvy.

Recognizing this, there are a number of retailers and distributors now developing what they call "corporate brands" within their own organizations, in which all of their chains stock that brand. While this is a viable name for their private label or exclusive brand, it also is confusing. One of the leading authorities on branding strategies, Professor David A. Aaker of the Haas School of Business at the University of California at Berkeley, identifies corporate brands as manufacturers brands. In clarifying this in his book, "Building Strong Brands," however, Aaker also notes that retailer brands or private-label brands "are competitive with national brands in quality and marketing support, but have substantial cost advantages—in part because the cost of the brand management team, sales force, and advertising is lower and can be spread over hundreds of product classes and in part because of logistical advantages." (Aaker 1996)

Four Assets of Brand Equity

He points to "four assets that underlie brand equity—awareness, perceived quality, brand loyalty, and brand association." (Aaker 1996) While name brands do not necessarily require the last asset, private label most certainly does. He recommends capitalizing on that asset. . .

"These retail brands often rely on packaging cues and customer trial to establish perceived quality and brand loyalty. Organizational associations, however, could also be a good vehicle to communicate quality both credibly and distinctively. Organizational associations are sensible because, after all, the retail chain is an organization. Further, any organizational associations used to enhance store brands will likely also help develop store loyalty." (Aaker 1996)

The organizational associations he refers to include the company's "particular set of values, culture, people, programs, and assets/skills to deliver a product or service. These organizational characteristics can provide a basis for differentiation, a value proposition, and a customer relationship..." (Aaker 1996)

This marketing perspective, or marketing strategy, is something that European retailers have practiced for decades. It's an import into the Americas, which not too many people are aware of today.

It seems inevitable that the 21st century will see explosive growth for exclusive brands. The future may, in fact, turn into a no-brand scenario as advertising becomes less important to consumer choice than "organizational" or retailer brand loyalty.

One technologically-derived scenario has consumers programming their needs from a voice-activated, user-friendly, computerized system in the store or in their homes. They can custom-order the ingredients, flavorings, package size, ethnic preferences, etc., allowing for any health or dietary requirements. They rely upon a medical and/or nutritional reference guide as well as suggestions for best beverage complements to a meal. Indeed, consumers may even have fun creating their own packaging or recipes, including ingredient searches for options in a meal presentation. The execution of shoppers' orders is constrained within certain parameters to keep costs down. There are also marketing opportunities in the form of recipe contests/exchange, in-store sampling, incentive contests, etc. This scenario is interactive between retailer and consumer, via Internet/World Wide Web linkage. As for the ongoing competition between name brands and exclusive brands, consumers of the future will buy the store of their choice. Patronage will depend on how well they are served and on relationship loyalty. Ultimately, their choice will be tilted toward the exclusive brands of the store, since that's where the retailer will exercise the greatest influence.

It is appropriate that this book closes with a short essay by one of the architects of private label and premium store-brand packaging, Don Watt, a top executive at Cott Corp. and the firm he founded, The Watt Group, both in Canada. This author approached Mr. Watt, asking him to comment on private label growth and change in North America. His analysis follow.

The Retail Brand Revolution Where It Is Today? Tomorrow?

By Don Watt

Prior to 1992, conventional wisdom in the United States believed that premium quality products could only be marketed to the American consumer under a national brand identity. These national brands capitalized on two technological advances to co-opt the consumers' TRUST—Network Radio in 1920 and Network TV in 1950.

By 1964, 9 out of 10 "decisions to buy" were made before the consumer entered her food or drug store. In that environment, premium retail brands could not have survived the weight of mass media arranged against them.

BUT THINGS CHANGE…

In 1972, scanning and the Universal Product Code (UPC) put information into the hands of retailers first. In 1973, when OPEC revalued oil and shattered our complacency, everyone—manufacturers and retailers alike, rushed to take costs out of their businesses.

Manufacturers lost a measure of trust at this time, and a fundamental power shift in favor of retailers began. Retailers examined private label options to improve their profit margins and differentiate themselves from competitors. "No Name" became the symbol for the time, when Loblaws in Canada used it to gain control of price in consumers' minds.

By the early 1980s, consumers were prepared to trade up; and Loblaws offered "President's Choice," a premium retail brand, to meet consumers' new wants. All this happened in Canada, where a few retailers were able to establish a balance with manufacturers and create a "test market" for the United States.

In the United States, the power of the brands still intimidated the retailers, until Wal-Mart and Wegmans embraced the idea of PREMIUM RETAIL BRANDS. Then the dam broke. These two retailers, respected in their channels, adapted the President's Choice concept to their own cultures and triggered a revolution.

Cott Corporation, with its license to use the RC cola formula as a basis for various adaptations for many retailers, helped to drive the revolution by providing a product preferred in blind tests over Coke and Pepsi. (Ironically, RC had proved its formula superior to Coke and Pepsi in blind tests since 1940, but had never been able to reach critical mass with its message through "traditional mass media.")

Today, many retailers have embraced what they think is the premium revolution, but have not taken the steps to reconfigure their business to capitalize on the opportunity. They are caught in the middle of a field, without understanding the "religion" that could lead them to the "promised land."

TOMORROW?

It is clear that many retailers have experimented with premium retail brands, some with more success than others. But traditional retailers need to find ways to improve profitability, or even to survive. Premium Retail Brands allow them to manage the mix between national brands and two levels of private label, to ensure that each category is profitable.

Will traditional thinking sink those retailers? Or will a few enlightened businesses find the way to reach new heights, building a new level of consumer trust—with aggressive prices on national brands, and real value in their retail brand programs?

REFERENCES/CITATIONS

Aaker, David A. 1996. "Building Strong Brands." The Free Press, New York, pp. 28-29.

____ , pg. 35

____, pg. 124

____, pg. 115

Exclusive Brands Magazine, "A National Brand Private Label." Vol 1, No. 1, 1997. Exclusive Brands LLC, New York

Lancaster, Bill 1996. (Phone interview with executive at Associated Wholesale Grocers, Inc., Kansas City, KS.)

Trout, Jack with Steve Rivkin 1996. "The New Positioning, The Latest on the World's #1 Business Strategy." McGraw-Hill, Inc., New York, pg. 42.

Upshaw, Lynn B. 1995. "Building Brand Identity, A Strategy for Success in a Hostile Marketplace." John Wiley & Sons, Inc., New York, NY., pp. 8-9.

APPENDIX

Cornell University Special Research Project:

Private Label Strategies of Branded Manufacturers

The purpose of the study was to investigate the current strategies employed by brand manufacturers regarding the production of private label. During the summer of 1996, several senior executives from over a dozen leading branded manufacturers were interviewed regarding their company's strategic initiatives toward the production of private label.

This study is the result of those efforts. Special thanks go to Gene A. German, Ph.D, professor of food marketing, and Debra J. Perosio, Ph.D. in food marketing, The Food Industry Management Program at Cornell University, Ithaca, NY, who both helped manage and write this report.

Introduction

Private label products are produced for retailers and wholesalers by manufacturers that specialize in producing store brand merchandise and also by manufacturers of nationally-advertised branded goods. For those firms that are dedicated to producing private label products, this activity is the main focus of their business; however, for manufacturers of branded products, it is a secondary activity and presents several marketing dilemmas.

Branded manufacturers face two basic dilemmas. First, they must decide whether or not they should produce a product line that competes with their own brand. Second, they must determine whether or not they are willing to lose private label sales (and perhaps market share) to another manufacturer. Most brand manufacturers, however, are quick to agree that their first priority lies with the marketing and growth of their own brands. Branded manufacturers view store branding opportunities as complementary and subordinate to their primary objective of promoting the sale of their branded items. More and more of these same firms nevertheless are engaging in the production of private label products.

One manufacturer insists that deciding on a private label strategy should be a long-term commitment on the part of the retailer. The marketing director put it this way: "We have to go through a lot of tedious meetings with these customers to insure that our product meets their (the retailer's) specifications, whether it is in packaging, ingredients, whatever it may be, it is a long process. You just don't turn on a private label and then turn it off. It's a long-term investment for us as well."

According to research* conducted by Cornell University, Ithaca, NY, the production of private label products, for retail or wholesale groups, provides a number of benefits for manufacturers of advertised branded products. These benefits include:

- Production efficiency
- Expanded product mix for their customer
- Extension of shelf space for the company
- Opportunities for strategic alliances
- Some fixed costs in manufacturing are amortized
- Maintenance of market share
- Better relationships with retail customers
- Transportation efficiencies
- The potential to leverage national brand products with specific customers.

Typically, manufacturers of branded products report entering the private label market for a number of reasons—to fill unused manufacturing capacity, to increase market share, and/or to survive in a mature market. The primary reason given by national brand manufacturers for providing private label products to various retail customers is related to the vendor's manufacturing capacity. The final decision, however, is usually based on a combination of factors, which include company marketing strategies, available production capacity, and cost issues.

This Cornell research report finds that although the existence of excess plant capacity is the primary concern for national brand manufacturers to produce private label, it may be a dangerous attitude for manufacturers since it lacks a "market-oriented stance." David Nichol, a former president of a Canadian retailer-wholesaler, Loblaw (Canada's leading food retailer and wholesaler) and the developer of the President's Choice upscale private label line, also feels that the primary focus for branded food manufacturers should be the wants and needs of the consumer market. The decisions to produce a private label product should not be based solely on available plant capacity. He says that "national brand manufacturers tend to think about filling their plant capacity first, but we think of market needs before everything else. This is the reason why we could succeed in developing the President's Choice brand."

However, questions remain. Do national brand manufacturers use private brands as a positive leverage to support their own brands in response to market needs? Do they produce private brands simply because there is excess production capacity? Do they use private label as a defense mechanism in order to keep out competitors?

Private Label Strategies

National brand manufacturers typically adopt one of three basic marketing policies relating to the production of private label products, for their retail or wholesale customers. The three policies are:

1) Not to produce private label products under any circumstances.
2) To selectively produce private label products.
3) To actively solicit private label business and produce as much as possible.

As part of an ongoing research effort relating to private label marketing, Cornell researchers interviewed a wide range of national brand manufacturers regarding their company policy, as it relates to the production of private label products. The executives from these national brand companies described the various strategies that their companies had adopted regarding private label manufacturing.

Strategy 1: No Private Label Production

Manufacturers that adopt this policy typically have the number one market position for all—or a high percentage of their products. Because of their strong market position, these national brand manufacturers choose not to produce private label products in order to direct their marketing, sales, and promotional energies (as well as dollars) toward their own national brands.

They offer the following specific reasons for committing exclusively to their core national brand business:

- Since they have a strong market share, they do not want to disrupt this position by competing against themselves.
- Some national brand manufacturers fear private label could damage their highly-valued brand reputation. They do not want to compromise the brand equity of their products, by producing private label products which may not have the same quality levels.
- Because of their strong market share, these firms seldom have excess plant production capacity.

These same national brand manufacturers admit there are conditions under which they would consider entering the private label business. The factors that might precipitate a change in strategy include:

- if sales declined and there was a need to fill plant capacity,
- if a tremendous shift occurs in consumer opinion, i.e. increased interest in private label products and an increase in private label sales,
- if overall private label business continues to grow substantially.

One executive with a national brand manufacturer, who currently is not engaged in private label production, summed up the competitive strategy of their firm against private label as, "not to sell on price but to sell on value." An executive from another manufacturer concurs: "Product quality and value are typically the way we compete. We talk about the benefits that our product has to offer in some cases; for example, in comparing our product to a private label, we will show a comparison that the private label may cost less to buy, by the package. Typically, our product has some combination of lower cost per use or greater value per use to offset that perceived price difference."

Strategy 2: Produce Private Label on a Selective Basis

A number of the executives, who were interviewed as part of the Cornell research project, indicated that their companies had a policy, or marketing strategy, to produce private label products on a selective basis. There were some variations to this policy of selectively producing private label products; but their strategies tend to fall into four categories:

1) Produce private label for select products or product categories. Executives, who were interviewed from national brand manufacturing firms, indicated that their company would produce private label products for certain products, or product categories where they had a weak market position, or low market share.

In other cases, these same executives indicated that the decision to produce private label products was sometimes prompted by the sales level of private label products in a category. If private label sales were strong in a given category—indicating strong consumer acceptance—they said their company would likely produce private label products for retail and wholesale customers.

2) Produce private label for select customers. Another strategy that was described by national brand executives was one of producing private label for certain retail or wholesaler customers, in order to:

- improve the existing relationship,
- obtain a new customer for a particular product line, and
- lower shipping costs by combining private label product with the firm's national brand items.

Executives from several national brand firms indicated that their company policy was not to produce private label products; however, they made exceptions for a few "special" retail customers, who worked very closely with them.

In most cases, these firms had very little excess production capacity. The executives interviewed indicated that their companies were not in a position to produce private label on an expanded basis.

3) Produce a private label, but control the brand through licensing. A number of national brand manufacturers have used a licensing strategy in a variety of ways. This is a marketing activity whereby the manufacturer maintains ownership of the brand, but licenses its use on a market-by-market basis. This strategy usually involves global brand marketers, who will license a major retailer in a country where the manufacturer does not have any significant marketing presence. In the strictest sense, this is not a private label, under the definition presented in this book. The classic example of this strategy, used by a retailer or wholesaler, is seen in the marketing of the "Presidents Choice" line by Loblaw. This premium quality line of products is licensed or franchised to non-competitive retailers outside of Canada in a market area on an exclusive basis. It then becomes that retailer's private or exclusive brand; but ownership of the brand lies with the label owner, Loblaw in this case, and not with the retailer.

4) Producing private label products as plant capacity permits. This is a strategy that may be combined with one or two of the marketing strategies already mentioned; but this is typically a short-term reaction, rather than a long-term strategy. Although it can be a profitable strategy for the manufacturer, if it moves a production facility closer to full capacity, it has a serious weakness, since it is based on available "production" capacity, and not on consumer demand.

Strategy 3: Actively Solicit Private Label Business

A number of nationally-based manufacturers actively pursue private label business. One example is a well-known manufacturer that enjoys an extremely high market share in a very narrow product line. Because their market share is so high, the number two brand in most markets, where this firm competes, is private label. The market strategy of this national brand manufacturer is summed up in this statement from an interview with a Cornell researcher: "Since we have the number one brand in every market where our product is sold, we find our product competing primarily with private label. So, for our company to grow, we can either work to take share away from private label, or we can produce the private label for our retail customer—we have chosen to aggressively seek out new private label business."

---

*This research project, conducted by Cornell University's Food Industry Management Program, was commissioned by the Flickinger Family, expressly for use in this textbook.

Index

B

C

D

E

F

G

H

I

J

K

L

M

N

O

P

Q

R

S

T

U

V

W

X

Y

Z